# A CRITICAL INTRODUCTION
# TO THE OLD TESTAMENT

D1613288

# A CRITICAL INTRODUCTION TO THE OLD TESTAMENT

### GEORGE W. ANDERSON, F.B.A.

*Emeritus Professor of Hebrew and Old Testament Studies in the University of Edinburgh*

**SECOND EDITION**

**DUCKWORTH**

Second edition 1994
First published 1959
Reprinted 1960, 1962, 1964, 1966, 1968, 1971, 1974

All rights reserved

© George W. Anderson 1959, 1994

Published by Gerald Duckworth & Co. Ltd.
The Old Piano Factory
48 Hoxton Square
London N1 6PB

ISBN 0 7156 2603 5

Produced in Great Britain
by Booksprint, Bristol

## PREFACE TO THE SECOND EDITION

Apart from a relatively small number of minor corrections, the original text of this book is unaltered in this edition. To take account of recent work the bibliography has been revised and brought up to date. There are, however, some recent contributions to the critical study of the Old Testament for which a mere bibliographical reference will not suffice. The most important of these studies relate to the composition and dating of the Tetrateuch/Pentateuch and involve challenges both to solutions previously offered and to the methods used in reaching these solutions. A brief account of these and of some recent work on the prophetic literature is given in an appendix.

September 1993                                  G.W. Anderson

## PREFACE TO THE FIRST EDITION

THE late Dr. G. Buchanan Gray's *Critical Introduction to the Old Testament* was first published in this Series in 1912. In many ways the situation in this, as in other fields of Old Testament study, is far more difficult to assess to-day. The present volume attempts to describe and appraise the most important theories which have been advanced about the nature and composition of the Old Testament books. The scope of the Series has made it necessary to omit much that would rightly find a place in a larger volume, and sometimes to dismiss in a sentence or two hypotheses which have been advanced by their authors with detailed supporting arguments. I have tried to be as fair as the requisite brevity permitted.

But the book is also intended to be an introduction to the Old Testament itself, and to give the reader some impression of the structure and contents of the several books. It is impossible either to understand or to estimate the soundness of the various hypotheses without a grasp of the texts. Moreover, if the hypotheses do not help us to a deeper understanding of the Old Testament itself, they are better forgotten.

The writing of this volume has taken far longer than I expected when I undertook the task. I wish to thank the General Editor of the Series, Dr. Nathaniel Micklem, for the great patience which he has shown during long delays and for his unfailing courtesy and helpfulness. To Professor H. H. Rowley I am indebted for the constant encouragement and help which he has given me in this as in other enterprises. He has read a considerable part of the typescript and given me the benefit of his discerning criticism. But the demerits of the book and any errors which it may contain are not to be laid at his door. My thanks are also due to Mrs. M. Noble who shared with my wife the task of preparing the typescript for the printer, and to Mr. Martin Reid, who checked the references and helped in the preparation of the indexes. At almost every stage I received encouragement and help from the one to whose memory the volume is dedicated.

G. W. ANDERSON.

# CONTENTS

IN PIAM MEMORIAM
UXORIS CARISSIMAE

# I.—INTRODUCTORY

OLD TESTAMENT introduction falls into three parts: the history of the Canon, the history of the text, and the study of the structure, date and authorship of the various books. The first two subjects are commonly grouped together as *general introduction,* to distinguish them from the third, which is known as *special introduction.* It is with the problems of special introduction that this book is in the main concerned, though some account of the Canon must also be included in it. The purpose of the book is to introduce the Old Testament itself rather than the study of Old Testament introduction; but something ought to be said at the outset about the history of scholarship in this field.

Two factors make this desirable. First, the number and variety of new or supposedly new theories have added to the complexity of an already difficult subject; and it may help to clarify the position if we attempt to describe the chief tendencies and methods which have to be reckoned with. Secondly, there is a feeling abroad in many quarters that the subject is in large measure irrelevant to the religious and theological interpretation of the Old Testament, and may safely be disregarded by the theological student and working minister, a view which cannot be intelligently held by anyone who has even the slightest knowledge of the interaction between literary analysis and the study of Hebrew history and religion.

The origins of the subject lie in the attempts made (long before the appearance of Biblical criticism in the modern sense) to provide the inquiring reader with useful information about various parts of Scripture, including some account of the circumstances in which the books were written. But it is

1

only since the Reformation that scientific study has been systematically devoted to the data. To the renewed interest in the Bible which came with the Reformation there was added the audacious enthusiasm for free inquiry which the Renaissance and the *Aufklärung* stimulated. The Scriptures could no longer be effectively shielded by ecclesiastical pronouncements from impartial investigation, any more than the chosen people could be thought of as having lived in a historical and cultural vacuum. Already in the 17th century, important pioneer work was done by two philosophers, the Englishman Hobbes, and the Dutch Jew Spinoza. During the latter half of the century and throughout the 18th the new science began slowly to find its bearings, until at last the first great critical introduction to the Old Testament was produced by the German scholar J. G. Eichhorn (*Einleitung in das A.T.*, 5 volumes, 1780–1783).

To begin with, the methods used were chiefly linguistic and literary; but, during the 19th century, it became increasingly clear that history and religion were involved. To no part of the Old Testament was so much attention directed as to the five books which were traditionally ascribed to Moses and regarded as the authoritative basis of religious life in ancient Israel. As a result of the cumulative labours of several scholars (and, in particular, of the persuasive advocacy of Julius Wellhausen on the Continent and William Robertson Smith in this country) the view came to be widely accepted that these books were a compilation from four main sources, all of them much later than Moses, and themselves spanning a period of centuries and reflecting successive phases in Hebrew life and religion.

The effect of this theory on the religious and theological understanding of the Old Testament can hardly be overestimated. Diehard traditionalists might be affronted by the suggestion that Moses was not the author of the Pentateuch, but here was a theory which was not content to deny Mosaic authorship and assert composite authorship. It put the Pentateuch towards the end instead of at the beginning of the history of Old Testament religion, and laid bare the development which led up to it. The impressive structure of religious law and custom contained in the first five books of the Bible was no longer regarded as the grand depositum delivered to the wilderness generation through Moses, but as the product of almost a millennium of evolution. It was as if excavators had dug beneath the floor of one building and had shown it to be in fact the roof of another.

Now, to accept the main outlines of this theory does not commit one to complete agreement with the view of Hebrew religion which some of its exponents held. But, once accepted, the literary analysis ruled the traditional view out of court.

The new view was effectively presented, and rapidly gained the assent of leading scholars; hence the serious encounters between 'orthodoxy' and 'criticism' which took place (in this country at least) during the latter part of the 19th century. The interpretation of Israel's religion in terms of development was incompatible with older views of the inerrancy of Scripture and the equal authority of its several parts. The theory of progressive revelation had a widespread vogue; and whatever its defects, it must be admitted that it brought to many a welcome relief from the yoke of traditionalism. This was but one result of the new estimate of the Old Testament which the documentary hypothesis had helped to make possible. In the whole history of Biblical scholarship probably no other critical theory has had such far-reaching effects. It involved a reassessment not of the Pentateuch alone, but of the entire Old Testament. And to-day, when the student is urged, as he so often is, to by-pass the supposedly arid waste of literary criticism and press on to understand the message of the Old Testament, it is necessary to recall that any religious or theological interpretation of the Old Testament must come to terms with the documentary hypothesis of the origin of the Pentateuch, or else find something more satisfactory to put in its place.

It seemed, then, towards the end of the 19th century that critical scholarship had won a double victory, over its

traditionalist opponents and over its complex subject-matter.
A general critical position had been established which was
likely to stand the test of time and to serve as a firm basis
for such further investigation as remained to be carried out.
Literary and historical criticism was being applied, not only
to the Pentateuch, but also to the historical and prophetical
literature, to the Psalter, and to the other books in the Canon.
Manuals of introduction were in the main concerned to present the results of this analysis, taking each book in turn, and
reducing it to its component parts. Some, however, adopted
a chronological treatment, beginning with the earliest fragments and reviewing in turn the literary production of each
successive age.[1] A volume which adopts this approach is less
an introduction to the Old Testament than an attempted
history of Israelite literature. Any such attempt must reckon
with two difficulties. We possess only partial remains of
ancient Hebrew literature; and from the pre-exilic period
there survive only such documents as theological censorship
and the vicissitudes of history have spared.[2] Again, the precise dating of many parts of the Old Testament cannot be
decided with certainty. The incompleteness and uncertainty
are, of course, equally real no matter how the results of
critical study are presented; but this particular approach
emphasizes them and is hampered by them.

Early in the present century, the German scholar Hermann
Gunkel introduced into Old Testament study a new technique
which has had important effects on many questions of introduction. He pointed out that it was impossible to carry
through an exact chronological treatment of Israelite literature, and that there could be no question of a complete biographical account of the outstanding authors of successive
periods, since the modern interest in the personality behind

---

[1] The most recent example of this method is the masterly volume by
Professor A. Lods, *Histoire de la littérature hébraïque et juive des
origines à la ruine de l'état juif (135 après J.-C.)*, 1950.

[2] It ought, however, to be said that, on the whole, scholars to-day
attribute more of the contents of the Old Testament to the pre-exilic
period than did those of an earlier generation.

the book was practically non-existent in ancient Israel. Particularly in the early stages, the personal and individual factors
in literature were far less prominent than in modern times.
There were certain typical, conventional forms of literature
which were appropriate to particular occasions. Gunkel held
that it was the function of literary history to recognize and
classify their forms (*Gattungen*), to relate each to its setting
in life (*Sitz im Leben*), and to trace their historical development. This development leads from the simple, short, literary
unit, produced and preserved by the oral tradition of which
the community is the custodian, on to the blending and interaction of different *Gattungen* in more sophisticated ages. In
this later phase, more must be attributed to the conscious,
creative effort of individual authors; and we pass from the
simple to the complex, from the oral to the written, from the
community to the individual.

Linked with this technique there was a new awareness of
the relation between Israel and its neighbours. Broadly speaking, the earlier analytical criticism had studied the Old Testament in isolation. But archæological discoveries in Egypt,
Babylonia, Asia Minor, and elsewhere, were making available
an increasing mass of new material relating to the life and
literature of ancient Near Eastern peoples; and Israelite
literature could now be seen against that background. If in
Babylonia or Egypt there existed at an early date psalms and
wisdom writings similar (in spite of the difference of religious
emphasis) to those in the Old Testament, it was no longer
necessary to date the Psalms and the Wisdom Literature as
late as some had done. In this and in other ways, the new
perspective and the new technique led to the modification of
some earlier conclusions; but the older approach was supplemented, not supplanted. Gunkel did not want to dispense
with literary analysis, but rather, assuming its general conclusions, to go on to a new synthesis of the material. It must
also be admitted that, while Gunkel's method deals admirably
with the smallest units (which he regarded as the oldest parts
of the literature), it is less applicable to the larger elements,

where unity of conception and the creative gifts of individual
writers count for so much.

Gunkel himself did not produce a full-scale treatment of
Israelite literary history. In a number of short studies[1] he
explained the main principles of the new approach; and in
his commentary on Genesis and his treatment of the Psalms
he demonstrated in detail its application.[2] Here, however, as
in other fields of Old Testament study, his work was un-
usually stimulating. His influence may be traced in the attempts made by some investigators to-day to go behind the
sources, of which some of the literature is composed, to the
earlier history of the material which they contain (traditio-
historical research). Again, Gunkel emphasized the oral
character of the beginnings of the literature; and in recent
years a good deal of attention has been directed to the
character and influence of oral tradition. A group of energetic
and able Scandinavian scholars claim that the oral tradition
of the Old Testament was continued to a comparatively late
date, and was reliable to a remarkable degree. They argue
that a critical approach which thinks in terms of actual
written documents is irrelevant to much of the Old Testament, and that first and foremost the critic must have in
mind the process of oral transmission. To them it seems that
Wellhausen's methods are antiquated and his theories demolished. But since it is in documentary form that the Old
Testament has come down to us, it is in the first instance as a
collection of documents that we must read it. Our inquiry will
often lead us behind the stage of literary transmission and
composition to a time when songs, stories, laws, prophetic
teaching, and the like were handed down by word of mouth.

[1] *Die israelitische Literatur* (in *Die Kultur der Gegenwart* I, vii, pp.
51-102); 'Die Grundprobleme der israelitischen Literaturgeschichte'
(in *Reden und Aufsätze*, pp. 29-380); art. 'Bibelwissenschaft'; I,C,
'Literaturgeschichte Israels' (in *R.G.G.*[1]); art. 'Literaturgeschichte,
biblische' (in *R.G.G.*[2]).

[2] *Genesis übersetzt und erklärt* (H.K.A.T.); *Die Psalmen übersetzt und
erklärt* (H.K.A.T.); *Einleitung in die Psalmen* (H.K.A.T.), completed by
J. Begrich.

But that does not mean that the tools of literary analysis can safely be discarded. They are still indispensable.

On the other hand, it may be freely admitted that these tools have often been used unimaginatively and pedantically. Superficial contradictions and unimportant stylistic variations have been used as evidence for the existence of a succession of editors and subsidiary sources. Some critics have required in the ancient writers a standard of consistency and an avoidance of repetition of which they are themselves not always capable. Nor have they always made sufficient allowance for Hebrew psychology.[1] But such criticism of the critics involves the improvement, not the abolition, of their methods. Both old and new techniques will be the more effectively used when common sense and sound judgement are given their rightful place.

The study of the literary types and of their setting in life has led to a keener appreciation of the relationship between Old Testament literature and life. There is a heightened interest in the liturgical character of the Psalms (and perhaps also of prophetic and other passages), in the influence of sanctuaries on law, legend, etc., and in the preservation and growth of the prophetic books, not merely by scribal activity, but within the life of prophetic communities.

In addition to these newer modes of approach, we must reckon with the researches of scholars who have continued to work in the old tradition of literary analysis. Their investigations, too, have led to the modification or amplification of earlier theories; and as a result of all these developments, the present situation in the study of Old Testament introduction is more complicated than it was half a century ago. It is sometimes stated that there has been a 'conservative reaction' in contemporary criticism. There is some ground for this. The tendency in many quarters to date a substantial part of the Psalter in the pre-exilic period is perhaps the most obvious instance of such a change. But the use of such terms as

---

[1] For an interesting scrutiny of critical method, see Pedersen, *Israel* I–II, pp. 521–523; and cf. further, *Israel* III–IV, pp. 725–757.

'conservative' and 'radical' in this connexion can be misleading. The aim of the scholar should be to establish the truth,
and not to defend 'conservative' or 'radical' conclusions.

Again, there are those who speak of the rejection or modification of particular theories as if 'criticism' itself was discredited. This is not so. The tendencies in scholarship outlined
above do not involve the abandonment of the critical principle, that matters which are properly the subject of scientific inquiry cannot be satisfactorily settled on the ground of
tradition, or by authoritative ecclesiastical pronouncement,
but by the scrupulous weighing of the evidence. If the views
of earlier scholars have been rejected, it is because, rightly
or wrongly, their methods have been judged unscientific.
Particular critical hypotheses have been discarded and
new methods introduced; but 'criticism' itself has not been
jettisoned. Indeed, it seems rather that some defenders
of traditional views are to-day more willing than formerly
to support their position by arguments rather than by
assertion.

On the other hand, it is possible to have no doubts about
the general validity of critical method and yet to question its
relevance to the religious and theological study of the Bible.
Our generation has seen a remarkable revival of interest in
biblical theology, in the major problems of interpretation, and
in the relation of the Old Testament to the New Testament.
The various introductory disciplines are only prolegomena to
such study. But they are indispensable prolegomena. It is,
perhaps, not superfluous to recall two facts which ought to
be familiar, but seem often to be forgotten. The first is that
the results of the critical movement challenged the doctrine
of the verbal inerrancy of Scripture. We can hardly dismiss
as theologically irrelevant a branch of study which did so
much to break the tyranny of the old dogmatic approach to
the Bible. In the second place, the very nature of the Old
Testament makes it folly to treat critical introduction as
valueless. The Old Testament tells of a revelation given in and
through history; and the revelation cannot now be adequate-

ly understood if it is abstracted from history.[1] The theologian
and exegete will misunderstand and misinterpret the Old
Testament, if he fails to hear in it 'the sound of running
history'. To prevent such misinterpretation is one of the
functions of criticism. Leaving aside details of theory, one of
the supreme merits of the critical movement is that it has
sought to put the documents into their original context, and
so to present the Bible as a living book.

A comparison of some recent volumes of introduction shows
that one of the most difficult problems confronting the writers
is the presentation of the material. Should each book be dealt
with in turn; or should the results of analysis be assumed, and
the contents of the Old Testament surveyed as nearly as
possible in chronological order? How much space should be
devoted to the study of literary forms, and at what point in
the discussion? The present volume is intended to be an introduction to the Old Testament rather than a literary history.
No attempt is therefore made at the outset to follow chronological order. Furthermore, it seems, on the whole, a sounder
method, and simpler for the student, to begin with the
material in the form in which we now have it, rather than to
pick out the now disjointed and fragmentary literary remains
of the earliest period. What we have in the Old Testament is
not primarily a literary collection, but a canon. The materials
have been produced, selected, and arranged within the life of
a religious community. This is a simple matter of fact, with
which the investigator must reckon, whether or not he himself has any religious convictions.

We begin, then, with the collection, and with the arrangement of the books within it. We proceed to examine each
book or group of books in turn. There follow brief accounts
of the main literary forms and of literary history, and, finally,
a discussion (for which, presumably, no apology is needed
in a series of Studies in Theology) of the place of the Old
Testament in the Christian revelation.

[1] Cf. C. R. North, *The Old Testament Interpretation of History*, pp. 153 ff
('. . . the historical circumstances are an integral part of the revelation').

## II.—THE CANON OF THE OLD TESTAMENT

THE Old Testament contains a wide variety of literary material, which, as arranged in the English Bible, falls into two main groups. The first five books, traditionally ascribed to Moses, contain *the Law* and form the basic, authoritative document of Judaism. There follow twelve narrative works (Joshua–Esther), grouped together as *history*, five *poetical* books (Job–the Song of Songs), and seventeen books of *prophecy* (Isaiah–Malachi). This arrangement according to contents or literary character has its defects. The term 'history' cannot be applied with any exactness to some of the books in the second group; there is a very considerable quantity of poetry outside the third group; and the book of Daniel finds a place among the prophets only if its character is misunderstood.

The Hebrew Bible contains the same books rather differently arranged in three main divisions: the Law (*Tôrâh*), the Prophets (*Nᵉḇî'îm*), and the Writings (*Kᵉṯûḇîm*). The first of these is identical with the opening section of the English Bible; and its normative religious significance can hardly be over-estimated. For orthodox Judaism all else, in the Bible and outside it, is subordinate to these five books.

The second group contains much more than we normally understand by the term prophecy. It is divided into two sections, the Former Prophets (*Nᵉḇî'îm Rîšônîm*) and the Latter Prophets (*Nᵉḇî'îm 'Aʰᵃrônîm*). The Former Prophets are the four books, Joshua, Judges, Samuel, and Kings,[1]

[1] In the Hebrew enumeration, the books of Samuel and Kings each appear as one, because in Hebrew, which was originally written without vowel signs, one roll of manuscript was sufficient for each. But when

10

which to the modern reader are history rather than prophecy. But it seems likely that at a fairly early date they were believed to have been written by prophetic personalities. Joshua was held to have written the book which bears his name, Samuel to have written Judges and Samuel, and Jeremiah to have been the author of Kings. The classification could also be justified on the ground that, in the form in which we now have these books, they are neither bald chronicle nor an impartial factual survey of Hebrew history from the settlement to the exile, but a religious interpretation and evaluation of events and leaders, an interpretation closely related to the teaching of the great prophets. The connexion is of the utmost significance. Hebrew historiography cannot be understood apart from the prophetic movement. We note, too, that Ruth is not included here as a coda to Judges, with which its only link is that it narrates events in the same period. In literary character, the two books are markedly different; and the insertion of Ruth at this point separates Judges from its natural continuation and culmination in Samuel.

The books of the Latter prophets, like the Former, are four in number: Isaiah, Jeremiah, Ezekiel, and the Twelve (Hosea, Joel, Amos, Obadiah, Jonah, Micah, Nahum, Habakkuk, Zephaniah, Haggai, Zechariah, and Malachi). It is significant that Lamentations and Daniel are not included. The twelve so-called Minor Prophets count as one, for the quite practical reason that they could be written on a roll of manuscript roughly the same size as those required for the three Major Prophets.

The third group is a miscellaneous assortment of writings. First come Psalms, Proverbs, and Job. These are traditionally known as the Poetical Books. But, as we have seen, even the larger group of poetical books in the other arrangement does

they were rendered into Greek, in which vowels are written, four rolls in all were required. The titles 1, 2, 3, 4 Kingdoms (or Reigns) were given in Greek to the resulting four books. Jerome, however, preferred to use the titles 1, 2, 3, and 4 Kings, whence come the sub-titles in the English Authorized Version: 'The First Book of Samuel, Otherwise Called the First Book of the Kings', etc.

not exhaust the poetry of the Old Testament. There follow
five short books known as the Five Scrolls (*Megillôt*): Ruth,
the Song of Songs, Ecclesiastes, Lamentations, Esther. For
many centuries these books have been associated with festivals:[1] the Song of Songs with Passover, Ruth with the Feast
of Weeks, Lamentations with the Ninth of Ab (the feast
which commemorates the destruction of Jerusalem), Ecclesiastes with the Feast of Tabernacles, and Esther with Purim.
Daniel comes next, followed by Ezra and Nehemiah (counting
as one book), and, finally, 1 and 2 Chronicles (also counting
as one book). It is an interesting fact that the book of Ezra–
Nehemiah, which is the chronological sequel to Chronicles,
precedes it in the Hebrew arrangement. In all probability
these books originally formed one consecutive history. But
when the third section of the Canon was being formed, Ezra–
Nehemiah was added first, and Chronicles omitted, because
it narrated events already dealt with in the earlier historical
books. But, later, Chronicles was added, presumably because
of its distinctive point of view. The overlap of some two and
a half verses between the end of 2 Chronicles and the beginning of Ezra is a relic of the original connexion between the
two books.

Thus there are eleven books in the third section of the Hebrew Bible, making, together with the five books of the Law
and the eight books of the Prophets, a total of twenty-four.

It has generally been held that this three-fold arrangement
corresponds to three stages in the formation of the Canon.[2]
Against this it has been argued that there was, in fact, no
Canon of Hebrew Scriptures until, at the end of the first
Christian century, a synod of rabbis at Jamnia (or Yabneh,
a few miles south of the modern Tel Aviv) defined its extent.
This latter view has been maintained by Oesterley and

[1] The earliest evidence comes from the 6th century of the Christian
era. See Eissfeldt, *Introduction*, p. 570; Weiser, *Introduction*, p. 345.

[2] The word 'Canon' is derived, through Greek and Latin, ultimately
from a Semitic word meaning 'reed'. The Greek κανών came to mean not
merely any sort of rod, but a carpenter's rule, and hence a norm or
standard, and, finally, a normative collection of writings.

Robinson (*Introduction*, pp. 4–8), following the contentions of Gustav Hölscher. But this seems to attribute too much to an assembly the evidence for which is neither precise nor complete. That the rabbis were disputing the exact limits of the Canon during the Jamnia period is indisputable and understandable. The calamitous result of the conflict with Rome, the rise of the Christian Church, and the diffusion of apocalyptic literature (which made considerable pretensions to antiquity and authority) may well have compelled them to define more precisely the regulative documents of Judaism. But to create and to define a Canon are not necessarily synonymous. Synods and councils only put the finishing touches to a task already largely achieved by the common judgement of the faithful. About the majority of the books there can have been no need to argue: their authority had been recognized for generations, or even for centuries. The territory had already been occupied: it remained only to define its frontiers. It was the latter task which was carried out towards the end of the first century.

The process which led to this latter task cannot be traced with anything like precision: but some general indications of the development are to be found in the Old Testament and the extra-canonical Jewish literature. It is clear that, from an early date, short law codes such as the Decalogue had binding authority, though some, at least, would originally be local rather than national in their application. In 2 Kings xxii–xxiii we are told of the discovery in the temple of a religious law-book, which became the law of the land through the energetic policy of King Josiah. It is widely held that this book was the code of law contained in Deuteronomy; and if this view is correct, we have in these chapters of 2 Kings the first significant step in the establishment of the Torah as an authoritative religious document. The next comparable step in the development seems to have been the coming of Ezra to Jerusalem with a book of law which was accepted as normative by the Jewish community in and around the capital (Ezra vii. 10, 25 f; Neh. viii). Unfortunately, there is

nothing like universal agreement about either the date of
Ezra's activity or the identity of his law-book. Some scholars,
adopting the traditional chronology, put these events in
the middle of the 5th century B.C.; others put them at the
beginning of the 4th century. Some hold that Ezra's law-book
was the five books of Moses in approximately their final form;
others that it consisted of only a part of the Torah. But it is
clear that, whatever its extent may have been, the document
was regarded as specially authoritative: and it is equally clear
that, if the entire Torah was not so recognized on this occasion, its position must have been assured, at the latest, soon
after Ezra's lifetime. For it was during this period that the
Samaritans finally broke away from Judaism and became a
separate religious community.[1] Now, the Samaritans took
over as Holy Scripture the five books of Moses, and them
alone. They are not likely to have accepted them from the
hated Jews *after* the schism, or in the preceding period of
tension to have welcomed a comparatively recent Jewish in-
novation. It appears, then, that these books must have been
already firmly established as in some sense canonical, but
that the remainder of the Old Testament was not yet
similarly recognized.

For the prophetic literature, the evidence is still less precise. The spoken word was from early times held to have
divine authority; and when a prophet or his disciples committed his teaching to writing (Isa. viii. 16; Jer. xxxvi), a
similar authority would be attributed to the written word.
The first clear indication of the existence of a prophetic
corpus comes from the early part of the 2nd century B.C.
Writing c. 190–180 B.C., Jesus ben Sira gives an impressive
review of the achievements of the great men of his nation's
past. In this synopsis, the main events in Joshua, Judges,
Samuel, and Kings are followed by allusions to the three

[1] The exact date is unknown. In the book of Nehemiah (recording
events which took place in the third quarter of the 5th century) there
are signs of an impending breach. The Jewish historian and quisling,
Josephus, puts the schism in the time of Alexander. It can hardly have
taken place much later.

major prophets and the 'twelve prophets' (Ecclus. xliv–xlix). The Hebrew text of xlix. 9 refers to the Job, who is mentioned in Ezekiel; and i. 9; ii. 10; and iv. 10 seem to imply knowledge of the book of Job. Nehemiah is mentioned; but nothing is said of Ezra, Daniel, Esther, or Ruth. Presumably, then, the son of Sira had before him at least the Law, and the Former and Latter Prophets.[1] Further evidence of the authoritative position which the prophetic literature had attained is provided by the book of Daniel (usually dated 165–164), in which Jeremiah is clearly classed as sacred Scripture (Dan. ix. 2).

Ben Sira's grandson, who translated his book (132 B.C.), speaks in the prologue which he prefixed to it of 'the law, the prophets, and the other books of our fathers', 'the law, and the prophets, and the others that have followed in their steps', 'the law itself, and the prophecies, and the rest of the books'. These expressions suggest that in his day the third section of the Canon was beginning to take shape. It is a curious fact that this third section does not contain the Psalms of Solomon, which were written in the first century B.C.; and some have concluded that the Canon was practically complete by then. However that may be, two New Testament passages seem to point to the completion of the Canon as we know it. Luke xxiv. 44 refers to the Law, the Prophets, and the Psalms, the Writings being designated by the name of the first and most important book in the collection. In Matt. xxiii. 35 (=Luke xi. 51) there is an allusion to the incident in 2 Chron. xxiv. 20–23. 'From Abel to Zachariah' means from Genesis to Chronicles, the entire range of Old Testament Scripture. The fact that the New Testament does not quote Obadiah, Nahum, the Song of Songs, Ecclesiastes, Esther, and Ezra-Nehemiah proves nothing about the date when these books were accepted.

---

[1] It has been argued that passages like Ecclus. xxiv. 33; xxxix. 12; l. 27, in which ben Sira seems to class himself with the great men of the past, show that, though the books referred to were venerated, they had not yet acquired canonical authority. See Oesterley and Robinson, *Introduction*, pp. 6 f.

There was, as we have seen, discussion among the rabbis about disputed books. Doubts existed about Esther, Proverbs, Ecclesiastes, the Song of Songs, and Ezekiel; but these doubts seem at times to have touched not the question of canonical status, but that of suitability for use in public worship. The uncertainty is not difficult to account for. Esther, so often criticized to-day because of its enthusiastic nationalism and lack of any obvious piety, was suspect on the rather different ground that it sanctioned the non-Mosaic Feast of Purim. Proverbs was questioned because of internal contradiction (xxvi. 4 f), and Ezekiel because the contents of the last nine chapters were difficult to reconcile with the Torah.[1] Ecclesiastes presented the stumbling-block of a scepticism which, fortunately, was more than offset by its supposed Solomonic origin. The allegorical interpretation saved the Song of Songs from exclusion, though there were irreverent literalists who sang these poems in taverns at the time when Akiba was passionately claiming that they were 'the holiest of all'.

The Jamnia period did not see the end of all discussion; but in all essentials the final fixing of the limits of the Canon had been achieved by A.D. 100. Writing about the same time, Josephus (*Contra Apionem*, i. 8 (41)) states that the sacred writings are limited in number, that they were written within a specified period, and that their text is unalterable. According to him, they are twenty-two in number, like the letters in the Hebrew alphabet: five books of the Law, thirteen prophetic books, and four containing hymns to God and moral precepts.[2] The time-limits, from Moses to Artaxerxes, seem

[1] Hananiah ben Hezekiah, a 1st-century rabbi, is said to have retired to his room equipped with 300 measures of oil, and to have wrestled triumphantly with the discrepancies.

[2] How these figures are reached is not clear. It is commonly assumed that the four books in the third section are the Psalter, the Song of Songs, Proverbs, and Ecclesiastes, that all the remaining books are included in the prophetic corpus, and that the number twenty-two is reached by linking Ruth with Judges and Lamentations with Jeremiah. This last point suggests the arrangement in the Greek Bible. But the Greek Bible contains Apocryphal books, which are not included in the

to be fixed in order to exclude certain apocalyptic works which claim a pre-Mosaic origin.

The age of Ezra is also indicated as the *terminus ad quem* of the creation of canonical literature in two passages which represent very different trends in Judaism. The first, of approximately the same date as Josephus, is 2 (4) Esdras xiv. 19–48, which attributes to Ezra and five associates the re-creation of the Canon after the havoc wrought by the fall of Jerusalem and the Exile. At Ezra's dictation, the five scribes copied out ninety-four books, twenty-four of which (i.e., the Old Testament as we know it) were for public use, the remainder being reserved for the enlightened aristocracy of the faithful. The second is a frequently quoted passage from the Talmud (Baba Bathra 14b, 15a), which includes some astonishing assertions about the authorship of individual books, but also provides further evidence that the above-mentioned Scriptures in the threefold arrangement were generally accepted.

The books which were thus being mobilized or petrified as part of the defence of Judaism against Christianity were taken over as authoritative by the Christian Church. The Old Testament was the first Christian Bible. But from an early period the Church was predominantly Greek-speaking and used a Greek rendering of the Old Testament. Into the involved question of the origin and history of this version it is not possible to enter here.[1] According to the traditional story, a rendering of the Law was made in Egypt during the reign of Ptolemy II Philadelphus (285–247) and under his patronage. The name Septuagint (LXX), commonly given to this translation, is derived from the legend that it was

---

above reckoning. Further, the Greek Bible combines Samuel with Kings as Kingdoms (or Reigns), which would again upset the reckoning. Perhaps Josephus left out two of the disputed books. (I am indebted to Professor H. H. Rowley for drawing my attention to the difficulties of this passage.)

[1] For fuller treatment see B. J. Roberts, *The Old Testament Text and Versions*, pp. 101-187 and E. Würthwein, *The Text of the Old Testament*, pp. 34-56.

produced by seventy-two scholars. Leaving legend aside, it is quite understandable that during this period Greek-speaking Jews should have required and produced a translation of the Torah in the language with which they were most familiar. It is, however, within the Christian Church that the Greek Bible has been handed down to us. There are two important differences between it and the Hebrew Canon. First, the books outside the Torah are arranged rather differently, as history, poetry, and prophecy; and second, these three sections contain books and parts of books which are not included in the Hebrew Bible. It seems likely that, in the Jewish communities in which the Scriptures were read in Greek, the Torah was the Canon, and no sharp distinction was made between the Prophets and the Writings (as recognized in Palestine) and some other more or less edifying literature. The additional material, which corresponds roughly to what we know as the Apocrypha,[1] was taken over by the Church, and passed from the Greek into the Latin Bible. There was some discussion among the Fathers about the authority of these additional books. At the time of the Reformation the question was revived; and the Reformers were disposed, in the main, to relegate them to an inferior position. English Bibles usually either do not contain these books, or print them separately, but give the books of the Hebrew Canon in the Greek arrangement. But the threefold grouping has distinct advantages in any study of the Palestinian Canon; and accordingly it is followed here.

[1] But 2 (4) Esdras is not part of the Greek Bible

## III.—THE PENTATEUCH

### 1. *Contents*

THE Torah or Pentateuch (ἡ πεντάτευχος, the five-volume work) consists of five books known to us by their Græco-Latin names: Genesis, Exodus, Leviticus, Numbers, Deuteronomy. In Hebrew these books are each designated by a word in the opening verse: 'In the beginning' (*Berēšiṯ*), '(the) Names (of)' (*Šemôṯ*), 'And (the Lord) called' (*Wayyiḳrā'*), 'In the wilderness (of Sinai)' (*Bemiḏbar*), and 'Words' (*Deḇārîm*). They contain a considerable amount of legal material, and some ancient poems, set in a framework of narrative.

Genesis falls into two parts: i–xi; xii–l. The first eleven chapters describe the creation of the world and of man as the crown of creation, and go on to tell of the conflict between the human will and the divine. The disobedience in the garden, the first murder, the iniquity of Noah's contemporaries, and the presumptuous building of the tower and city of Babel lead to divine punishment, but also to the covenant made through Noah with succeeding generations and to the promise made to Abraham. From xii to the end of the book, the promise begins to be fulfilled in the providential guidance of the Patriarchs, Abraham, Isaac, and Jacob; and a sequence of divine choice and rejection, from the story of Noah onwards, culminates in the concentration of interest on Jacob-Israel and his descendants. Through the misfortunes and success of Joseph, the chosen family finds security in Egypt in time of famine. Varied as its contents are, the book has an impressive unity, which is emphasized by its very incompleteness. All its leading events and characters look forward to a hitherto unrealized goal.

In Exodus the situation changes. The Hebrew tribes suffer oppression in Egypt under a new regime; but God raises up Moses to make known both to them and to Pharaoh His will for His people. Nine plagues fail to have any lasting effect on Pharaoh; but the last and most dreadful of them makes him let Israel go. On the night of their escape, the Israelites celebrate the first Passover festival. At the Sea of Reeds, they are almost overtaken by Pharaoh's army; but God brings them safely over; and their enemies are destroyed. They march on to the Mount of God, where they enter into covenant with Him. His will is revealed in the Decalogue (xx. 1-17) and in a collection of laws known as the Book of the Covenant (xx. 22-xxiii. 33). Then follows the ratification of the Covenant (xxiv). Most of the closing chapters of Exodus (xxv-xxxi; xxxv-xl) deal with the construction of the Tabernacle and its equipment, and with the priests and their vestments. Sandwiched between these two groups of chapters, which are closely allied in theme and outlook, there come the incident of the golden calf, the setting up of the Tent of Meeting outside the camp (xxxii. 1-xxxiv. 9) and the giving of another brief law code (xxxiv. 10-26).

Leviticus is almost exclusively legal; and the small amount of narrative is subservient to legal interests. i–vii contain regulations for sacrifice and offering; viii–x describe the institution of the Aaronic priesthood; xi–xv deal with laws about the clean and the unclean, and are followed by the account of the ritual of the Day of Atonement in xvi. xvii–xxvi form a distinct code, in which ritual and ethical precepts are combined. The dominant theme is expressed in the formula, 'Ye shall be holy: for I the Lord your God am holy' (xix. 2); and these laws are commonly known as the Holiness Code. The last chapter of the book (xxvii) contains regulations for the commutation of vows and tithes.

The variety of material in Numbers, and the absence of any clear principle of arrangement or coherent sequence of events, make it difficult to characterize or summarize. The title of the book is derived from the account of the census with which it opens. The disposition of the camp is then described; and there follow laws mainly concerned with priests and Levites, and with points of ritual (i. 1–x. 10). The section x. 11–xvii. 18 describes events during the wilderness wanderings, including the bestowing of the spirit on seventy elders, the vindication of Moses against the jealousy of Aaron and Miriam, the reconnaissance of Palestine, and the revolt of Dathan and Abiram and of Korah and his followers. Within this narrative framework comes a group of laws in xv. xviii contains laws about priests and Levites. xix, which is something of an erratic boulder, is concerned with the removal of pollution caused by contact with the dead. A narrative section follows (xx–xxv), relating, *inter alia*, the punishment of Moses and Aaron and the death of Aaron, the plague of fiery serpents, the victories over Sihon, king of the Amorites, and Og, the king of Bashan, and the fruitless attempts of Balak to induce Balaam to curse Israel. The remainder of the book (xxvi–xxxvi) is composed of miscellaneous narratives and laws.

In contrast with the rather formless variety of Numbers, Deuteronomy presents a remarkable unity of theme and a recognizable pattern. The name of the book is derived from an erroneous Greek translation of a phrase in xvii. 18. The Hebrew means 'a copy of this law'; but the Greek Bible renders, 'this second lawgiving' (τὸ δευτερονόμιον τοῦτο). Almost the entire book purports to be a long address delivered by Moses to the Israelites on the eve of their entry into the Promised Land. It can be divided into three main sections: (a) i–xi; (b) xii–xxvi; (c) xxvii–xxxiv. The first of these consists of two prefaces, i. 1–iv. 40 [1] and iv. 44–xi. 32, in which past history is appealed to as a witness to God's love for Israel, a love to which Israel must respond by obedience. These chapters are, in fact, expositions of the historical events and the general principles on which the specific laws of the central part of the book are based. Two passages are of special significance. In v there is a version of the Decalogue which differs significantly from Exod. xx at two points. In vi. 4 f we have the great summary of the Law. The central part of

---

[1] iv. 41–43 does not fit into the context.

the book contains specific laws, religious, civil, and criminal. Amid all the multiplicity of detail, two characteristics stand out: Israel's worship is to be centralized at one legitimate sanctuary; and its religion is to be purged of all heathen contamination. The third section contains two chapters of blessing and curse (xxvii. f), two chapters of reminders and warnings (xxix. f), Moses' farewell (xxxi), the Song of Moses (xxxii), the Blessing of Moses (xxxiii), and the narrative of Moses' death (xxxiv).

## 2. *Analysis*

The division of the Torah into five books goes back at least to pre-Christian times, for it is found in the Greek Bible. That the books have a literary unity is assumed by the traditional Jewish and Christian belief that Moses was their author. No such claim is made in the books themselves, though in one or two passages Moses is said to have made specific written records (Exod. xvii. 14; xxiv. 4; xxxiv. 27; Num. xxxiii. 2; Deut. xxxi. 9, 24), or to have 'spoken' certain passages (Deut. i. 5; iv. 45; xxxi. 30). But many features in the books cannot be reconciled with Mosaic authorship.

First, some passages imply the standpoint of a much later age. The statement in Gen. xii. 6 (cf. xiii. 7) that 'the Canaanite was then in the land', is presumably later than the Canaanite régime in Palestine. Gen. xiv. 14, which mentions Danite territory in the north of the country, must be later than the migration of the tribe during the period of the Judges (Josh. xix. 47; Judges xviii. 29). Gen. xxxvi. 31 ff refers to Edomite kings, who reigned before the establishment of the Hebrew monarchy; and therefore it cannot be earlier than that date. The Israelite occupation of Canaan is implied both by Deut. i. 1 (cf. Gen. l. 10 f; Num. xxii. 1), which refers to Transjordania from the standpoint of one living west of Jordan, and also by Deut. ii. 12, which speaks of 'the land of his (Israel's) possession, which the Lord gave unto them'.

Second, there are features which suggest that these five books are not the product of a single author or of a single age. The same events are sometimes described more than once, with significant differences; and plain contradictions occur even within single stories, in such a way as to point to the interweaving of varying traditions or written records.

Gen. i. 1–ii. 4a gives a different account of creation from that contained in Gen. ii. 4b–25. In the one, plants and animals are created before man, and man and woman are created together. In the other, man is formed first, and only after plants and animals have been made is he provided with 'an help meet for him' in woman.

In the story of the Flood, Noah is in one place told to take into the Ark one pair of each kind of animal, but in another he is told to take seven pairs of each kind of clean beast and one pair of each unclean species (Gen. vi. 19 f; vii. 2 f). The Flood is said to have lasted a year and ten days (Gen. vii. 11, 24; viii. 13a, 14); but elsewhere its duration is reckoned as forty days, plus three periods of seven days, making a total of only sixty-one days (Gen. vii. 4; viii. 6–12).

We are twice told that Abraham passed his wife off as his sister, once in Egypt (Gen. xii. 10–20) and again in Gerar (Gen. xx). A similar story is told of Isaac and Rebekah in Gerar (Gen. xxvi. 6–14). There are also two accounts of how Hagar was driven out from Abraham's household (Gen. xvi. 4–14; xxi. 8, 21); and, although it is not impossible that two separate incidents are described, the points of similarity are remarkable.

Again, the naming of Beersheba and Bethel are each referred to two distinct occasions (Gen. xxi. 22–34; xxvi. 26–34; xxviii. 19; xxxv. 14 f).

In the story of Joseph, we read that *Reuben* tried to save Joseph's life by persuading the brothers to put him into a pit alive, and that *Judah* also sought to prevent murder by suggesting that Joseph should be sold to a passing caravan of *Ishmaelites*. But the immediate sequel speaks of *Midianites*, who took Joseph out of the pit, and, as it appears from the present form of the narrative,[1] sold him to the Ishmaelites,

[1] It is probable that the original subject of the verb 'sold', in Gen xxxvii, 28, was not the Midianites, but Joseph's brothers.

who then took him to Egypt (Gen. xxxvii. 18–28). Later, however, we are told that it was the *Midianites* who sold him into servitude (Gen. xxxvii. 36; cf. xxxix. 1). Meanwhile, Reuben, apparently unaware of Judah's proposal and its sequel, returned, as he had intended, to rescue Joseph from the pit, only to find it empty. The confusion of the story is explained, if we suppose that two accounts of the events have been fused, in one of which the brothers, on Judah's advice, sold Joseph to the Ishmaelites, who then took him to Egypt, whereas, in the other, Reuben's attempt to save Joseph was foiled by the unexpected arrival of the Midianites, who, unknown to the brothers, removed Joseph from the pit and carried him off.

These examples are all taken from Genesis; but similar duplicate passages and inconsistencies occur in the legal and ritual parts of the other books of the Pentateuch. Exod. xxxiii. 7–11 describes a Tent of Meeting, which was erected outside the camp, and was entrusted to Joshua's care (cf. Num. xi. 16 ff; xii. 4 ff); but there is also an account of a much more elaborate structure, attended by a large staff of Levites, and always placed in the centre of the tribes, whether they were encamped or on the march (Exod. xxv–xxxi; xxxv–xl; Num. i. 50–iv. 49). Exod. xx. 24 presupposes a number of altars in different parts of the land; but, according to Deut. xii. 13 f, sacrifice may be legitimately offered at only one place. In Deut. xviii. 6–8, we read that all Levites may perform priestly functions; and this is assumed throughout Deuteronomy; but in Exod. xxviii. 1 ff, only those Levites who belong to Aaron's house are regarded as priests; and in Num. iii. 5–10, the offering of a sacrifice by any others is made a capital offence.

One of the most significant discrepancies concerns the use of different terms for God. In Exod. vi. 2 f, we read, 'And God appeared to Moses and said to him, "I am Yahweh; and I appeared to Abraham, to Isaac, and to Jacob as El Shaddai; but by My name Yahweh I did not make Myself known to them".' But Gen. iv. 1 and 26 imply the use of the name

Yahweh from very early times; and in Gen. xv. 7 and xxviii. 18 God says to Abraham and to Jacob, 'I am Yahweh'. We note, too, that in some passages *'Elōhîm* is used for God, and the name *Yahweh* does not occur; whereas in others *Yahweh* is the term employed.

This leads to the third important fact, namely, that there are differences in vocabulary and style in various parts of both the narratives and the laws. Arguments based on such linguistic and literary factors are often regarded as subjective and inconclusive. Admittedly, they must be judiciously applied. An author's style will vary considerably according to his subject, and may well be appreciably modified during the course of his life. Again, an author may, on occasion, deliberately assume a style appropriate to the period about which he is writing, a device which is perhaps employed by the unknown author of the book of Ruth. But the striking thing about the variations of style and vocabulary in the Pentateuch is that they correspond with other differences, and therefore strengthen the case for diversity of authorship.

In Gen. i. 1–ii. 4a, the style is formal, precise, clear-cut, and dignified, though somewhat repetitious. In ii. 4b–25, it is more free and vivid. In the one account *'Elōhîm* is used for the Deity; and His activity is several times described by the distinctive term *bārā'*, 'he created', as well as by the more general term *'āśâh*, 'he made'. In the other, *bārā'* does not occur at all; but we find instead the word *yāṣar*, 'he formed', which depicts the work of a craftsman, such as a potter. This later account refers to God as *Yahweh 'Elōhîm*.

The word *mîn*, 'kind', which is never used in ii. 4b–25, occurs several times in i. 1–ii. 4a. It is found in only a few passages in the Old Testament; and its next appearance is in the story of the Flood, in two places (vi. 20; vii. 14), where we recognize the precise, repetitious, formal style of Gen. i. In the first of these passages (vi. 9–22), we notice, too, the expression 'male and female' (*zākār ûneḳēbâh*), and the word *'Elōhîm*. We have already seen that the number of the animals to be taken into the Ark, as given in vi. 19 f, cannot

easily be reconciled with vii. 1–5. It is, therefore, the more
significant that, in the latter passage, 'the male and his
female' represents a different Hebrew phrase (*'iš weištô*), and
that *Yahweh*, not *'Elōhîm*, is the term for the Deity. Further,
the beginning of vi. 9–22 repeats in part the sense of vi. 5–8,
but differs from it in using *'Elōhîm* instead of *Yahweh*, and
*hišhît*, 'he destroyed', instead of *māhâh* (lit. 'he blotted out').

These are but a few of the ways in which repetitions and
discrepancies in substance correspond with variations in style
and vocabulary.[1] By contrast, another important feature is
the homogeneity and consistency of Deuteronomy. If we
omit the poetical passages at the end, and possibly a few
other sections, we find that the book is written in a distinctive
style, in which an essentially simple diction is used with the
maximum of emphasis and rhetorical effect. Here, as nowhere else in the Pentateuch, the unity of God's being is
presented with uncompromising clarity. Here, too, sacrificial
worship is limited to one un-named sanctuary (Deut. xii. 14,
contrast Exod. xx. 24); and the legitimate priesthood is
identical with the Levites (Deut. xviii. 7; contrast Exod.
xxviii. 1; Num. iii. 5–10). By its internal consistency and by
the significant ways in which it differs from the rest of the
Pentateuch, Deuteronomy may be seen to have a distinctive
character.

From the above data we may conclude:

1. that the Pentateuch in its present form comes from a
later age than that of Moses;
2. that it is not a homogeneous work, but contains
different strata;
3. that the bulk of Deuteronomy probably forms a
special source.

In recent years, many rival theories have been advanced as
solutions of the problem of the Pentateuch; and the claim

---

[1] For further detail, reference should be made to S. R. Driver's *Introduction to the Literature of the Old Testament* or to any of the more
detailed commentaries on the books of the Pentateuch.

has often been made that 'the higher criticism of the Pentateuch' has been demolished. But, whatever differences of
opinion there may be about the character of the strata
(whether written or oral), their extent, date, and origin, the
first two conclusions just mentioned must form the basis of
any reasoned theory about the Pentateuch; and the third is
scarcely less fundamental.

The diversity of contemporary theory is more easily understood and assessed in the light of the history of scholarship.
There are certain well-marked phases in the study of the
Pentateuch during the past three or two centuries. In the
latter part of the 17th and practically the whole of the 18th
centuries various forms of *the older documentary hypothesis*
were advanced. These were based on the kind of data mentioned above, which were held to indicate the use of more
than one documentary source in the production of the
Pentateuch. Some combined this theory with belief in Mosaic
authorship, the sources being held to be earlier than his time.

At the end of the 18th and the beginning of the 19th
centuries there was, for a time, a change of approach. Many
passages in the books may be treated as self-contained; and
this led to the formulation of *the fragment hypothesis*, according to which the Pentateuch had been put together out of a
large number of fragments of varying length. This theory
took full account of the diversity of material, but hardly
did justice to the architectonic quality, which, for all their
diversity, the books reveal.

Adequate allowance was made for this factor by *the supplement hypothesis*. On this view, the bulk of the Pentateuch
consists of a single document (*Grundschrift*), which uses
'*Elōhîm*, and which is supplemented by later material, in
which *Yahweh* is used. In its strictest form, this theory fails
to account for the consecutive character of the *Yahweh*
passages.

During the third quarter of the 19th century, rapid ad-
vances were made in the delimitation of the sources and the
determining of their dates. Previously, the general tendency

had been to separate the passages in which $'El\bar{o}h\hat{\imath}m$ is used from those in which $Yahweh$ occurs, and to regard the former as of earlier origin. But now it was argued by some (reviving an earlier suggestion) that the $'El\bar{o}h\hat{\imath}m$ passages were not homogeneous, but belonged to two different sources. These passages do not all reveal the formal and exact style, which, as we have seen, characterizes the opening chapter of Genesis; and many divergences in character and content point to the existence of two Elohistic strands. Thus it came to be held that *four* main sources had gone to the making of the Pentateuch: the two sources which use $'El\bar{o}h\hat{\imath}m$ (now known as P and E), the source which uses $Yahweh$ from the beginning (now known as J), and the bulk of Deuteronomy (commonly referred to as D). Thus emerged *the new documentary hypothesis*.

In this phase of the discussion, further important developments took place. It was recognized that the problem was not only a literary one in the narrower sense, but a historical one. Granted that these sources existed and could be partly reconstructed by analysis of the texts, was there any evidence of their age? It had been assumed that the Elohistic source which appears in Gen. i (P)[1] was the oldest of all, an assumption which is particularly evident in the supplement hypothesis, and that the Yahwistic source was later. The book of Deuteronomy had for long been associated with the book of the Law which was found in the temple in the reign of King Josiah (2 Kings xxii), since its contents seemed to agree with the main features of the reform which the king subsequently carried out. The identification of Deuteronomy with that Law book was not new. It had been made by Jerome and Chrysostom; and it is, of course, possible to make the identification and yet to hold that this book was written long before, but, having been hidden or lost, was rediscovered in the reign of Josiah. But it was now held that the book had been produced only a short time before its discovery; that it

[1] The symbols J, E, D, P, had not yet come into use, but are employed here in the interests of clarity.

was, in fact, a 7th-century composition. Clearly, if this theory could be substantiated, an important point of dating would be established.

Historical criticism was also applied to a much wider range of evidence. The testimony of the historical books to the worship and religious institutions of Israel at different periods was compared with the contents of the various codes of law in the Pentateuch; and it was concluded that the Elohistic source, which had hitherto been regarded as the oldest of all (P), was, in fact, the latest; that the source which used Yahweh (J) was the oldest; that the other Elohistic source (E) came second, and Deuteronomy (D) third.

The main arguments in support of this position are as follows. Deuteronomy forbids sacrificial worship except at one central sanctuary. The laws in J and E appear to know nothing of such a prohibition. The historical narratives seem to show that, in the time of the judges and the early monarchy, pious Israelites like Samuel and Elijah knew nothing of it either, since they offered sacrifice and even erected altars in various parts of the country (e.g., 1 Sam. vii. 9 f; xvi. 5; 1 Kings xviii. 32 f). This gives the impression that this law was unknown during the greater part of the period of the monarchy; and the emphasis laid on the law in Deuteronomy does suggest that it is comparatively new. In the laws in the other Elohistic source (P), however, the restriction of sacrificial worship to one sanctuary is not explicitly prescribed, but tacitly assumed, which suggests that it was now a well-established usage. This seems to point to the chronological order mentioned above.

Again, in Deuteronomy, priests and Levites are identified: all priests are Levites and all Levites are priests. This identification is not made in J or E; and again, in the historical narratives of the period of the Judges and the early monarchy, we find that, although it may have been desirable that a priest should be a Levite, it was by no means essential (Judges xvii. 5; 2 Sam. viii. 18; xx. 26). On the other hand, the other Elohistic source (P) limits the priesthood to those

Levites who belong to the house of Aaron (Exod. xxviii. 1;
Num. iii. 5–10). In the last nine chapters of Ezekiel, which
describe the religious institutions which are to be established
in the restored Israel, the priesthood is limited to the family
of Zadok (Ezek. xl. 46; xliii. 19; xliv. 15). This appears to
be an attempt to limit the priesthood more narrowly than
Deuteronomy had done. But the attempt was not successful;
for the Aaronid priesthood is the one we find established in
post-exilic Israel. This arrangement is in accord with P, a
further indication that it is the latest source.

Thus there was established, to the satisfaction of a large
number of scholars, the view that the Pentateuch contains
four main sources, J, E, D, and P, which are to be dated in
that order, with D, as the fixed point, assigned to the 7th
century. This chronology, reversing the earlier view that P
was the oldest of the sources, is the Graf-Wellhausen theory,
so called from the names of the two scholars (Karl Heinrich
Graf and Julius Wellhausen) who advanced it with such
cogency.

Later scholarship, in so far as it has not been directly
opposed to this theory, has been concerned with more precise
delimination and analysis of the sources and with the attempt
to discover the process by which they came into existence,
were transmitted, and, finally, were combined to give us the
Pentateuch as we now have it. In spite of considerable
diversity of view on such points, comparatively few scholars
would deny the existence of these four main blocks of
material. We therefore examine their extent and characteristics.[1]

The source which uses the divine name Yahweh from the
beginning is called the Yahwistic or Jahvistic source, and is
indicated by the symbol J. The material attributed to it
includes the following: the Creation (second account), the

[1] In the account of the sources given here, the lists of passages are not
exhaustive; but are intended to indicate only the main contents. For
details, the commentaries and larger introductions should be consulted.
An asterisk denotes conflation of the sources.

Fall, Cain and Abel; the sons of God and the daughters of men; parts of the Flood story; Noah and his sons; parts of the table of nations; the Tower of Babel; the call of Abraham, his journey into Egypt and return to Palestine; his separation from Lot; Yahweh's promise to Abraham and His covenant with him; Sarah and Hagar; Abraham's divine visitors and the destruction of Sodom and Gomorrah; the story of Rebekah; the birth of Esau and Jacob; Isaac and Abimelech; Isaac's blessing of Jacob and Esau; Jacob at Bethel; Jacob in Haran; Jacob and his wives; his wrestling at Peniel and his meeting with Esau; the outrage at Shechem (in part); the selling of Joseph into servitude (in part); Judah and Tamar; Joseph and Potiphar's wife; Joseph in power (in part); the blessing of Jacob; the burial of Jacob; the oppression in Egypt (in part); parts of the story of Moses' early life, exile, call, and return to Egypt; the turning of the water into blood; the plagues of frogs, flies, murrain, hail, locusts, darkness, and the death of the first-born (in part); the Passover (in part); the Exodus and the crossing of the sea; Moses' song; manna; water given at Massah; arrival at Sinai; Moses and elders on Sinai; the Levites' zeal; Moses' intercession; Moses' converse with Yahweh; the giving of the Law; the departure from Sinai; the spies (in part); the revolt of Dathan and Abiram (in part); the waters of Meribah (in part); the by-passing of Edom and battles against the Canaanites (in part); parts of the Balaam story; the apostasy at Shittim (in part); the settlement east of Jordan (in part); and possibly parts of the concluding chapters of Deuteronomy (Gen. ii. 4b–iv. 26; vi. 1–4; vi. 5–viii. 22*; ix. 18–27; x. 8–19, 25–80; xi. 1–9; xii* and most of xiii; most of xv; most of xvi; xviii and xix; xxiv; xxv. 21–84; xxvi; xxvii; xxviii. 18–16; xxix. 2–14, 81–35; xxx*; xxxii. 1–xxxiii. 17; xxxiv*; xxxvii*; xxxviii; xxxix; xliii–xliv; xlvi. 28–34; most of xlvii; xlix. 1–27; l. 1–11; Exod. i. 8–12; ii–v*; vii–xi*; xii. 21–89*; xiii–xiv*; xv*; xvi*; xix*; xxiv*; xxxii. 25–85; xxxiii. 12–28; xxxiv. 1–28; Num. x. 29–82; xiii*; xiv*; xvi*; xx*; xxi*; xxii–xxiv*; xxv. 1–5*; xxxii*; (?) Deut. xxxiv*).

As we have seen, these passages are marked by special characteristics and style. The name Yahweh is used from the beginning; the Mount of God is called Sinai; the pre-Israelite inhabitants are called Canaanites; and the third patriarch's name is given as Israel, rather than Jacob. The narrative style is one of the most brilliant and effective in the whole Bible. Light, vivid, and graceful, it presents the action with masterly economy and simplicity. The Yahwist has an uncanny power of suggesting a scene without actually describing it in detail, of taking us to the heart of a human situation by the sheer brevity and directness of his narrative (see, e.g., the story of Rebekah in Gen. xxiv, and that of Joseph and Potiphar's wife in Gen. xxxix). The greatest of the Gospel stories trace their literary ancestry to him.

This artistry is matched by a profound religious and theological insight. Moderns have often commented on the boldness of the Yahwist's anthropomorphisms: God, like a craftsman, fashions man (Gen. ii. 7). He walks in the garden when the heat of the day is tempered by the cool breeze (iii. 8); He shuts the door of the Ark (vii. 16), smells the pleasant odour of Noah's sacrifice (viii. 21), and comes down to see the tower of Babel and to punish its builders (xi. 5, 7). This should not be attributed to any theological naïveté in the Yahwist. Anthropomorphism, in one form or another, appears throughout the Old Testament, and is one of the means by which God is presented as personal and as accessible to man. It is true that the instances just quoted differ from the anthropomorphism of metaphor and simile. But these vivid simplicities (some of which, at least, belong to the raw material inherited by the Yahwist) are redeemed from theological crudity by the spiritual insight which marks the J material as a whole.

That material may be divided into four categories: myth, clan history, national history, and law. The clan history includes traditions about the fathers as individuals; but sometimes it is the experiences and achievements of clan and nation that are presented in individual terms (e.g., Gen.

xxxiv). These traditions are bound together by the sense of
Israel's vocation, expressed in the promises to the fathers and
God's providential direction of their wanderings, and finding
its fulfilment in the national deliverance from Egypt and the
settlement in Canaan.

This narrative is given a universal setting by the remarkable series of myths from the Creation to the Tower of Babel.
Non-Israelite traditions underlie these passages. But in their
Israelite context they are made to express the conflict of
the human will with the divine, the pride, self-will, and self-
sufficiency of man. Each catastrophe in the sequence of myths
is followed by a divine promise; and thus the promises to
Abraham and Israel are presented as part of God's providential and redemptive dealings with all mankind.

The living religious interest of the Yahwist appears in his
many references to the connexion of the fathers with sanctuary sites (e.g., Gen. xii. 7 f; xiii. 4, 18; xxvi. 25; xxxv. 14),
which are not merely antiquarian records, but reflect the
religious practice of his day.

He has also included the so-called Yahwistic Decalogue
(Exod. xxxiv. 12–26), a predominantly ritual code, which
appears in places to have been expanded. To make a decalogue of its present form requires either arithmetical or textual
juggling. It resembles the Decalogue of Exod. xx and Deut. v
in some of its requirements, but its content is ritual rather
than ethical. Hence it is often called the Ritual Decalogue, and
regarded as much earlier than the other. H. H. Rowley has
argued persuasively that it represents an ancient Kenite code,
modified to suit agricultural conditions, and preserved among
southern tribes who assimilated Yahwism from Kenite
neighbours.

The material is almost certainly of southern origin. (Hence
the symbol J is often connected with Judah.) A number of
references are made to the great southern sanctuary at
Hebron (Gen. xiii. 18; xxxvii. 14). The patriarch Judah plays
a prominent part in the Joseph stories (cf. also the story in
Gen. xxxviii). In the Blessing of Jacob there appears to be an

allusion to the hegemony of the tribe of Judah under David (Gen. xlix. 8 ff; cf. Num. xxiv. 17).

The question of date is not easily settled, since due allowance must be made for older elements and later accretions. Arguments based on its place in the evolution of religious thought are nowadays given less weight than formerly. Though it cannot be denied that some religious ideas were more characteristic of one age than another, the evidence does not support any tidy theory of evolutionary development.

What has been said about the southern origin of J suggests that it is not earlier than David; and this is borne out by Gen. xxxvi. 31. Many have accepted *c.* 850 B.C. as a likely date. A rather earlier period is probably nearer the mark. The stories reflect a robust national confidence, appropriate to the age of liberation and expansion. There appears to be no reference to the disruption of the kingdom or to the existence of the temple. Gen. xxvii. 40 may well refer to the subjugation of Edom under David and the subsequent revolt against Solomon (2 Sam. viii. 14; 1 Kings xi. 14–22). The reign of David and the early part of the reign of Solomon appear, like the Elizabethan age, to have been a time of both material and literary achievement; and perhaps part of its legacy to us is the work of the Yahwist. The concentration of interest on the South may, however, suggest the period after the Disruption.

Of the two sources which avoid the name Yahweh before the time of Moses and use instead the word *'Elōhim,* one is known as the Elohistic source, and is designated by the symbol E. It is somewhat harder to determine the passages which may be attributed to it, partly because the stylistic distinction between J and E is a subtle one, and partly because the E material seems often to have been used merely to supplement the J narratives. But the following is probably a fair summary: parts of the story of God's covenant with Abraham; Abraham and Abimelech; Abraham, Sarah, and Hagar; the covenant with Abimelech at Beer-sheba; the offering of Isaac; Jacob at Bethel (in part); Jacob and his wives; Jacob and Laban; Jacob at Bethel and Shechem; the

selling of Joseph into servitude (in part); Joseph in power
(in part); the blessing of Ephraim and Manasseh; from the
death of Jacob to the death of Joseph; the oppression in
Egypt (in part); parts of the story of Moses' early life, call,
and return to Egypt; the turning of the water into blood; the
plagues of hail, locusts, and darkness, and the prediction of
the death of the first-born (in part); the Exodus and the
crossing of the sea (in part); the Song of Miriam; the waters
of Marah; Meribah; the defeat of Amalek; Jethro's visit; the
theophany at Sinai (in part); the Decalogue and the Book of
the Covenant; Moses on the Mount of God; the golden calf;
Moses' converse with Yahweh (in part); the guiding Ark;
complaints in the wilderness; the seventy elders; the rebellion
of Aaron and Miriam, and the vindication of Moses; the spies
(in part); the waters of Meribah (in part); the by-passing of
Edom, and battles against the Canaanites (in part); parts of
the Balaam story; apostasy at Shittim (in part); and possibly
parts of the concluding chapters of Deuteronomy. (Gen. xv*;
xx; xxi; xxii; xxviii*; xxix*; xxx*; xxxi; xxxv. 1–8;
xxxvii*; xl–xlii; xlv. 1–xlvi. 5; xlviii. 1 f; 8–22; l. 15–26;
Exod. i. 15–22; ii–v*; vii–x*; xiii*; xiv*; xv. 20–27; xvii*;
xviii; xix*; xx–xxiii; xxiv*; xxxii. 1–24; xxxiii*; Num. x.
33–36; xi. 1–6; xi. 16–30*; xii. 1–15; xiii*; xiv*; xvi*; xx*;
xxi*; xxii–xxiv*; xxv. 1–5*; (?) Deut. xxxiii*; (?) xxxiv*.

The widely-held view that the E material begins with the
patriarchal stories has been challenged by S. Mowinckel, who
holds that there are traces of E in Gen. i–xi. But there does
not appear to be sufficient evidence to justify this conclusion.
The same scholar had previously advanced the view that the
E is simply a revision of the J traditions; and Volz and
Rudolph (the latter less radically) have also denied that E is
a separate stratum. It is true that the E material is sometimes
difficult to distinguish from J, and, when it has been identified, often seems to consist of fragmentary variations of the
J stories. But, as we shall see, there are probably historical
reasons for this; and, though less seems to have been preserved of E than J, the passages listed above point to the

existence of an independent sequence of traditions, with a distinctive emphasis and outlook.

The diction of E is marked by the use before Exod. iii of *'Elōhîm* or *hā'Elōhîm* for the Deity. The pre-Israelite inhabitants of Canaan are called Amorites; the Mount of God is referred to as Horeb.[1] Jacob is the name used of the third patriarch. The difference in style between E and J is a subtle one, and easier to sense than to describe or define. A good example of E is Gen. xl–xlii. Even at its best, E is inferior to J in strength and vividness.

The core of the religious teaching of E is identical with that of J: the story of God's special purpose for Israel, of their deliverance from Egypt, and His providential leading of them to Canaan.

The importance of the central events in this epic of salvation is emphasized in a number of ways, of which the most striking is the revelation to Moses of the name Yahweh, the implication being that it was previously unknown to the Hebrews. The miraculous element is heightened in the stories of the plagues (Exod. iii–v; vii–x); and the traditions about the work and character of Moses are more detailed. There are signs of theological and ethical reflection, God's converse with man is less direct than in J, His message being conveyed by dreams, by His angel, and by prophets. He also instructs man by testing him (Gen. xxii. 1 ff; Exod. xv. 25b; xx. 20). His judgements in history have a moral character (Gen. xv. 16; Exod. xxxii. 34). Moral blemishes in the conduct of the patriarchs are toned down (Gen. xx. 12; xxi. 11–14; xxxi. 6 f). There are warnings against the danger of alien worship (Gen. xxxv. 2, 4; Exod. xix. 5 f; xxxii. 21); and although the stone pillars which were characteristic of Canaanite worship are not condemned, their pagan associations seem largely to have been lost (Gen. xxviii. 22; Exod. xxiv. 4).

E includes a form of the Decalogue, which is probably of considerable antiquity, and may well be in substance Mosaic.

[1] This has been contested by Noth, *Ueberlieferungsgeschichtliche Studien I*, p. 20, n. 4.

The reason given for observing the Sabbath is clearly connected with the P story of Creation; but this is evidence of later expansion of this law, not of late authorship of the entire code.

E also contains the interesting short law book known as the Book of the Covenant (Exod. xx. 22–xxiii. 33), which presupposes the conditions of a settled agricultural community. Similarities between this code and the Code of Hammurabi have often been noted; and, more recently, it has been argued that its affinities, not only with Babylonian but with Hittite and Assyrian codes, ultimately go back to Sumerian law. It seems probable that some Canaanite code was the immediate source from which Israel borrowed much of the content of the Book of the Covenant; but it is significant that the familiar form of the civil law of the ancient Near East, 'if a man . . .', 'if thou . . .' (casuistic law) is here blended with the categorical form, 'thou shalt', 'thou shalt not' (apodictic law), in which the individual is confronted by the divine authority.[1]

E probably comes from the Northern Kingdom. There are many signs of special interest in the northern and central tribes, and especially in Ephraim (with which the symbol E is often connected), the more influential of the two Joseph tribes. We hear more about Jacob than in J, and less about Abraham. Much of the Joseph story comes from E; and Reuben (not Judah, as in J) is specially prominent among Joseph's brothers. The sanctuaries at Bethel and Shechem are mentioned; and we also hear of Beersheba, which, as Amos implies (v. 5; viii. 14), was frequented by the central tribes, though it was in the far south.

Since the Northern Kingdom fell in 721 B.C., it seems likely that E should be dated earlier than that event. Probably fugitives from the north came to Judah bringing their religious traditions with them. When these traditions were combined with those of Judah, it would be natural for the latter to form the basis, and for additions from the northern

---

[1] Cf. A. Alt. *Die Ursprünge des israelitischen Rechts*, 1934, now reprinted in *Kleine Schriften* I, pp. 278–332.

material to be used when some interesting variant had to be preserved or some gap filled. This seems to be a likely and adequate explanation of the fragmentary character of many of the passages.

But when did E originate? The protest against pagan religious practice echoes the kind of protest which was made in the Northern Kingdom at least as early as Elijah, and probably earlier. There seem to be no allusions to the Assyrian menace. Weiser has suggested the period of comparative calm in the early part of the eighth century. This is as likely a period as any.

Few traces of the Deuteronomic source (D) are to be found in the first four books of the Pentateuch.[1] To it is attributed the bulk of Deuteronomy, the exceptions commonly made being xxvii; xxix; xxx; xxxi. 1–8, 14–30; xxxii–xxxiv.

The diction of D is fundamentally simple; but the same familiar words and phrases, recurring frequently, are nearly as characteristic as a more *recherché* vocabulary might be: 'to observe to (and) do', 'take heed to thyself', 'a mighty hand and a stretched out arm', 'which I am commanding thee this day', 'that thy days may be long'. This use of ordinary words in characteristic phrases produces an impressive rhetorical simplicity and emphasis, which appear not only in the hortatory sections in the opening chapters, but also in the explanatory comments which accompany the laws.

The narrative and hortatory preambles (i–iv; v–xi) describe Yahweh's past goodness to Israel, and present Him as the one Lord, who claims of His people undivided allegiance, as one who loves Israel[2] and claims an answering love towards Himself and towards others, especially towards the needy and defenceless. This teaching is reflected in the laws (xii–xxvi).

Israel's allegiance to Yahweh must be expressed in a pure cult, free from heathen contamination. A vigorous polemic is

---

[1] Exod. xii. 24–27; xiii. 1–6; xxxii. 7–14; Num. xxi. 32–35; cf. Deut. iii. 1–3.

[2] The verb used is *'āhēb*. It is noteworthy that 'choose' (*bāhar*) is also one of the characteristic words. Israel's election is given clear expression in D.

waged against Canaanite and other pagan religious practices
(xii. 29–31; xiii; xiv. 1 f; xvi. 21 f; xvii. 2–7; xviii. 9–14).
In this, D carries further the religious teaching of E. The
similarities and differences between many of the laws in D
and those in the Book of the Covenant are clear and significant. Not only does D represent later development; it adds
to the laws some religious comment and exhortation (cf.
xv. 12 ff with Exod. xxi. 2–6; and xix. 1–18 with Exod.
xxi. 12 ff). One interesting and distinctive feature in D is the
legislation about kings and prophets, which is clearly based
on experience and aimed at maintaining religious purity (xiii.
1–5; xvii. 14–20; xviii. 9–22).

Doubtless it is also to preserve the purity of the cult that
sacrificial worship is limited to one legitimate sanctuary,
where Yahweh has chosen to cause His name to dwell. This is
stated at the beginning of the code (xii. 1 ff), a clear sign of
its importance; and it is frequently echoed or alluded to. It
appears strikingly in the command to observe the Passover,
which had been, as it was later, a domestic festival (xvi. 1–8).

This law had two important sequels. Previously the
slaughter of domestic animals had been a sacrificial act; and
only after the fat and the blood had been offered might the
flesh be eaten. But now that there was only one legitimate
place for sacrifice, a distinction was made between slaughter
for sacrifice and slaughter solely for food (secular slaughter).
The latter was permitted anywhere, provided the blood was
not consumed but poured out on the ground (xii. 20–27).

The second sequel affected the priests. We have seen that in
D all Levites are priests. Now, the suppression of local sanctuaries deprived the provincial priests of their living. Provision
was therefore made for any who came to the central sanctuary
to perform priestly functions there and to receive priestly
dues (xviii. 6–8). The economic consequences of the law of
centralization also account for the frequent commending of
'the Levite that is within thy gates' to the charity of the
Israelite.

Concern for the needy is a frequent theme in D. This

humane spirit contrasts sharply with the implacable attitude
adopted to apostasy. Apostasy means contempt of what
Yahweh has done for Israel. To care for the needy is to copy
Yahweh's saving love to Israel, and to reflect His own care
for the afflicted (see especially x. 18 f). The humanitarianism
of Deuteronomy has a firm theological foundation.[1]

The entire religious emphasis of D suggests that it represents an attempt to systematize and unify the religious traditions of Israel. Its theme has been neatly summarized in the
German phrase, *ein Gott, ein Volk, ein Kult*. But the systema-
tization is no mere pedantic exercise. No word is more
characteristic of Deuteronomy than 'to-day': it asks for
choice, response, obedience now. The results of obedience or
apostasy are national prosperity or disaster. This is made
plain in terms which are echoed in the historical books, and
which, rigorously applied to the individual, provide part of
the theme of Job.

The identification of D with the law book found in the
temple in the reign of Josiah is not an exclusively modern
view (for it was held by some of the Fathers), nor does it
necessarily involve belief in the 7th-century origin of the law
code. But these two positions, previously advanced by de
Wette, were, as we have seen, of central importance for the
Graf-Wellhausen hypothesis.

The arguments for the identification of D (or part of it)
with Josiah's law book are clear. The consternation caused by
the reading of the book (2 Kings xxii. 11, 13, 16 f) is in keeping with the curses which D invokes on the disobedient and
apostate. The religious measures adopted by Josiah correspond to leading features in the Deuteronomic legislation: the
suppression of local sanctuaries (2 Kings xxiii. 8 f. 19; cf.
Deut. xii. 13 f), of the worship of the heavenly bodies (2 Kings

---

[1] It is, of course, true that some laws which seem to be prompted by
humane motives originally had a very different basis in primitive religious thought (e.g. xx. 1–9). But the original point of such rules may
not always have been as plain to the Israelite as it is to the modern
scholar. It is sometimes a mistake to credit the Biblical writers with
detailed knowledge of the comparative study of religion.

xxiii. 11 f; cf. Deut. xvii. 2 ff), of sacred prostitution (2 Kings xxiii. 7; cf. Deut. xxiii. 18), of divination and necromancy (2 Kings xxiii. 24; cf. Deut. xviii. 10 ff), and of child sacrifice (2 Kings xxiii. 10; cf. Deut. xviii. 10); and the celebration of the Passover at the temple (2 Kings xxiii. 21 ff; cf. Deut. xvi. 1–8). The law about the status of provincial priests (Deut. xviii. 6 f) was not carried out (2 Kings xxiii. 8 f); but practical difficulties (and possibly the exclusiveness of the Jerusalemite priests) may well account for this.

Some of the features just mentioned suggest that in its present form the code can hardly be much earlier than the 7th century. Child sacrifice and star worship were both rife in the bad days of Manasseh. The law of the single sanctuary was clearly unknown to pious Israelites of earlier ages. Many features in the code reflect the conditions of urban life: note especially the recurring phrase 'within thy gates'. The laws about prophets imply some experience of the prophetic movement; and the protest against Canaanite cult objects and practices is more detailed and radical than in the teaching of the great 8th-century prophets. The Deuteronomic teaching about the love of God suggests a connexion with Hosea. Some hold that a passage like xv. 1–18 implies the conditions of an earlier age, before the creation of the large estates which the prophets condemn. That some parts of the legislation in such a code should be older than others is quite natural. But we need not, therefore, date all of it so early. We have seen that the substance of many of the laws is already found in the Book of the Covenant; but the laws are modified, and explanatory comments are added. These additions are in the distinctive Deuteronomic style, which, on the whole, does not appear in the earlier Prophets, but is common in the book of Jeremiah and later.

The finding of a book which leads to a reform which corresponds to the laws; distinctive legislation which seems to have been unknown even to the pious before the end of the 8th century, and some of which applies particularly to 7th-century conditions; a distinctive style which is previously unknown, but which, from the last quarter of the 7th century, is commonly used in some circles: the evidence may not suffice for irrefutable demonstration; but it at least makes alternative theories improbable; and most scholars are content to hold that D is the code of the Deuteronomic reform, and that it came into its present form some time during the century preceding its discovery in the temple. But, during the past generation, other views have been suggested. G. Hölscher holds that Josiah sought to purify, and not to centralize the cult, and that the law of the single sanctuary would have been practicable only in a community occupying a limited territory. Accordingly he dates D about 500 B.C. Against this, it has been pointed out that the law continued to apply in later times, when the Jewish community in Palestine was again larger and more widely dispersed. Further, Hölscher's view forms part of a complex of theories, in support of which he has had to subject some of the Biblical documents to drastic handling, a fact which tells against the theories.

R. H. Kennett[1] also maintained that D must be later than the time of Josiah, and suggested that it was brought to Jerusalem by priests from Bethel, thus accounting for some features in the book which suggest northern origin.

The northern affinities of D were emphasized by A. C. Welch in an impressive plea for a much earlier date.[2] He held that the law of centralization appears only in xii. 1–7 ('the place which Yahweh your God shall choose *out of all* your tribes'), which he regarded as a later addition connected with Josiah's reform, and that in xii. 14 and elsewhere the legislation applies to the Yahwistic sanctuary in any given locality (interpreting the Hebrew phrase as 'the place which Yahweh thy God shall choose in *any* one of thy tribes'). A similar view was advanced by T. Oestreicher. On this earlier dating, the code aimed at the purification of the cult and the reform at

[1] *Deuteronomy and the Decalogue* (1920) = 'The Origin of the Book of Deuteronomy' in *The Church of Israel* (1933).
[2] *The Code of Deuteronomy* (1924).

its centralization. On Hölscher's dating, the reform aimed at purification and the code at centralization. On the latter view, 2 Kings xxiii. 8a, 9 has to be treated as a later addition. On the earlier dating, Deut. xii. 1–7 is secondary. Welch's study is remarkably stimulating; but his interpretation of the phrase in xii. 14 and elsewhere has not carried conviction. His view that the code contains much old material is not incompatible with the theory that it was put into its present form in the century before 621 B.C.

A still earlier date has been advocated by E. Robertson.[1] He thinks that Deuteronomy was put together, under the direction of Samuel, to serve as a coherent system of legislation when the monarchy was established. The varying traditions and usages of the local sanctuaries, now to be superseded, were collected and prefaced to Deuteronomy: hence the inconsistencies and repetitions of Genesis–Numbers. Solomon provided the central sanctuary which the code required; but his policy led to the split in the kingdom for which the code was intended. Its rediscovery in 621 coincided aptly with the hope of the reunion of all Israel.

The importance of sanctuaries in the formation of the sources has been increasingly recognized in recent years; and it is a further merit in the above theory that it recognizes that some inconsistencies may reflect the usage of different places rather than different periods. But, even if 1 Sam. x. 25 were sufficient evidence of Samuel's work as a compiler of laws, it would still be difficult to identify his new code with D. Why does D show knowledge of E, but not of the distinctive legislation of P; and why does P take D's law of centralization for granted?

These rival theories have been mentioned because they are representative of criticisms made of the central point in the Graf-Wellhausen hypothesis. General acceptance of any of them would mean the establishment of another critical theory, and not, be it noted, the vindication of the unity or the Mosaic authorship of the Pentateuch. But, in fact, all

[1] *The Old Testament Problem* (1950).

these theories involve greater difficulties than the one they
rival, though some of them include features which must find
a place in any final view of the code.

Like the other codes, D contains material from different
periods. It has undoubted affinities with the Northern Kingdom: the parallels with the Book of the Covenant (E); the
use of the term 'Amorites' for the pre-Israelite inhabitants of
Canaan, and of 'Horeb' for the mount of God (as in E); the
links with Hosea. But parts of it also reflect conditions in
7th-century Judah. Some of these features would be difficult
to account for on the view, which some have advanced, that
the book was a forgery, foisted on the nation at the time of
Josiah's reform. They can be more easily understood, if we
take into account two other events. The fall of the Northern
Kingdom in 721 must have driven south fugitives who were
pious Yahwists, who had memories of the bitter conflict with
paganism, who saw in their country's fall Yahweh's judgement on apostasy, and who brought with them northern
traditions. We have seen that E probably represents some of
that material; part of it may also be included in D. In the
same generation, Hezekiah carried through a programme of
cultic purification and centralization (2 Kings xviii. 3 f; there
is no need to question the historicity of this record), but
Hezekiah's reign was followed by an age of apostasy, in which
loyal Yahwists were persecuted. It may well be that in that
dark age the aims of Hezekiah's reforms were not only recorded, but adapted to the grosser paganism of the 7th
century, that the document was hidden, and then lost, only
to be rediscovered in the eighteenth year of Josiah. How
much of our present book of Deuteronomy was discovered is
uncertain: certainly the legislative kernel (xii–xxvi), and
almost certainly v–xi, which is so intimately linked with it.
The closing chapters contain material added later from other
sources. The narrative in i–iv, though Deuteronomic, may be
connected with the framework of Joshua–2 Kings (see below).

The importance of Deuteronomy in the history of Hebrew
religion can hardly be over-estimated. It gathered up some of

the best traditions of a Yahwism militant against pagan corruption. It proclaimed certain judgement on apostasy. When, for a time, Assyria's weakness made possible an independent policy, so that reform could be achieved and men might even dream of a reunited Kingdom, it summoned all Israel to the high standards of a Yahwism enriched by the prophetic movement. The liberty was shortlived. The work of the reform was undone. The stroke of judgement fell. But the reform had set a standard; and the book survived. Against the loose assertion that Josiah's reform failed must be set one plain historical fact: the finding of the book and the work of the reformers meant that the exiled community had standards other than those of Manasseh's reign.

The following are the chief passages assigned to P (the Priestly source, so called because of its dominant cultic interest): the Creation (first account); the genealogy Adam–Noah; parts of the Flood Story; parts of the table of nations; the genealogy Shem–Abraham; God's covenant with Abraham, and the institution of circumcision; the birth of Isaac; the purchase of the cave of Machpelah; the death of Abraham and the generations of Ishmael and Isaac; Jacob's departure to Paddan-aram; the outrage at Shechem (in part); God's promise to Jacob; Jacob's sons; the generations of Esau; Jacob's descendants; Jacob's adoption of Ephraim and Manasseh; Jacob's last words and death; the oppression in Egypt; God's revelation to Moses; Moses and Aaron sent to Pharaoh; water turned to blood; plagues of frogs, gnats, boils, and the death of the first-born; regulations for the Passover; the giving of manna and quails; instructions about the tabernacle, vestments, priests, offerings, etc.; Moses' descent from Sinai; the making of the tabernacle and its furniture, etc.; the priestly vestments; all Leviticus (laws about sacrifice, the priesthood, uncleanness and purification, holiness and the commutation of vows); the census; the duties of Levites; miscellaneous laws, including the ordeal of jealousy and the Nazarite rule; the offerings of the tribal leaders; the dedication of the Levites; Passover law; the spies (in part);

sundry ritual laws; revolt of Korah; vindication of the
Levites; status and prerogatives of Levites; ritual of the red
heifer; waters of Meribah (in part); the zeal of Phinehas; the
second census; the daughters of Zelophehad; Moses and his
successor; offerings at sacred seasons; women's vows; holy
war against Midian; the settlement of the Transjordanian
tribes; account of the route from Egypt to Jordan; laws for
the occupation of Canaan; and possibly part of the end of
Deuteronomy (Gen. i. 1–ii. 4a; v. 1–28, 30–32; vi. 9–ix. 17*;
x*; xi. 10–27; xvii; xxi. 3–5; xxiii; xxv. 7–20; xxvii. 46–
xxviii. 9; xxxiv*; xxxv. 9–13, 22b–29; xxxvi; xlvi. 6–27;
xlviii. 3–7; xlix. 28–33; Exod. i*; vi. 2–30; vii. 1–13; vii.
14–xi. 10*; xii. 1–20, 40–51; xvi*; xxv–xxxi; xxxiv. 29–35;
xxxv–xl; Lev. i–xxvii; Num. i–x; xiii*; xiv*; xv; xvi*; xvii–
xix; xx*; xxv. 6–xxxvi. 13; (?) Deut. xxxii*; (?) xxxiv.*

The distinctive style of this material is more obvious in
translation than its equally distinctive vocabulary. As examples of the latter we may note the verb 'to create' (*bārā'*);
the expression 'to *establish* (the) covenant' (*hēkîm bᵉrît*; contrast the usual *kārat bᵉrît*, 'to cut a covenant'); 'congregation'
('*ēdâh*); 'these are the generations of' ('*ēlleh tôlᵉdôt*). As in E,
'*Elōhîm* (not Yahweh) is used of God before the revelation to
Moses; but El Shaddai (commonly translated as 'God Al-
mighty') is also used. As in J, the Mount of God is called Sinai.

The precise, formal style has already been noted. Lists,
genealogies, exact measurements, and numbers occur frequently. Such details replace the vivid touches found in the
J narratives. A special group of lists is connected with the
expression 'these are the generations of', which *ends* the
creation story (Gen. ii. 4a), but *introduces* the references to
the progeny of Noah (Gen. vi. 9 f), Shem (Gen. xi. 10–26),
Terah (Gen. xi. 27), Ishmael (Gen. xxv. 12–17), Isaac (Gen.
xxv. 19 f), Esau (Gen. xxxvi), Jacob (Gen. xxxvii. 1, 2a);
compare also the reference to the generations of Aaron and
Moses (Num. iii. 1 ff).

Though similar to J in general narrative outline, P is very
different from it in outlook and approach. The transcendence

of God is emphasized. Gen. xxxv. 9 ff (cf. Exod. vi. 2 ff)
describes a theophany comparable to some found in the
earlier sources; but elsewhere in P God's presence is often
indicated by His Glory (*kābôḏ*), veiled by cloud (Exod. xxiv.
16 f; cf. xxxiv. 33–35). Anthropomorphisms are, on the whole,
avoided (but note, e.g., that God is said to *rest* on the seventh
day; Gen. ii. 2 f). The verb to create (*bārā'*) emphasizes the
distinctive character of the divine action in creation. The use
of the verb to establish (*hēḵîm*), with God as subject, makes
less of the reciprocal character of the covenant, and draws
attention to the divine initiative.

The transcendent God is approached through the mediation
of the priesthood and the ritual of the cult. In P, the priests
are the members of the House of Aaron (Exod. xxviii. 1); to
other members of the house of Levi subordinate duties at the
sanctuary are assigned. Ritual interest is prominent in P. Not
only is the greater part of it concerned with cultic legislation,
but many of the stories are explicitly connected with some
point of religious observance. The creation story leads up to
the institution of the Sabbath; the covenant with Noah is
connected with the prohibition of bloodshed, and the covenant with Abraham is linked with circumcision. In the stories
about the pre-Mosaic period, when the Law had not yet been
given, there is no reference to sacrifice or to the distinction
between clean and unclean. Thus history is related and
adapted to ritual instruction.

A distinctive style and outlook characterize Lev. xvii–xxvi
(the Holiness Code, H), which forms a special unit within P.
We have already noted the appeal for holiness which dominates this interesting collection of ethical and ritual precepts,
addressed to priests and people alternately. Its ethical
emphasis is summed up in the command 'Thou shalt love thy
neighbour as thyself' (xix. 18).

Though included in P, it has points of contact with D and
with Ezek. xl–xlviii, which raise intricate questions. The place
of this code in the history of Hebrew law cannot at present be
determined with anything like certainty. To mention only one

obvious difficulty, Lev. xvii. 8 ff emphatically forbids secular slaughter but assumes the centralization of the cult. D permits the former and enjoins the latter. It might be argued that H must be earlier than D, since it states the law of slaughter as it held before D. But against this it may be said that the emphatic prohibition of secular slaughter looks like a deliberate reversal of the law of D, and that it is therefore the later. This accords with the assumption in H of cultic centralization as something to be taken for granted. The difficult question of the relation of H to Ezek. xl–xlviii cannot be discussed here. It calls for detailed examination; and no really convincing theory has yet been offered.

How old is P? Before attempting to answer this question it is well to ask what it means. Any document which contains legal material of the kind and scope which we find in P is unlikely to be entirely the product of a single generation, but will include material of varying antiquity and reflect the usage of many generations. To show that any individual law or custom is of great antiquity is not decisive for the date of the entire source. To determine the latter, we must ask when the material was assembled and given its present general character. However old certain individual elements in P may be, the case for dating the process of codification in the period after the Exile is strong.

The evidence for putting P later than D and not earlier than Ezekiel xl–xlviii has been stated above (p. 80). These latter chapters (whether attributed to Ezekiel or to another) cannot be earlier than the 6th century. On the other hand, the book of the Law which Ezra brought with him to Jerusalem at least included P. In Ezra's time, the Feast of Tabernacles lasted for eight days (Neh. viii. 18), which agrees with P (Lev. xxiii. 86), but differs from D (Deut. xvi. 18). Neh. x. 82 mentions a temple tax of a third of a shekel. Nowhere in the Pentateuch except in P (Exod. xxx. 18, where the amount is half a shekel) is any temple tax mentioned. Perhaps Ezra's Law book included more than P. His opposition to mixed marriages (Ezra ix. 1 f; x. 1–8) agrees with passages in the

Pentateuch outside P (Exod. xxxiv. 12, 15 f; Deut. vii. 2 ff). It is, therefore, at least possible that when Ezra came to Jerusalem (457 or 397 B.C.; see above, p. 14) P had already been combined with the other Pentateuchal sources, and this would suggest that it had been in existence for some time. The absence of political interest in P deprives us of historical allusions which might have made possible a more precise dating.

## 3. *Growth*

Apart from the attempt to eliminate E, and the rival views about the date of Deuteronomy (see above, pp. 35, 42 f), the most important recent theories about the Pentateuch are concerned with the way in which the material reached its present form. Some scholars have carried the work of literary analysis further, arguing that the main sources were themselves produced by the conflation of earlier documents. Some have emphasized the influence of sanctuaries and of cultic practice in the formation and preservation of the material. That oral tradition played a part is widely recognized; and by some it is regarded as of supreme importance.

It is clear that none of the sources recognized above is a complete document written at one time. They all contain units of material which did not originally belong to their present contexts.

First, there are sundry passages in metrical form. In Num. xxi. 14 f there is a snatch of poetry about places in Moab, introduced by the statement that it comes from the Book of the Wars of Yahweh. Later in the same chapter (Num. xxi. 27–30), a short poem about an invasion of Moab by Sihon, king of the Amorites, is stated to be from the traditions of the bards. It seems likely that several other poems in the Pentateuch are also derived from written collections or from oral traditions, and that most of them are older than their present contexts.

The Song of Lamech (Gen. iv. 23 f) is an ancient poem of tribal vengeance. The Song of the Well (Num. xxi. 17 f) may

originally have been a working song or an incantation. A
number of blessings and oracles describe the character and
destiny of tribes or nations, often in individual terms: the
Blessing and Curse of Noah (Gen. ix. 25–27); Isaac's words
about his sons (Gen. xxvii. 27 ff, 39 f); Jacob's Blessing of
Ephraim and Manasseh (Gen. xlviii. 15 f); the Blessing of
Jacob (Gen. xlix); the Blessing of Moses (Deut. xxxiii); the
oracle to Rebekah about her children (Gen. xxv. 23); and the
Balaam Oracles (Num. xxiii–xxiv), to which are appended
three apparently independent oracles on Amalek, the Kenites,
and Asshur (Num. xxiv. 20–24). The ancient hostility of Israel
to Amalek is expressed in the oath against Amalek (Exod.
xvii. 16). Num. x. 35 f, which, in its present context, refers to
the wilderness journeys, probably preserved the formulas
used when the Ark went forth and returned in the campaigns
of the armies of Israel. Another ancient formula, from
Hebrew worship, is preserved in the beautiful Aaronic Blessing (Num. vi. 24 ff). The Song of Miriam (Exod. xv. 21)
celebrates the crossing of the Red Sea, a theme which is
linked with subsequent history in the Song of Moses and
Israel (Exod. xv. 1–19), a poem of later date. The Song of
Moses in Deut. xxxii is a religious poem, probably from the
6th century.

Second, we have already seen that the sources include independent law codes: the ritual or Yahwistic Decalogue in J
(Exod. xxxiv. 10–26), the two forms of the ethical Decalogue
in E and D (Exod. xx. 1–17; Deut. v. 1–21); the Book of the
Covenant in E (Exod. xx. 22–xxiii. 33); the series of twelve
curses in Deut. xxvii. 15–26 (probably not D); the Code of
Holiness (Lev. xvii–xxvi).

Third, the story in Gen. xiv, of Abraham's military exploit
(a passage which bristles with problems) cannot be attribu.ted
to any of the four main sources. Although it has often been
regarded as late, it may well be early, and is almost certainly
so in substance, if not in its present form.

Apart from the existence of these self-contained units, it is
argued that, as the Pentateuch may be analysed into sources,

the sources may be further analysed into subordinate strands.
This is not a particularly new trend, but there have been
special developments of it during recent decades.

In J, for instance, some passages near the beginning of
Genesis seem to imply ignorance of the Flood story (e.g.,
Gen. iv. 16–24; vi. 1–4). Such apparent inconsistencies led
earlier critics to divide J into $J^1$ and $J^2$. More recently,
O. Eissfeldt has assigned many of the $J^1$ passages to a source
which he traces through the Pentateuch and the books of
Joshua, Judges, and Samuel. He holds that it reflects the
primitive nomadic ideal; and because its interests are so far
removed from P, he calls it L (*Laienquelle*, Lay Source). He
dates it in the 9th century. What others have called $J^2$, he
labels J, holding it to be an 8th century source.

Some of the passages from Genesis assigned by Eissfeldt to
L are included in what R. H. Pfeiffer calls S (=Seir or South),
a supposed Edomite source from the 10th century. In the
stories about Moses, J. Morgenstern finds a Kenite source
(K), which also overlaps L, and which he dates at the beginning of the 9th century. The view of Mowinckel, mentioned
above (p. 35), that E is to be found in Gen. i–xi, also comes
under this head, since what he there calls E approximates to
$J^2$ or Eissfeldt's J.

Attempts have also been made to analyse D into sections
which use 'thou' and 'you', or into laws which involve
centralization and others which do not. In the Priestly source,
von Rad has distinguished two documents ($P^A$ and $P^B$) which
have been combined with other material. Other critics have
offered more elaborate analyses.

Carried to extremes, this kind of criticism would amount to
a revival of the fragment hypothesis. It is sometimes argued
that the artificial results obtained by some scholars reveal the
fundamental unreality of the methods of literary criticism,
and that therefore the hypothesis of four main sources is in-
secure and ought to be discarded. But, although the methods
may be the same, the amount of evidence for these more
minute analyses is less than that for the existence of J, E, D,

and P, and the supposed remains of the subordinate strata are usually fragmentary. Accordingly, the improbability of the more extreme analytical refinements does not affect the general probability of the main theory. We may readily admit the presence of varied material from different periods in all the sources; but precise definition of its extent and development remains conjectural.

At the other extreme are those Scandinavian scholars (chiefly the so-called Uppsala school) who reject the usual theory of sources. They maintain that the analysis of the material is based on a western standard of logical consistency, which does not do justice to Hebrew psychology or to the technique of the oriental story-tellers; that the belief in documentary sources fails to allow for the importance and reliability of oral tradition; and that the dating is derived from an untenable, evolutionary view of Israel's development. I. Engnell, for instance, holds that in Genesis–Numbers we have a large collection of various traditions, of which the narrative parts were mostly transmitted orally, whereas the law codes were written down at a fairly early stage. Only at a late stage was the entire work committed to writing. The core of the collection is the Passover legend (Exod. i–xv; Engnell here follows the Danish scholar J. Pedersen). This is ultimately derived from a liturgical text used in the cult in the celebration of Yahweh's deliverance of His people, but, as we now have it, is less like a liturgy and more like a story. Engnell refers to Genesis–Numbers as the 'P-work'. He believes that it comes from a circle of traditionalists, who combined their own inherited material (apparently roughly equivalent to what literary critics call P) with other material; but he thinks that we cannot now analyse the latter into J and E. Similarly, he holds that there is a 'D-work' (Deuteronomy–2 Kings) distinct from the other, but, like it, combining written laws derived from various centres with narratives, most of which had been transmitted orally. Both the 'P-work' and the 'D-work' reached their final form in the age of Ezra and Nehemiah.

The separation of Genesis–Numbers as a Tetrateuch, originally distinct from the Deuteronomic history (Deuteronomy–2 Kings), is also advocated by the German scholar M. Noth. He points out that there are very few traces of D in the Tetrateuch: the JE material has been fitted into the framework of P; but there is no indication that these sources were interwoven with D. Many scholars have held that J, E, and P are continued in the historical books and are combined there with Deuteronomic material. But, apart from some verses at the end of Deuteronomy, and some insignificant traces in the later books, Noth holds that J, E, and P end with Numbers, and that Deut. i–iv is the beginning of the Deuteronomic history (Deuteronomy–2 Kings), in which has been embodied the hortatory and legal material which follows Deut. iv. To the bearing of this view on the historical books we must return. Meanwhile it should be noted that, whereas Engnell regards the documentary analysis as demolished, Noth takes it as the foundation of his researches.

G. von Rad also uses the study of the history of tradition as complementary to documentary analysis. Behind all the written sources lies the story of how Yahweh brought His people out of bondage into Canaan, found briefly expressed as a cultic confession of faith in Deut. xxvi. 5 ff (cf. Deut. vi. 20–24; Joshua xxiv. 2–13), and used in the ritual of the feast of Weeks at the sanctuary at Gilgal. This theme is the core of the Pentateuch. To it J added the tradition about Sinai, which belonged to the ritual of the autumnal festival (at which the covenant was renewed) at Shechem. He further enriched the record by adding the stories of the patriarchs, and by prefixing to the whole the primeval history. The details of von Rad's theory are open to criticism; but his general approach is illuminating and sound.

### 4. Conclusions

In the face of this welter of conflicting theory, it may seem futile to attempt to draw any useful conclusions. But some conclusions can be drawn.

In spite of all that has been said about the importance of oral tradition, the Pentateuch is a written document; therefore the methods of literary criticism must be used. We can examine what still exists; and we may draw conclusions about what used to exist; but we have no first-hand knowledge of the latter. We must argue back to the stage of oral tradition primarily on the basis of our written documents.

If, then, we begin with the three basic statements made above (p. 26), that the Pentateuch is post-Mosaic and composite, and that the bulk of Deuteronomy is a special document, we may further conclude, with a high degree of probability, that four main sources, of the kind described above, have been combined. What we know of the methods of ancient Eastern historians, and the way in which the author of Chronicles used Samuel and Kings, shows that there is nothing unreal or improbable in the idea that written sources were thus combined. The criticism made by some of the Scandinavians, that inconsistencies and repetitions do not justify source analysis, is a useful warning against defining the limits of the sources too sharply or subdividing them too minutely. But it does not demolish the general theory of sources, which is based, not merely on a few inconsistencies, but on a wealth of interlocking evidence of different kinds. Engnell has renewed the attempt to discredit the evidence from the varying use of the divine names, on the ground that the Greek text often disagrees with the Hebrew. Against this may be set two facts: (a) forty years ago, John Skinner decisively demonstrated the reliability of the Hebrew text in this regard; (b) Engnell himself rightly regards the Hebrew text as generally superior to the Greek.

The plea that the material should not be fitted into a preconceived evolutionary pattern is also by no means groundless. Varying usages may have existed at the same time in different places. Further, all the sources contain material from different periods; and to date any one of them is not to date every item in it, but to decide the most likely period at which the source as a whole was given its present general form and character. This being granted, the relative dating of the sources, indicated above (p. 29), was no mere doctrinaire conjecture, but was based on a combination of evidence drawn both from the Pentateuch and from other books of the Old Testament. Its general probability has not been seriously shaken, even if the view of Hebrew religion with which it was once associated may need revision. The absolute dating of Deuteronomy has been challenged, but not disproved. The absolute dating of the other sources is more open to question: we must be content to suggest the most likely general period for each.

But, if the newer views have not seriously discredited the general framework of the source hypothesis, they have shown that behind the sources lies a long period of growth, in which oral tradition must have played an important part. We cannot return to the hair-splitting analyses which were fashionable about half a century ago, but must be content sometimes to leave the lines of demarcation between the sources vaguely defined.

Recent study has also brought out clearly the vital connexion of the Pentateuchal material with the life and worship of ancient Israel. The study of tradition history is the attempt to go behind the written record and to discover the factors which moulded the traditions which it contains. In such study, a fair measure of conjecture is involved, and the conclusions are sometimes far from certain. But, detailed conclusions apart, the great gain of this approach is the recognition that the Pentateuch is far more than a scribal compilation. It embodies the experience of a worshipping community.

An interesting parallel may be drawn with the New Testament. Behind the diversity of New Testament literature lies the apostolic *kerygma*, which tells of God's saving acts in Jesus Christ. This may be reconstructed in concise form from allusions in the Epistles, and from the records in Acts of the apostles' preaching. In the four Gospels, the outline of the *kerygma* reappears, very considerably expanded by the addition of miracle stories, parables, and the like. Similarly, in

what von Rad has called the *confessio* in Deut. xxvi. 5 ff
there is a brief presentation of the saving acts of God towards
Israel. The pattern recurs frequently, in longer or shorter
form, as the ground of the prophetic appeal (Amos ii. 9 ff;
Micah vi. 4 ff), in the Psalms (lxxviii; cxxxv; cxxxvi), and
elsewhere. It also appears, in greatly extended form, as the
framework of the four main sources and of the entire Pentateuch together with Joshua. Just as, for example, St.
Matthew's Gospel expands the *kerygma* by the addition of
miracle stories and blocks of teaching, so, in the Pentateuch,
the outline of the saving acts is expanded by codes of law,
the stories of the Patriarchs, and the primeval history. As the
Sermon on the Mount and the parables need the context of
the saving acts of God, if they are to be understood, so we
cannot appreciate what the laws meant for Israel unless we
remember their setting, a setting which many of them doubtless had in worship long before they were given their present
context in the Pentateuch. There is, it is true, this difference,
that, unlike the Gospel material, the myths in Genesis and
many of the laws were borrowed from Israel's neighbours;
but such material took on a new meaning, both by Israelite
revision and also because of its new setting in the life of
Yahweh's people and in the record of His dealings with them.
It is significant that the Decalogue (for which no alien origin
need be sought) begins, not with command, but with affirmation: 'I am Yahweh thy God, who brought thee forth out of
the land of Egypt, out of the house of slaves'. In the cult, the
Israelite experienced this anew; and although much, perhaps
most, of the Pentateuch may be several stages removed from
actual cultic situations, it links us with that experience, in
which the past became contemporary, when the Israelite
heard words such as these: 'Not with our fathers did Yahweh
make this covenant, but with us, even us, who are all of us
alive here to-day' (Deut. v. 3). '*To-day*, O that ye would hear
His voice!' (Ps. xcv. 7).

The Pentateuch is the Torah; but its place in the Old
Testament is that of the Gospels in the New.

# IV.—THE FORMER PROPHETS

## I. Joshua

### 1. Contents

The book of Joshua is a sequel to the end of Deuteronomy, and carries the story forward from the death of Moses to the death of Joshua. The contents fall into three parts: (*a*) i–xii, the conquest of Canaan; (*b*) xiii–xxii, the partition of Canaan among the tribes; (*c*) xxiii–xxiv, Joshua's last words and death.

(*a*) After the death of Moses, Joshua is commanded by Yahweh to lead the people into Canaan (i). Spies are sent to Jericho (ii); and, after their return, the people cross the Jordan, the waters of the river being cut off (iii). Memorial stones are erected to commemorate the event (iv). The males are circumcised and the Passover celebrated (v). Then Jericho is taken and put to the ban (vi). The Israelites advance on Ai, but are repulsed; and when it is discovered that this defeat is the consequence of Achan's breach of the ban, Achan is put to death (vii). Ai is then taken by means of a ruse (viii. 1–29). Joshua builds an altar on Mount Ebal (viii. 30–33). By deceit, the Gibeonites make a covenant with Israel (ix), which leads five kings from the south to strike at Gibeon; but Joshua swiftly intervenes, and routs the allies in the battle of Aijalon (x. 1–27). Further successes in the south are recorded (x. 28–43). In the north, Joshua defeats Jabin, king of Hazor (xi. 1–15). Joshua's successes are enumerated (xi. 16–23); and the section ends with a list of defeated kings (xii).

(*b*) This part of the book begins with a list of districts not yet conquered, and of the parts allotted to the tribes east of

Jordan (xiii). Eleazar and Joshua prepare to divide the land by lot; and Caleb makes good his claim to Hebron (xiv). Then follow accounts of the boundaries of Judah, Manasseh, Ephraim, Benjamin, Simeon, Zebulun, Issachar, Asher, Naphtali, and Dan (xv–xix). Three cities on either side of Jordan are appointed as places of refuge for innocent homicides (xx); and forty-eight cities are allocated to the Levites (xxi). After the division of the country, the two and a half Transjordanian tribes are free to return to their own territory. They build an altar there, and when the other tribes reproach them, explain that it is not intended for sacrifice, but solely as a witness to their unity with the rest of Israel (xxii).

(*c*) This section contains two speeches by Joshua to all Israel. The first is a general warning against apostasy (xxiii). The second is an address to a national assembly at Shechem, recalling Yahweh's past mercies (cf. Deut. xxvi. 5 ff), and appealing for individual allegiance to Him; the people pledge themselves to obedience (xxiv. 1–28). The book ends with the death and burial of Joshua, the burial of Joseph's bones, and the death and burial of Eleazar (xxiv. 29–33).

### 2. *Analysis and Growth*

According to Jewish tradition, the book was written by Joshua. This tradition is untenable. The statement in xxiv. 26, that 'Joshua wrote these words', refers only to the immediate context. As in the Pentateuch, there are signs that Joshua comes from a later period and that it is a composite work.

The closing verses, which describe Joshua's death and burial, can hardly be from his own hand. Some passages (e.g., iv. 9; v. 9; vii. 26; ix. 27; xv. 63; xix. 47) betray the outlook of a period long after the conquest. xix. 47 mentions the capture of Leshem (Laish), which, according to Judges xviii, took place after the Danites had moved from the region in which they first settled. The poetic apostrophe to the sun and the moon in x. 12 f is said to be taken from the book of Jashar, which included David's lament over Saul and Jonathan (2 Sam. i. 18), and cannot have been earlier than the monarchy.

A number of repetitions and inconsistencies occur, which are unlikely to have belonged originally to the same narrative. The crossing of Jordan is described twice (iii. 17 and iv. 10 f). In iv. 8, 20, twelve stones are carried from the river and set up at Gilgal; but in iv. 9, they are set up in the midst of the Jordan. The story of the capture of Jericho (vi) seems to combine two accounts: in one, the Israelite host marched round the city in silence seven times, and then gave the war cry and attacked; in the other, priests headed the procession, blowing trumpets, and after the seventh circuit the walls fell down. The duration is in one account only one day; but in the other, it is seven days. In viii. 3, Joshua sends 30,000 men west of Ai to lie in ambush; but in viii. 12, he sends 5,000 to the same place for the same purpose. x. 26 and 37 both tell of the death of the king of Hebron. Hebron itself is said in x. 36 f to have been taken by Joshua and its inhabitants exterminated; but in xv. 14, it is taken by Caleb. The general impression given by the book as it now stands is that the entire country was conquered and occupied during Joshua's lifetime (xxi. 43–45); and the accounts given of the various engagements imply swift campaigns under a unified command. But, scattered throughout the book, there are tell-tale allusions to the existence for a long time of pockets of Canaanite resistance, and to the protracted struggles which had to be carried on by the Hebrews in different parts of the country. This latter account of the conquest agrees with the description in Judges i.

Thus it can hardly be doubted that Joshua is a composite work. But can consecutive sources be reconstructed, and can these sources be identified with those found in the Pentateuch? The fact that Joshua is the sequel to the Pentateuch might lead us to expect this; and many hold that J, E, D, and P are continued in it. But the question is complicated; and among scholars there is nothing approaching a common mind about the details of the analysis.

In i–xii, it is fairly clear that we have a composite narrative within a Deuteronomic framework. The diction, style, and outlook of Deuteronomy are evident in i, with its emphasis on the law and the land which Yahweh is about to give; and again, in ii. 10 f; iv. 21–24; viii. 30–35 (cf. Deut. xxvii. 1 ff); ix. 1 f; and elsewhere, the echoes of Deuteronomy are plain. There are also a few traces of the interest and manner of P (e.g., iv. 15–19; v. 10–12; ix. 15–21). But there does not seem to be any strong evidence enabling us to identify parts of the stories with J, and E. A. Alt and his disciples have argued that most of the stories in ii–ix are ætiological, i.e., that they were told to account for customs or local features (e.g., iv. 9, referring to the memorial stones; v. 9, on the name of Gilgal; ix. 27, explaining the position of the Gibeonites), that x and xi. 1–9 are war stories, originally local rather than national in character. The ætiological element is present; but it would be a mistake to over-emphasize its importance. As in the Pentateuch, so here, attempts to trace the pre-literary history of the material must remain in the realm of rather precarious conjecture. All that we can say with any confidence is that in this part of the book we have old traditions from more than one source, which have been used by a Deuteronomic writer, and that minor additions (P) were made later.

In the second part of the book, most scholars would agree that the incidental references to the gradual occupation of the land come from an old source (many would say J), since they reflect a realistic account, which seems to be nearer to the facts than the later, somewhat idealized picture of a swift, complete conquest under a unified command. It is argued that much of the material is akin to P, whose characteristic features appear in the lists and in some other passages. A good example is xiv. 1–4, where the priest Eleazar, Aaron's son, is named before Joshua in the preparation for apportioning the land (cf. xxi. 1 ff). In xxii. 9–34, we have a longish narrative in the Priestly style. But it can be argued that although opening and closing formulas may be from P, the actual content of the geographical and other lists may well be very much older. Indeed, Alt has argued that xiii–xix is derived from a document earlier than the monarchy, except that xv comes from a list of the provinces in Josiah's kingdom. There are also Deuteronomic passages in this part of the book (e.g., xiv. 6–15; xxi. 43–45); but the proportion of P seems to be larger than in the first part.

In the third section, xxiii is unmistakably Deuteronomic in style and in content. xxiv is usually attributed to E (note the importance of Shechem and the reference to Joseph), though there are Deuteronomic touches in it (e.g., v. 13). It contains an enlarged form of the story of God's saving acts (cf. above, pp. 53, 56).

Summing up, we may say that the book appears to be a Deuteronomic work (probably 6th century) incorporating much older material from more than one source; and that it subsequently (in the 5th century) received Priestly additions, especially in its latter half. In substance, it is the sequel to the Pentateuch; but in literary form, it is more accurately described as the sequel to Deuteronomy. P provides the framework in Genesis–Numbers, but that is not continued through Deuteronomy and Joshua, for the framework of the latter book connects it with Deuteronomy. Because of this, and because of the difficulty of identifying the older material in Joshua with J and E, the practice of referring to Genesis–Joshua as the Hexateuch is at least questionable.

## 8. *Historical Value and Religious Content*

As we have seen, the general picture of a swift, complete, unified conquest, which Joshua gives, is at variance with sundry hints in the book itself. It is also improbable in itself. If there had been so great a slaughter of the Canaanites, it would be difficult to account for the persistent influence of their culture and religion on Israel during the succeeding centuries. Other historical difficulties are present. Archæological evidence suggests that the site of Ai was not occupied at any period at which the Israelites are likely to have entered Palestine. It may be that the story of the fall of some neighbouring town (Bethel?) was transferred to Ai. Some have also questioned the accuracy of the story about the defeat of Jabin and his allies. In Judges iv, Jabin's defeat is attributed to a later age. Moreover, at this period, there were still important Canaanite strongholds on a line across the country from Carmel to the Jordan valley. The Hebrews were at their best in the hills; in the plains they were at the mercy of the Canaanite chariotry. Could a substantial force of them have made their way past the strongholds, across the plains of Esdraelon, and into the highlands of Galilee? The suggestion has been made that the battle was part of an independent invasion, not under Joshua, made north of the Sea of Galilee.

But we should beware of under-estimating the historical value of Joshua. The picture of a swift, complete conquest is Deuteronomic. The substance of most of the narratives belongs to the older traditions, which are much nearer in time to the actual events; and they should not be rejected except on really strong grounds. Too much should not be made of the ætiological factor. The fact that a story (rightly or wrongly) was connected with some feature or custom does not prove that the story is untrue. In fact, the crossing of Jordan, the swift attack on Jericho, the thrust into the hill-country, the fear of the southern kings that Joshua might gain control of the Gibeonite cities which occupied a position of strategic importance on the east–west line from Jericho to the coast, and Joshua's swift surprise attack—all these, in their essentials, form a coherent and credible account of a campaign which gave Israel control of certain essential strategic points.

That the Deuteronomic historian should sharpen the outlines, amplify the details, and heighten the colours is understandable. The conception of a united Israel is a prominent feature in Deuteronomic thought; and so the conquest is described as complete. Canaanite ways are an abomination; and Canaanites ought to have been exterminated: the words on the banner carried by Cleland at Bothwell Brig, 'No quarters for ye active enemies of ye covenant', sum up the

Deuteronomic theory of what should have happened. But it was a theory prompted by a hatred of pagan corruption, not by a lust for blood.

The story might easily have been told as an epic of national achievement; but it is told, not to the glory of Israel, but to the glory of Yahweh. The supreme quality required in the national leader is religious (i); and the closing appeals are for national religious faithfulness. Thus the historian, who is three parts preacher, recounts the triumphs of the past, not to stimulate the spirit of jingoistic nationalism, but to summon Israel to faithful obedience, to arouse, not national pride, but trust in Yahweh.

## II. JUDGES

### 1. Contents

The book of Judges falls into three main sections: (a) i. 1–ii. 5, fragmentary records of the conquest of various parts of Canaan; (b) ii. 6–xvi. 31, a general preface, followed by the stories of national heroes, who 'judged' Israel; (c) xvii–xxi, an appendix containing two detached stories.

(a) tells of the achievements of Judah, Simeon, and the 'house of Joseph', and of the failure of Manasseh, Ephraim, Zebulun, Asher, Naphtali, and Dan to dislodge the Canaanites and Amorites from certain regions. This is at variance with the general impression given by Joshua, that the conquest was swift, complete, and carried out under a unified command. Here it is gradual, partial, and effected by separate tribes or groups of tribes acting independently. This corresponds to the fragmentary references in Joshua which have been referred to above; and, in fact, some verses in Judges i are almost identical, word for word, with the corresponding parts of Joshua. Compare, for example, i. 20b, 10b–15 with Josh. xv. 14–19, i. 21 with Josh. xv. 63, i. 27 f with Josh. xvii. 12 f, i. 29 with Josh. xvi. 10.

In (b) we have the stories which have given the whole book its name. There appear to be twelve judges. Some are mentioned quite briefly; others performed exploits which are

described at greater length. Accordingly they are usually
described as major and minor. The six minor judges are
Shamgar (iii. 31), Tola (x. 1 f), Jair (x. 3–5), Ibzan (xii. 8–10),
Elon (xii. 11 f), Abdon (xii. 13–15), and the major judges,
Othniel (iii. 7–11), Ehud (iii. 12–30), Deborah or Barak
(iv–v), Gideon (vi–viii), Jephthah (x. 6–xii. 7), Samson
(xiii–xvi).

These latter were judges in the sense of deliverers (cf. the
phrase 'to judge the widow and the orphan', which means to
vindicate their cause, restore to them their rights). Othniel
the Kenizzite saved his people from the tyranny of Cushan-
rishathaim. In a daring and cunning enterprise, Ehud, single-
handed, disposed of the Moabite oppressor, Eglon. In the
north of the country, where the Hebrews were menaced by
the Canaanites of the plain of Esdraelon, Deborah arose,
summoned Barak and the tribes to war, and so became leader
of a rising which ended in the victory of hillmen over chariots
in the rain-sodden plain. This story is told twice: in prose
(iv), and in poetry (v). In the central hill country, distress
was caused by the periodical incursions of Bedouin tribes
from the east; but Yahweh raised up Gideon, through whose
faith, courage, and resourcefulness the invaders were routed.
On another occasion, when danger came from the more
settled people living east of Jordan (the Amorites), Jephthah
was raised up to restore the situation, though his very ardour
impelled him to make a fateful vow, which led to the sacrifice
of his daughter. Finally, a new danger emerged in the
southern reaches of the coastal plain: the well-equipped and
growing power of the Philistines, whom Samson was raised
up to resist. Different in some respects from the other Judges,
Samson shares with them the essential feature of divine
appointment and endowment with the spirit.

In this sequence of stories there is preserved a record of the
temporary and local kingship of Gideon's half-Canaanite son,
Abimelech. It was unscrupulously gained, unpopular, and
short-lived. Although it may seem to have affinities with the
position of the hero-judges just mentioned, there is this

decisive difference, that Abimelech became king by means of a *coup d'état* carried out in his own interest, whereas the judges were raised up to be instruments of the divine purpose to save Israel.

These stories are set in a framework which contains a chronological scheme and religious comment. The theme and pattern of this comment are given *in extenso* in a general preface to this section of the book (ii. 6–iii. 6); the apostasy of the people, punishment in the form of foreign oppression, repentance and prayer to Yahweh for succour, Yahweh's compassion for His people, shown in the raising up of a deliverer. This preface and framework provide (i) a chronological scheme (note the periods of twenty, forty, eighty years); (ii) a national setting for the events (which in the narratives themselves are local or tribal in scope), thus implying that the judges had national authority, and (iii) a religious interpretation of the events, in terms of the Deuteronomic principle of reward and punishment. The beginning and ending of the story of Abimelech and the notices of the minor judges do not conform to this pattern.

The two detached stories in (*c*) differ from the central part of the book in that they tell of no judge and are not fitted into the same chronological scheme or accompanied by the same kind of religious comment. The first of them (xvii–xviii) tells how Micah, the Ephraimite, made a private sanctuary and hired a Levite to serve as priest. A party of Danites, looking for new territory for their tribe, passed that way; and later, when the entire tribe migrated, the Levite was persuaded to leave Micah and become priest at their new sanctuary in Dan. The story is told with what seems to be deliberate humour in order to ridicule the great northern shrine which was regarded in Judah as apostate. The Levite was a grandson of Moses; but someone who thought this unfitting has inserted the letter 'N', turning Moses into the hated name 'Manasseh' (see R.V. margin).

xix–xxi begins with the grim story of the Levite's concubine and of the vengeance taken by Israel on Benjamin.

Later, sympathy with the offending and now-decimated tribe prevailed; and two expedients were adopted to provide the surviving Benjamites with wives: first, after Jabesh-gilead had been punished for absence from the assembly, the un-married girls from that place were given to the Benjamites; and then arrangements were made to steal the maidens of Shiloh, in order to circumvent the oath taken by the rest of Israel, that they would not give their daughters in marriage to the Benjamites.

## 2. *Analysis and Growth*

Most of the first section is of great antiquity, for it repre-sents the old, realistic view of the conquest, and corresponds to the fragments contained in the second half of Joshua. Many have labelled it J; but there does not seem to be sufficient evidence to establish the identity. The opening words ('And it came to pass after the death of Joshua . . .') are inappropriate if, as the parallels in Joshua suggest, some of the events took place in Joshua's lifetime. The closing verses (ii. 1–5) express the view that the Canaanites should have been exterminated.

In the main part of the book it is clear that we have to do with material of two kinds: the stories and the framework. Most scholars find in the stories themselves traces of diverse origin. The most obvious example is the story of Deborah (iv–v), where the accounts, in prose and poetry, lie side by side. They do not exactly tally; and the differences are per-haps not entirely due to the poetic style of v. Jabin, king of Hazor (cf. Josh. xi. 1 ff), is not mentioned in the poem, where Sisera appears, not as a subordinate, but as the leader of the Canaanites. In the poem, too, a larger number of Israelite tribes is mentioned. In the story of Gideon, it has been maintained that vi. 2–6 and 7–10 are duplicate introductions, and that vi. 11–24 and 25–32 are parallel accounts of Gideon's call. viii. 4–21, which tells how Gideon pursued and killed Zebah and Zalmunna, is thought to come rather awkwardly after the story of the rout of the invaders and the death of

Oreb and Zeeb. (The complete analysis as sometimes made
is vi. 2–6, 11–24, 34; viii. 4–21, 23–27a, and vi. 7–10, 25–32,
36–40; vii. 1–viii. 3, 22 f, 27b). Two strands are found in the
Abimelech story, the account of Gaal's revolt (ix. 26–41)
being regarded as separate from the rest. In the Jephthah
story, a difficulty is caused by the fact that Jephthah's
message to the king of Ammon deals with Moabite territory
and cities, and refers (xi. 24) to the Moabite god Chemosh,
and here, too, the text has been analysed into two strands.
But, even if the composite character of these two passages
be taken as demonstrated, and even if the two strands are
held to show a general similarity to the Pentateuchal sources
J and E (note the occasional variation in the use of the divine
names: Yahweh in vi. 11 ff; 'Elōhîm in vi. 36–40), there is
insufficient evidence to prove that there once existed independent and continuous J and E narratives, extending from
the Pentateuch into Judges, and beyond. We should think
rather of material derived from more than one cycle of tradition, coming, it may be, from the same circles as J and E.

These stories describe local crises and local deliverances.
By giving them a national setting, the prefaces transform
local heroes into national deliverers, and make the entire
narrative a record of the history of all Israel, in which the
Deuteronomic doctrine of reward and punishment is amply
illustrated. The general preface (ii. 6–iii. 6) and the framework
are manifestly of Deuteronomic origin.

If the events described in the stories were, in fact, local in
their scope, then some of them may have overlapped in time,
and some of the judges may have been contemporaries. But,
when the crises are presented as national in scope, they must
be regarded as belonging to different periods; and, if the
judges judged all Israel, they cannot have been contemporaries. The framework presents them in sequence and fits
them into its chronological scheme, which gives a total of
410 years for the period. This is in itself too high, since the
Exodus cannot have taken place before the 15th century,
and the monarchy was established in the 11th. Moreover, it

cannot easily be reconciled with the statement in 1 Kings vi. 1 that 480 years elapsed between the Exodus and the founding of the temple: the wilderness wandering, the conquest, the period of Eli and Samuel, and the reigns of Saul and David are likely to have been more than seventy years. To reconcile the two figures, various devices have been adopted: the omission of the minor judges and Abimelech, or of the years of oppression and the régimes of Abimelech and Saul. But the 480 years of 1 Kings vi. 1 may well be an artificial estimate (twelve generations of forty years); and the frequently occurring periods of twenty, forty, and eighty years in Judges seem to be artificial or approximate. It therefore seems unlikely that the figures can be reconciled, or that those in Judges provide a reliable chronology of the period.

The notices of the minor judges include chronological data, but are not accompanied by Deuteronomic comment. It has, therefore, been held that they are a later addition to this part of the book; but it seems unnecessary to draw this conclusion until stronger evidence is forthcoming. The story of Abimelech also lacks the familiar framework, and is thought to have been rejected by the Deuteronomic writer as not sufficiently edifying, and added subsequently. In the story of Samson, the closing formula is found in xv. 20. The conclusion has therefore been drawn that the contents of xvi offended the Deuteronomist, and were rejected by him, but subsequently restored. There are undoubtedly some irregularities in arrangement; but that the Deuteronomist discarded such passages from some earlier document seems, at most, only a possibility; and that some later writer should have added them without edifying comment is a remote possibility.

Both stories in the third section of the book seem to embody ancient tradition. The conditions of life described in xvii–xviii are those of an early period; and, in substance, the narrative is presumably old. The motive of its present form is to ridicule the sanctuary of Dan, which points to some time after the Disruption of the kingdom. The end of xviii. 30 is later than the fall of the Northern Kingdom. Though the Deuteronomic style is not evident, the theme would commend itself to an enthusiast for the sanctuary at Jerusalem.

xix–xxi also contains very old material. The story of the outrage at Gibeah is no pious invention in the interests of edification. But xx–xxi bears clear marks of late influence. The tribes are depicted as acting in concert, without any human leader; and they are described as the 'congregation' ('*ēḏâh*). The connexion between Benjamin and Jabesh-gilead reappears in the story of Saul (1 Sam. xi; xxxi. 11–18; 2 Sam. ii. 5–7). Perhaps the picture of Benjamin as an offending tribe is connected with the criticisms of Saul which we find in some parts of 1 Samuel. If so, the Deuteronomist might well have made use of the story; but it has been modified by a later hand. Many have contended that the whole story, together with xvii–xviii, was added after the Deuteronomist had done his work; but the evidence does not seem to be conclusive.

Thus the book is, in the main, a Deuteronomic product, in which older materials have been used. There is no strong evidence for the view that it existed in a pre-Deuteronomic form; and it is safer to recognize that we do not know in what shape the older stories reached the Deuteronomist. Did they even form a sequence before he gave them their present framework?

The Deuteronomic book was probably part of a larger whole. ii. 6 ff repeats Joshua xxiv. 29 ff; and it is probable that i. 1–ii. 5 (which though mainly old, begins and ends with later matter) disturbs the original connexion of Joshua and Judges. Nor does the story of Samson end the narrative. Unlike the other judges, Samson did not decisively deliver his people from oppression. The Philistine menace continues in 1 Samuel. The opening chapters of that book describe the latter part of the age of the Judges (note the statement that Eli judged Israel forty years; 1 Sam. iv. 18), which is formally ended by Samuel's last speech as judge of all Israel (1 Sam. xii).

### 8. *Historical, Literary, and Religious Importance*

Judges is a source-book of great value for our understanding of Hebrew history. We have already seen that it contains ancient and reliable evidence about the character of the conquest and the settlement. The stories of the major judges illustrate vividly the social and religious conditions of the period, and show the working of those political forces through which the confederacy of tribes was led on to monarchy. They also show the supreme importance of religion in the survival and development of the Hebrew tribes.

The book is not merely a corpse to be dissected by the critics, or a source-book to be cited by the historian. It is great as a book. Most of the stories would rank high in any collection of the short stories of the world. The tale of Jephthah has more than a little of the spirit of republican Rome, and contains the stuff of a tragedy in the manner of Corneille. Its amazing brevity is characteristic. The Hebrew literary artist was at his best when he crammed action and emotion into a few sentences. Even in the most brutal passages, there is an austere dignity. In the pungent words of Jotham (ix. 7 ff), Judges has preserved almost the only fable in ancient Hebrew literature. But its supreme literary treasure is the Song of Deborah, a magnificent example of early Hebrew poetry, probably contemporary with the events which it describes. Even in translation, its sonorous quality and vivid narrative power are unmistakable.

The more bloodthirsty stories in Judges often present a stumbling-block to the modern reader. There is no need to pretend that the warriors of old Israel were any better than they are, in fact, made out to be. Such deeds were characteristic of the time; but with cruelty and violence there often went courage, faithfulness, and integrity. With all their shortcomings, the heroes were remembered, not solely as warriors, but above all, as agents of Yahweh. The whole sequence of events is lifted to a higher level of thought by being set in the Deuteronomic framework, which judges national life in terms of religious fidelity.

### III. 1 and 2 SAMUEL

1. *Contents*

We have already noted (p. 10 n.) that these two books form
one, according to the reckoning of the Hebrew canon. It may
be divided into the following parts:

(*a*) 1 Sam. i–vii. This tells the story of the birth of Samuel,
the double defeat of the Israelites by the Philistines, the loss
and restoration of the Ark, and the decisive defeat of the
Philistines during Samuel's régime.

(*b*) 1 Sam. viii–xv. The people ask for a king; and Yahweh
tells Samuel to grant their request. Saul is privately anointed,
publicly chosen by lot, and seen to be divinely endowed when
he leads the relief of Jabesh-gilead. Samuel makes a farewell
speech. Saul's campaign against the Philistines has scarcely
begun, when Samuel announces his rejection. Then follow
accounts of an engagement with the Philistines, in which
Jonathan distinguishes himself, and an expedition against
the Amalekites, after which Saul is again rejected for disobedience.

(*c*) 1 Sam. xvi–xxxi. David is secretly anointed. He becomes a member of Saul's bodyguard and gains fame as a
warrior. Saul's vindictive jealousy drives him into outlawry;
and later he decamps to Philistine territory. Saul is defeated
at the battle of Mt. Gilboa, and loses his life.

(*d*) 2 Sam. i–viii. For a time the land is divided between
David and Saul's son, Ishbaal (Ish-bosheth). After Ishbaal's
murder, David becomes king of all Israel. He captures
Jerusalem and makes it his capital. The Philistines are decisively defeated. The Ark is brought up to Jerusalem, where
David wants to build a temple for it. Through Nathan,
Yahweh rejects this plan, but promises to uphold David's
dynasty. Lists are given of David's campaigns and of his
ministers.

(*e*) 2 Sam. ix–xx. This section deals in the main with events
at David's court. David shows clemency to Jonathan's son
Mephibosheth. There is a protracted war against Ammon,

which provides the setting for David's seduction of Bathsheba and his virtual murder of Uriah. The rape of Tamar by her half-brother Amnon is followed by Absalom's murder of Amnon. Absalom is exiled but later brought back. He leads a revolt against David, but is defeated and killed. A revolt headed by Sheba is also suppressed.

The section does not really end at this point, but is rounded off in 1 Kings i–ii, which tells how Adonijah was set aside and Solomon made king.

(*f*) 2 Sam. xxi–xxiv. These chapters, which clearly interrupt the sequence of ix–xx and 1 Kings i–ii, may be divided into six parts: (1) the famine, and its removal by the sacrifice of Saul's sons (xxi. 1–14); (2) deeds of David's mighty men (xxi. 15–22); (3) a psalm of thanksgiving ascribed to David (xxii = Ps. xviii); (4) a poem called 'the last words of David' (xxiii. 1–7); (5) more deeds of David's mighty men, and a list of his heroes (xxiii. 8–39); (6) the census and the plague (xxiv).

## 2. *Analysis and Growth*

Jewish tradition ascribed the authorship of the books of Judges and Samuel to the prophet Samuel. The analysis of Judges given above shows that he cannot have written that book (unless E. Robertson's view of Deuteronomy is correct); and the very contents of Samuel (extending far beyond the prophet's death) make his authorship impossible.

There are many signs that the material is of diverse origin. This is most apparent in the stories about the establishment of the monarchy (1 Sam. viii–xii), which may be divided into two accounts: (*a*) ix–x. 16; xi. 1–11, 15; and (*b*) viii; x. 17–27; xii. In (*a*), the monarchy is represented as Yahweh's gracious gift to His people to save them from Philistine oppression (ix. 16); Samuel is a local seer, unknown to Saul and only vaguely known to Saul's servant; and the monarchy is inaugurated at Gilgal (xi. 15). In (*b*), the people's request for a king is regarded as an act of rebellion against Yahweh, and is granted as a concession, with solemn warnings (viii); Samuel is not merely a local seer, but the universally recognized leader of the Israelite tribes (viii. 4); and the king is chosen by means of the sacred lot at Mizpah (x. 17 ff).

Several other passages appear to be duplicates. The downfall of Eli's house is prophesied twice (1 Sam. ii. 31–36; iii. 11–14). There are two accounts of Saul's rejection (1 Sam. xiii. 7b–14; xv). David is twice introduced to Saul: in 1 Sam. xvi. 14–23, he becomes a member of Saul's personal entourage; yet, in xvii. 55–58, he appears to be unknown to Saul. David's flight to Philistia is described in xxi. 10–15 and in xxvii. 5–12; and two passages (xxiv; xxvi) tell how he spared Saul's life. Some of these duplicate narratives might be descriptions of similar but distinct events. But the number of them, combined with the clear divergences in 1 Sam. viii–xii, points definitely to the composite character of the book. By contrast, there is an unmistakable homogeneity of style and dramatic unity of theme in 2 Sam. ix–xxi; 1 Kings i–ii.

Many scholars have analysed the material into two main strands. Among the chief passages ascribed to the earlier are the stories of the Ark; the favourable account of the origin of the monarchy; David's sparing of Saul in the wilderness of En-gedi; the story of Nabal; most of the material about David's activities among the Philistines; the account of Saul's final defeat and death (but not 2 Sam. i. 1–16); the accounts of David's rule at Hebron and Jerusalem; the sacrifice of Saul's sons; the passages about David's mighty men. The later account is thought to include (*inter alia*) the story of Samuel's childhood, the unfavourable account of the origin of the monarchy, David's sparing of Saul in the wilderness of Ziph, the story of the witch of En-dor; the Amalekite's account of Saul's death. Linguistic evidence has been advanced to show that these two sources are generally similar to, or continuous with, the sources J and E in the Pentateuch.

There are many variations of theory, but we must specially note two points at which the above view has been disputed. (*a*) It has been held that there is evidence of more than two main strands. (*b*) The association of much of the material with

J and E has been challenged; and, in particular, it has been held that some of the later passages bear the stamp of Deuteronomic writing rather than of E.

O. Eissfeldt, who traces his Pentateuchal source L through Joshua and Judges, finds it in Samuel too. Closer examination of 1 Sam. ix–xii, for example, raises the question whether only two strata are to be found there. On three separate occasions Saul is made king (ix. 26–x. 1; x. 24; xi. 15). Moreover, xi. 1 ff, which tells how Saul delivered Jabesh-gilead from the Ammonites, could be regarded as independent of ix–x. 16, in which Saul is anointed to save his people from the Philistines.

But is a theory of three sources adequate for the whole book? It is noteworthy that, particularly in 1 Samuel, the material is grouped around certain themes or persons, and that when the disparate material is sorted out, there is neither the connected sequence of action, nor the amount of interlocking evidence, which, in the Pentateuch, justifies the theory of parallel sources. Only in 2 Sam. ix–xx, 1 Kings i–ii do we have a sustained sequence of events. It is generally admitted that this is a special source. With the exception of the intrusion of the appendix after 2 Sam. xx, it is not interwoven with other material.

It therefore seems best to adopt a view similar to that advanced by A. R. S. Kennedy (see p. 77, n. 1). He held that there were five main sources.

(i) A biography of Samuel (S), represented by 1 Sam. i–iii (except ii. 1–10 and 27–36), and probably xv. 1–xvi. 13 (perhaps 7th century).

(ii) A history of the Ark (A), part of which is found in 1 Sam. iv–vii. 1 (Does 2 Sam. vi also belong to it?) The religious beliefs reflected in it are early; and the source is therefore in all probability an old one (10th century?).

(iii) A source which is critical of the monarchy (1 Sam. vii. 2–viii. 22; x. 17–24; xii). Kennedy regards it as Deuteronomic and labels it D. As we have seen, others associate it with the Pentateuchal source E. There are, admittedly, some linguistic

affinities with E; and the polemic against Canaanite paganism is similar. Samuel's farewell speech in 1 Sam. xii has
been likened to Joshua's in Josh. xxiv, which is by many
labelled E. Moreover, the fact that there are two accounts of
the rejection of Saul suggests that the material which is
critical of the monarchy was not completely unified. On
balance, the likeness to Deuteronomy seems more pro-
nounced. The picture of Samuel as the theocratic judge of all
Israel corresponds to the presentation of the judges in the
framework of the book of Judges. The critical attitude to the
monarchy in 1 Sam. viii. 11–18 is, indeed, much stronger than
anything in Deut. xvii. 14–20. To this source we should also
ascribe 1 Sam. ii. 27–36, which alludes to the subordination
of the country priests to the house of Zadok as a result of the
centralization of sacrifice (note, again, that the situation
described is not that implied by the law in Deut. xviii. 6–8,
but rather that which actually resulted, as mentioned in
2 Kings xxiii. 8 f). 2 Sam. vii, which Kennedy attributes to
this source, raises problems. Does the contrast between the
house which Yahweh will build for David and the house
which He forbids David to build imply a criticism of the very
sanctuary which D venerated? And what is a prophecy of
the permanence of the Davidic dynasty doing in a source
which is critical of the monarchy? The matter is further
complicated by the relation of the chapter to 1 Chron. xvii
and Ps. lxxxix. Here we can only note the problems raised.

(iv) A source which is favourable to the monarchy (M). In
this, Kennedy includes not only the older parts of the story
of the origin of the monarchy (1 Sam. ix.–x. 16; xi. 1–11, 15),
but also most of the material from 1 Sam. xiii to 2 Sam. vi.
1 Sam. xv–xvi. 13 is omitted, as belonging to S. The passages
xvii. 12–31, 41, 50, 55–xviii. 5 (which do not appear in Codex
B of the Greek Bible) represent David as unknown to Saul
(by contrast with xvi. 14 ff), and, if omitted, leave a more
or less complete story (xvii. 1–11, 32–40, 42–49, 51–54):
Kennedy therefore (like many others) thinks that they were
added later. The story of Saul and David in the wilderness

of Ziph (xxiii. 14–xxiv. 22), and a number of shorter passages
are also excluded as variant traditions or editorial expansions.
M is contrasted with D, not only in its attitude to the
monarchy and its account of Samuel as a local seer-prophet,
and not a national judge, but also by its account of the
political situation. In vii. 13 f (D), the Philistine menace is
said to have been finally removed; but in M, Saul is made
king to save Israel from the Philistines, and he spends much
of his time in conflict with them. As in Joshua and Judges, so
here, the more realistic account is likely to be the earlier; and
the material in M may well go back to the 10th century.

(v) 2 Sam. ix–xx; 1 Kings i–ii, the history of David's court,
is represented by the symbol C, and dated in the 10th century.
Other scholars have held that these chapters were originally
continuous with what Kennedy calls M; Kennedy admits that
there is some evidence for this in the general similarity of
style; but his own preference is shown by his use of a separate
symbol. It seems probable that such likeness as exists
between M and C is to be explained by their origin in the
same period, rather than by a common literary origin. C is
not merely a sequence of narratives; it is one narrative, in
which the successive incidents are causally related to each
other. Its climax is the accession of Solomon; and it tells of
the elimination of Amnon, Absalom, and Adonijah. It is in
no sense a tendentious narrative. With uncanny penetration
it presents David's greatness, yet, at the same time, tells
quite objectively the sorry story of his own weakness and of
the conflicts in his household. The unity of the document is
obvious. An occasional apparent contradiction like xiv. 27, as
against xviii. 18; or the rare mark of a later hand, such as the
'unto this day' of xviii. 18 is quite insufficient to disprove it.
Here, too, we have the work of a contemporary author, not
the accumulation of popular tradition given shape and coherence by a later hand. This is clear from the scope and
sequence of the narrative, and from the first-hand knowledge
of events and persons at David's court which the document
reflects. Attempts have been made to identify the author. As

some would see the author of St. Mark's Gospel in the young man referred to in Mark xiv. 51 f, so, here, it has been held that xvii. 17–21 seems to contain personal reminiscence, and points to either Jonathan, son of Abiathar, or Ahimaaz, son of Zadok, as the author, and that xviii. 19–32 indicates the latter. The suggestion is an attractive one, and has at least a measure of probability.

The above are the main sources enumerated by Kennedy; but he also allows for sundry passages derived from tradition (T), chiefly variants of stories in M (e.g., 1 Sam. xxiii. 14–xxiv. 22); sections added after the book had taken shape (Z), such as the Song of Hannah (1 Sam. ii. 1–10) or the appendix, and minor editorial insertions (R). Kennedy's A + M + C amounts roughly to what some have called J, and his S + D + T to their E. Modifications in detail may be necessary. Perhaps M ought to be divided into a group of traditions about Saul and another about David. But Kennedy's analysis is substantially sound.[1]

His account of the process by which these various elements were combined is less convincing: a Deuteronomic compilation towards the end of the Exile of S, A, and M, omitting 1 Sam. xxviii. 3 ff and C (because insufficiently edifying), and summing up David's reign in 2 Sam. viii; a post-Deuteronomic edition restoring C, and repeating 2 Sam. viii. 16–18 in xx. 23–26, a process which was continued for some time in the addition of passages such as 1 Sam. ii. 1–10; xix. 18–24; 2 Sam. xxi–xxiv.

This reconstruction, which has been widely accepted, resembles the view that there was once a Deuteronomic edition of Judges which omitted the story of Abimelech and the end of the story of Samson. We have seen reason to doubt the latter; and we may question whether there is sufficient evidence to support the former. There is, it is true, practically no trace of Deuteronomic writing in C, by contrast with the earlier parts of the book. But the stringing together of groups

---

[1] Kennedy's views are set out in his excellent commentary on 1 and 2 Samuel in *The Century Bible* (1905).

of traditions offers more scope for editorial insertion and conflation than the use of a closely knit narrative like C. There was certainly no call for the Deuteronomic doctrine of reward and retribution in a document which demonstrated so plainly the effects of sin without indulging in pious comment.

The clear case of later insertion is the appendix, which separates 2 Sam. xx from the end of C. Of the items contained in it (see above, p. 72), the first (the famine) corresponds to the sixth (the census), the second corresponds to the fifth (David's mighty men), and the third (the psalm of thanksgiving) corresponds to the fourth (David's last words). It seems likely that (1) and (6) were added first, then (2) and (5) inserted between them as a continuous passage, only to be divided later by the interpolation of (3) and (4). The character of the stories in (1) and (6) shows that they contain ancient material; and there is no reason to doubt the antiquity of (2) and (5). (3) is a psalm of thanksgiving, and may well have been intended for use by a king of David's line. *Vv.* 21–25 could hardly have been used or composed by David himself without considerable mental reservation, and would be more appropriate, in language and thought, to the time of King Josiah. It is generally held that (4) is not by David, since it is difficult to believe that he would have described himself as 'the darling of Israel's songs'.

In the so-called Song (or Prayer) of Hannah (1 Sam. ii. 1–10) we have another poem which is a later insertion. Probably it was connected with its present context because the reference to the barren bearing children seemed appropriate to the story of Hannah. But the rest of the poem is not particularly relevant to her situation; and the reference in *v.* 10 to the king shows that it is no earlier than the monarchy. It is a psalm of thanksgiving for deliverance from dire distress.

The two other poems included in the book are David's lament over Saul and Jonathan (2 Sam. i. 19–27), which is said to have been contained in the Book of Jashar (cf. above,

p. 58), and David's lament over Abner. There can be little doubt that they are authentic examples of the poetic gift for which David was famous. It is rightly argued that if the former had been by a later writer, he would almost certainly have introduced some religious theme, in keeping with David's reputation as a psalmist. The second is also entirely in keeping with the situation to which it refers.

Summing up, we may say that the material was in all probability given approximately its present shape by a Deuteronomic writer, who used a variety of ancient traditional sources, and a superb historical document, to which he added later material, including a religious interpretation of past events in the Deuteronomic idiom. As the age of the judges does not end with Judges xvi, but continues into 1 Samuel, so the reign of David and the history of the succession do not end with 2 Sam. xx, but continue in 1 Kings. As in Judges, too, there is a later appendix inserted at the end. But there is this difference, that the Deuteronomic outline is by no means as prominent and formative in Samuel as in Judges.

## 3. *Historical, Literary, and Religious Importance*

The presence of really ancient and authentic material in Samuel gives the book a rare historical importance. But it would be a mistake to under-rate the value of the later passages. The later account of the origin of the monarchy, for example, may be a less accurate account of what actually happened. But it is more than a religious idealization of events. It shows what the monarchy sometimes became in the later period (1 Sam. viii. 11 ff), and it echoes the prophetic protest against tyranny and royal apostasy. The contemporary can never fully evaluate the events through which he lives, though he may record them accurately. 'He may not have known or suspected influences which have been later revealed.'[1] An enthusiastic admirer of Cromwell in the 17th

[1] C. V. Wedgwood, *The King's Peace*, p. 15. The whole passage (pp. 14 f) is relevant to the point made above.

century would not be able to appreciate the importance of
his work in the same way as a 20th-century admirer, who is
aware of subsequent developments.

It has been suggested that the later traditions about
Samuel are inaccurate at one important point, in that they
transfer to him what was originally the story of the birth of
Saul. Admittedly, the explanation of the name which is
given in 1 Sam. i. 20 suits the name Saul (='asked') better
than Samuel. But such popular explanatory etymologies in
the Old Testament are often inaccurate and more dependent
on sound than sense. Moreover, to fit Saul the Benjamite into
an Ephraimite environment raises difficulties and solves
none.

The supreme historical treasure of Samuel is the Court
History. This document stands midway between the old
traditional material, with its accretions from popular lore,
and the reflective, increasingly doctrinaire histories of later
times. It has the factual accuracy of contemporary chronicle.
But, unlike the mere annalist, the writer reveals the relationship of character with event, and of one event with another,
by the sheer skill of his narration. In the whole of the Old
Testament, only the work of the Yahwist is comparable with
the superbly simple prose of the Court History. As history, it
is unequalled in ancient Hebrew literature. At this period, and
for centuries afterwards, the neighbouring civilizations produced nothing comparable. The writer had seen history made
in David's reign; and when, probably in the reign of Solomon,
he wrote his narrative, he himself made literary history.

Of the poems in the book, the Song of Hannah and the two
psalms in the appendix belong to the literary and religious
tradition enshrined in the Psalter. The two laments (2 Sam.
i. 19–27; iii. 33 f) deserve attention, both as examples of
David's art and also because of their character. The one on
Abner is brief, and perhaps only fragmentary. It expresses
sorrow and respect, but no warm affection or deep sense of
personal loss. If, at Abner's funeral, David made no attempt
to display emotions which he did not feel, there is every

reason to suppose that the deep feeling expressed in the other lament was entirely sincere. Tradition apart, the haunting beauty of this passionate lament would suffice to establish David's reputation as a poet of rare power.

The ancient traditions about the Ark preserved in 1 Sam. iv–vi contain valuable evidence about Hebrew religion at an early stage. It is significant that, combined with early ideas about the dynamic holiness of Yahweh and His sacramental presence in the Ark, there is more than a touch of sardonic, sceptical humour in the attitude to Dagon. The older passages about the origin of the monarchy provide valuable evidence about the prophetic movement. In the story of Jonathan's enterprise (1 Sam. xiv), the character of the oath, the practice of fasting, the use of the sacred lot, and possibly substitutionary slaughter (xiv. 45) are illustrated. The practice of the ban appears in 1 Sam. xv. In the story of the witch of En-dor we catch a glimpse of the eerie pagan practices against which loyal Yahwists strove. Comparatively little is said about contemporary religious practice in the Court History; but the ethical insight is not less impressive because the author scarcely ever pauses to point a moral. In Nathan's denunciation of David (2 Sam. xii), what is elsewhere implicit becomes unforgettably explicit. Finally, the later passages gather together the varied strands of the story into the context of the Deuteronomic theology. If there was little of full-blooded apostasy to serve as an awful warning, it was at least possible to recall that even in the heroic age the way was opened to the tyranny and arrogance of later times.

## IV. 1 and 2 Kings

### 1. *Contents*

Like 1 and 2 Samuel, the books of Kings are reckoned as one in the Hebrew Canon (see above, p. 10 n.). The contents may be divided into four parts:

(a) 1 Kings i–ii. The end of the history of David's court, describing how Adonijah's *coup d'état* was foiled, David's last days, and the establishment of Solomon's position as king.

(*b*) 1 Kings iii–xi. The reign of Solomon.

(*c*) 1 Kings xii–2 Kings xvii. The Disruption of the Kingdom, followed by the reigns of the kings of Israel and Judah till the fall of Samaria in 721 B.C.

(*d*) 2 Kings xviii–xxv. The reigns of the kings of Judah from the fall of Samaria to the fall of Jerusalem in 586, with a closing reference to the release from prison of the exiled king Jehoiachin.

A more detailed examination of the contents of each section must be undertaken in our attempt to analyse the book.

### 2. *Analysis and Growth*

Little need be said here about (*a*). The document of which it is a part has already been discussed in the chapter on the books of Samuel. We should, however, notice the presence of Deuternomic style and thought in ii. 2b–4, 10–12, 27.

Near the end of the account in (*b*) of Solomon's reign there is a reference to 'the Book of the Acts of Solomon', to which the reader is referred for further information. It seems likely that that book has been used as a source for iii–xi; but it is probably wrong to conclude that all, or nearly all, the material in these chapters was derived from it. The marked variety of style and content suggests diversity of origin. It might of course be argued that, since this varied material has been assembled in Kings, it may equally well have been already assembled in the source-book referred to. But, as we shall see, such unity as the material now has, has been given to it by a Deuteronomic hand.

Only the closing chapter (xi) mentions Solomon's defects. The bulk of the section describes his merits and achievements (iii–x). The larger part of that is devoted to his building programme (v–ix. 14), in which the building of the temple has pride of place. It seems likely that temple records (or, as Montgomery suggests, the architect's specifications), have been drawn upon for this part of the book. But, in addition to the technical details, there are sections which refer to

Solomon's relations with Hiram and the general preparations
for the building. It is quite likely that these are taken from
the Acts of Solomon (v. 1, 6–11, (?)13–18; ix. 10–14).
Passages of a similar character describe Solomon's other
activities (e.g., parts of iii; iv. 22–28; ix. 15–28; x. 11–12,
14–29; xi. 14–25). There are also lists of officials and the like,
probably derived from the palace archives (iv. 1–19, 27 f).
Other stories have a more popular character, and present
Solomon as the pious young king asking for the gift of
wisdom (iii. 3–15), as the shrewd judge (iii. 16–28), as one
whose renown brought the Queen of Sheba to visit him (x. 1–
10, 13).

The story of Jeroboam (xi. 26–31, 40) is a straightforward,
realistic account, and probably quite old.

It seems that this varied material has been arranged so
that the story of the building of the temple should be central,
with stories about Solomon's wisdom before and after it, and
excerpts from the official chronicles and archives fitted in at
various points.

Running through the whole record is a thread of Deuteronomic comment (iii. 3, 6, 14; v. 3–5, 12; vi. 11–13; viii. 9;
xi. 41–43); and at some points the Deuteronomic material is
more substantial. The account of the dedication of the temple
begins with a narrative (viii. 1–13), which reads like part of
the royal records, touched up by Deuteronomic and post-
Deuteronomic hands.[1] It leads up to the long Deuteronomic
prayer (viii. 14–53) and Solomon's blessing (viii. 54–61). The
theophany which follows the dedication is also Deuteronomic.
These passages contain two clear references to the Exile
(viii. 46 ff; ix. 6 ff), which are no doubt later than 586 B.C.,
and therefore contrast with viii. 8 (note, 'unto this day').
Again, in xi. 1–13, Solomon's shortcomings are described and
denounced in Deuteronomic terms. It is significant that the

---

[1] *Vv.* 12 f contain an ancient poetic fragment, which may be a quota-
tion from the Book of Jashar. The Greek text has "the Book of the Song";
and it seems quite likely that the Hebrew consonants in 'song', *šyr*,
were originally *yšr* (*yāšār*).

religious consequences of his marriage with an Egyptian
princess are enlarged on. The political implications of that
event, which must have been very important, are not mentioned in this passage; but we get a hint of them in the older
source ix. 16. This emphasis on religion and neglect of important political factors is typical of the Deuteronomic approach. Finally, a paragraph of Deuteronomic comment is
included in the story of Jeroboam (xi. 32b–39). If, as seems
likely, xi. 36 is earlier than the fall of Jerusalem (contrast
viii. 46 ff; ix. 6 ff) the material is not all of one date.

In (b), then, we have material which has been derived, not
from a single, connected chronicle, but from different sources,
arranged, expanded, and edited by a Deuteronomic writer.

Parts (c) and (d) may be taken together. From 1 Kings xii
onward there are frequent references to two sources: 'the
Book of the Chronicles of the Kings of Israel' (1 Kings xiv. 19,
and sixteen other references), and 'the Book of the Chronicles
of the Kings of Judah' (1 Kings xiv. 29, and fourteen other
references). It seems likely that the many brief references to
the doings of the kings (their wars, their building and com-
mercial enterprises, and the like) are drawn from them.
Neither of these sources is to be identified with 1 and 2
Chronicles, which are probably dependent on those earlier
sources as well as on the books of Samuel and Kings. Nor are
they to be identified with the official palace records. The
account of the turbulent history of the Northern Kingdom,
for example, presents the sequence of intrigue and assassina-
tions with candour, and does not read like the work of a
court historian who had to write circumspectly. The references to the Book of the Chronicles of the Kings of Israel end
with the reign of Pekah (2 Kings xv. 31), the reign of Hoshea,
the last of the Northern kings, being left without such
comment. The Book of the Chronicles of the kings of Judah
is last mentioned at the end of the reign of Jehoiakim
(2 Kings xxiv. 5).

In some parts of the record, the temple features prominently (2 Kings xi. 4 ff; xii. 4 ff; xxii. 8 ff); and it may be that

the temple archives have been drawn upon. But, as J. A. Montgomery has observed,[1] there is no trace of the priestly style in these passages; and some of them are slightly critical of the priesthood. It is, therefore, unlikely that priests wrote these archives, though the temple may have housed them.

There is also evidence of the use of other sources, which are not named. One lengthy section (1 Kings xvii–2 Kings x) stands out from the general run of brief historical notices. It covers roughly a quarter of a century in sixteen chapters, giving special attention to the religious crises of the time. Leaving aside a few verses of the annalistic type (e.g., 1 Kings xxii. 44, 47–49; 2 Kings i. 1; viii. 20–22; x. 32 f), and certain Deuteronomic elements, which must be mentioned below, it contains three main cycles of stories, all clearly northern in origin.

(1) 1 Kings xx and xxii describe important incidents in the wars between Israel and Syria during the reign of Ahab. In xx, he appears as a heroic king, successfully resisting aggression, but merciful after his victory. xxii. 1–38 tells of Ahab's death in his last battle against the Syrians. He is described in a somewhat less favourable light, as self-willed and heedless of the word of a true prophet. Oesterley and Robinson hold that these stories are taken from a document which dealt with Ahab's achievements in the Syrian wars. They call it 'the Acts of Ahab'. Others think of it as a more general history of those wars. At all events, it seems to have been a historical source which gave some account of political and military events; and its general character suggests that it was written not long after Ahab's time. The story of the prophet who denounced the king's clemency (xx. 35–43; cf. 1 Sam. xv. 10–31) is usually regarded as a later addition. It is noteworthy that whenever a prophet appears on the scene, Ahab is presented in a less favourable light. This is so, as we have seen, in xxii. 1–40, where the prisoner, Micaiah, towers

[1] *A Critical and Exegetical Commentary on the Books of Kings* (I.C.C.), p. 38; cf. J. E. McFadyen, *Introduction*[2], p. 121.

in moral stature over the warrior king. There is some ground for thinking of that passage as primarily a prophetic story.

The other two cycles are clearly prophetic. They tell of the deeds of Elijah and Elisha, and were, in all probability, told and transmitted among the prophetic communities ('the sons of the prophets') to which there are several references in these very stories. They bear an obvious resemblance to the biographical parts of the Latter Prophets.

(2) The Elijah stories (1 Kings xvii–xix; xxi; 2 Kings i) tell of the drought, of how Elijah was sustained at Cherith and Zarephath, of the raising of the widow's son, the contest on Mount Carmel, Elijah's flight to Horeb, the affair of Naboth's vineyard, and Elijah's prediction of Ahaziah's death. The story of Naboth's vineyard appears to have been inserted before xxii, so that the prophecy of xxi. 19 might be linked with its fulfilment (xxii. 38).

In these stories, Ahab is not the national hero (as in xx), but the tyrant and corrupter of Israel. In xix. 17, Syria is the rod of Yahweh, rather than a foreign aggressor to be resisted. The point of view is thus very different from that in the account of the Syrian campaigns.

(8) The Elisha stories may be said to begin in 1 Kings xix. 19–21, which tells of Elisha's call. The main body of them begins with 2 Kings ii. 1–18, the story of the translation of Elijah, which might be included in the Elijah cycle, but is best regarded as the introduction to what follows. ii. 19–x contains stories, in most of which the wonder-working powers of the prophet play some part. In some, that is the main point: the healing of the waters (ii. 19–22); the story of the bears. (ii. 23–25); the widow's oil (iv. 1–7); the poisoned pottage (iv. 38–41); the miraculous feeding of a hundred prophets (iv. 42–44); the floating axe-head (vi. 1–7); the Shunammite's distress (viii. 1–6). Akin to these is the story of the life-giving power of the prophet's bones (xiii. 20, 21). (This, together with the account of Elisha's death-bed in xiii. 14–19, must originally have belonged to the cycle.) In others, the miraculous element is combined with a fine de-

lineation of character: the Shunammite woman and her son
(iv. 8–37); the healing of Naaman and the sin of Gehazi (v).
Others, again, bear on the military and political history of
the time: the campaign against Moab (iii. 4–27); the blinding
of the Syrian army (vi. 8–23); the siege of Samaria (vi. 24–
vii. 20); the story of Hazael (viii. 7–15); the anointing of
Jehu, and the revolution (ix–x. 28).

A number of these stories closely resemble some in the
Elijah cycle. But the miraculous element is much more
prominent in the Elisha narratives. Also, the stories about
Elijah have more coherence than those about Elisha, which
are linked together by little more than the personality of the
prophet. Both cycles were probably handed down by oral
tradition for some time before being written. As we have
seen, it is natural to think of the prophetic communities as
the appropriate milieu; but the popular character of the
Elisha cycle suggests that it circulated more widely and for a
longer period.

In one or two of the Elisha stories, the political and
historical interest is very marked (e.g., vi. 24–vii. 20); and
they perhaps come from a source similar to the so-called
'Acts of Ahab'. Again, in the brilliantly written account of
Jehu's revolution, Elisha appears only in the opening
passages. It may therefore have belonged to an independent
prophetic source. It is difficult to believe that it is not contemporary, or nearly so, with the events.

A prophetic source may also lie behind the narratives in
2 Kings xviii. 17–xx. 19, in which the prophet Isaiah plays
a significant part. They tell of Sennacherib's invasion, the
illness and recovery of Hezekiah, and the embassy from
Merodach-baladan. This passage is also found in Isa. xxxvi–
xxxix; but since it seems to be a later addition there, it is
unlikely to have formed part of the main body of traditions
about the prophet, preserved by his disciples.

It is instructive to compare this account of Sennacherib's
invasion with the summary statement (drawn, perhaps, from
the Book of the Chronicles of the Kings of Judah) which

precedes it. There has been much discussion of the question
whether xviii. 17–xix. 8 and xix. 9–37 contain two varying
accounts of the same visit of the Rabshakeh to Jerusalem, or
describe two different visits in the one campaign, or refer to
two quite distinct invasions. But there is no sufficient reason
for not taking the story as it stands: first, the Rabshakeh
comes to Jerusalem with a strong force; later, when the
Egyptian advance threatens Sennacherib's army, no strong
force can be spared, but the Rabshakeh returns to Jerusalem
to intimidate Hezekiah, lest he should co-operate with Egypt.

The passage also includes a prophetic oracle in the form of
a taunt-song (xix. 21–28).

In 1 Kings xiii there is a quaint story about the denunciation of the altar of Bethel by a man of God from Judah. It is
clearly late, for it refers to the cities of Samaria, implying
that Samaria was a province, as it was at a later period;[1] and
it is usually classed as a midrash (an edifying fiction based
on a historical theme). It may go back to some tradition
connected with the sanctuary at Bethel. It should certainly
not be classed with the prophetic narratives which we have
considered above.

1 Kings xiv, which tells how the prophet Ahijah foretold
the death of Jeroboam's son, may preserve old prophetic
material; but it has been much revised.

We have already noted the presence of Deuteronomic
elements in parts (a) and (b). These also appear in (c) and (d),
where they occur in three main forms: (1) a framework;
(2) short additions to the narrative or religious comments;
(8) one or two longer passages.

(1) The framework is in some ways similar to the one in
Judges, since it combines chronology with religious judgements. But, whereas in Judges the material within the framework consisted of disconnected stories, the histories of the
two kingdoms were parallel and continuous records. They are
combined by the following method: the reign of one king is

[1] In Jeroboam's time, the *city* of Samaria had not yet been built
(1 Kings xvi. 24).

narrated to its conclusion, then the reigns of all the kings who came to the throne of the other kingdom during that period. The reigns of the kings of Judah are introduced by a synchronism of the king's accession with the regnal year of the king of Israel, a statement of the king's age, the length of his reign, his mother's name, and a judgement on his reign; and they are rounded off by a reference to the Book of the Chronicles of the Kings of Judah, a statement about the king's death and burial, and the name of his successor. The synchronism with Israel does not appear, of course, after the fall of Samaria. The reigns of the kings of Israel begin with a synchronism with the regnal year of the king of Judah, a statement of the length of the reign, and a judgement on it; and they end with a formula similar to that used for the kings of Judah, except that the phrase 'was buried with his fathers' is never used. The concluding formula does not appear at the end of the reigns of Athaliah, Jehoahaz, Jehoiachin, and Zedekiah of Judah, and of Jehoram and Hoshea of Israel. There are other minor modifications, but the most interesting differences appear in the judgements on the reigns. All the kings of Israel (with the exception of Shallum, who reigned only a month) are said to have done evil. Of the kings of Judah, Hezekiah and Josiah are given unqualified commendation, because they did right and suppressed the high places; some are commended for doing right, with the reservation that the high places were not suppressed; the others are condemned (except that Judah, not Rehoboam, is mentioned in 1 Kings xiv. 22 f). Clearly, all are judged by Deuteronomic standards, and, in particular, by the law of the single sanctuary. It is characteristic that, after recording the political crisis which led to the Disruption, the Deuteronomist emphasizes the religious consequences of Jeroboam's policy, which he judges by Deuteronomic standards (1 Kings xii. 25 ff).

The chronology of the framework raises intricate problems. Before the Disruption and after the fall of Samaria, the reckoning is by the reigns of the kings in Jerusalem. But for

the period of the divided monarchy there is a double reckoning: by the synchronisms, and by the length of the reigns in
each kingdom. Unfortunately there are discrepancies between
the systems; and no simple solution is possible.[1]

(2) The short Deuteronomic additions are, for the most
part, easily recognizable. They appear in references to the
fulfilment of prophecy (e.g., 1 Kings xv. 29b; xvi. 7), in
religious comments and judgements (e.g., 2 Kings x. 29–31),
and sometimes in brief narratives with a religious point (e.g.,
1 Kings xii. 21–24, 25–31).

(3) The longer passages occur at crucial points in the
narrative: the lengthy comment on the fall of the Northern
Kingdom as the outcome of apostasy (2 Kings xvii. 7–23);
the account of the reign of Manasseh, the apostate king of
Judah (2 Kings xxi. 1–18); the story of the last years of the
kingdom of Judah, the fall of Jerusalem, the assassination of
Gedaliah and the release of Jehoiachin (2 Kings xxiv. 8–
xxv. 30).

From the above it appears that the material in Kings has
been put together from a variety of sources by a Deuteronomic
writer or writers. Some of the sources (e.g., the Elijah and
Elisha stories) must have been transmitted orally before being committed to writing; others (particularly the annals)
were, by their very nature, literary sources. It has been held
that J and E are to be found in the book; and Eissfeldt
traces L, J, and E.

The closing verses of the book show that the work was
completed about the middle of the 6th century, because
Jehoiachin was released from prison in 561 B.C. The date
cannot be brought much lower, since there is no allusion to
the fall of Babylon.[2] But there are Deuteronomic passages in
the book which seem to be earlier than the fall of Jerusalem
or even the death of Josiah (1 Kings viii. 8; xi. 36; 2 Kings

---

[1] For further information on this difficult subject, reference may be
made to J. A. Montgomery, *op. cit.*, pp. 45 ff, and to E. R. Thiele, *The
Mysterious Numbers of the Hebrew Kings; A Reconstruction of the
Chronology of Israel and Judah.*

[2] Some post-Deuteronomic elements may have been added later.

viii. 19, 22; xxii. 20). It is, therefore, usually held that there was more than one stage in the composition of the work.[1]

The traditional ascription of the authorship of Kings to Jeremiah is barely possible, and very improbable. Jeremiah was taken down to Egypt after the assassination of Gedaliah. It hardly seems likely that he was alive when Jehoiachin was released. But it was during his lifetime, or very soon after, that the books of the Former Prophets were composed.

## (3) *Historical, Literary and Religious Importance*

The book of Samuel covers a period of roughly a century. In Kings about the same space is devoted to more than four centuries. Accordingly a more summary treatment is to be expected. In fact, the amount of detail varies considerably in different parts of Kings. The reign of Solomon, the Disruption, the history of Northern Israel in the 9th century, the reign of Hezekiah, Josiah's reform, and the fall of Jerusalem are treated at length. Interest is concentrated on events and persons of religious importance. Much that must have been of great political and social moment is omitted. Omri, the founder of Samaria and the conqueror of Moab, was unquestionably one of the strongest kings of Northern Israel. Even after the extinction of his line, the Assyrians called Israel the land of Omri. But only six verses are devoted to his reign (1 Kings xvi. 23–28), whereas events from the reign of his son, Ahab, occupy as many chapters. Yet these chapters do not mention the important battle of Karkar (854 B.C.), in which Ahab provided a very strong contingent to the force of the western allies against Shalmaneser III, from whose inscription the battle is known to us.

More will be said later in justification of the Deuterono-

---

[1] The Greek text of Kings raises difficult problems. Apart from textual variations of the usual kind, it includes entire narratives which do not appear in the Hebrew text (e.g., following 1 Kings xii. 24). For details, reference should be made to the larger commentaries, such as that by J. A. Montgomery, quoted above, or C. F. Burney, *Notes on the Hebrew Text of the Books of Kings.*

mist's selection. Meanwhile, we may note that he has, in fact, preserved much material of great historical value.

In the account of Solomon's reign, the building of the temple is, naturally, given pride of place; but there is more than a hint of the policy which led to the Disruption. And if the Deuteronomist is concerned to emphasize the religious consequences of that event, he allows the older narrative to make plain the other factors involved.

At the other end of the period, the record again becomes more detailed, and provides useful and authentic information about the last years of the kingdom of Judah.

Most striking of all, however, is the fact that a work which glorifies the temple at Jerusalem includes so much from northern sources for the period of the divided monarchy. The historical importance of these narratives varies. Of Ahab's Syrian wars, the social and religious crises of his reign, and Jehu's revolution, we have memorable and authentic records. Some of the Elisha stories have been likened to medieval hagiography; but, even if the miraculous element were to be entirely removed, there would remain an illuminating picture of life in 9th-century Israel, quite indispensable for the social historian of the period.

The literary quality of several of these northern stories is outstanding. The dramatic power of the Elijah stories and of the Micaiah episode, the graphic narrative of Ahab's campaigns, the simplicity and pathos of the story of the Shunammite and her son, the delineation of character in the story of Naaman, and the brilliant realism with which Jehu's revolution is recorded, reflect the intellectual vitality of the Northern Kingdom and its prophetic communities.

Some of these stories are among the great documents of Old Testament religion; and, elsewhere in Kings, there are passages (e.g., Solomon's dream in 1 Kings iii; the stories of Sennacherib's invasion in 2 Kings xviii–xix) which have their own religious message. But to appreciate the theological value of Kings as a whole we must consider it together with the other Former Prophets.

## V. The Deuteronomic History

The books Joshua–Kings are more than a record of historical events; they are a record of the varying ways in which, up to the 6th century at least, the story of Israel's past was told and interpreted.

Much of the material, especially in Joshua and Judges and the early chapters of Samuel, is of the kind known as *saga*. These stories tell of historical events and persons; but they have passed through a process of popular oral transmission before being committed to writing; and in that process they have probably been refashioned, their contours sometimes sharpened, sometimes blurred, and their colours heightened.

In the Court History in 2 Samuel and 1 Kings, we at last reach a stage in which the events of history are recorded in a document; for, although that work may show slight signs of later editing, it bears none of the marks of popular transmission. The story has a goal: the secure establishment of Solomon on the throne. The skill with which the story is told itself provides the interpretation of the events. The biographical interest appears in the clear presentation of character and motive, so much so that some think of it as biography rather than history.

Documentary sources of different kinds are represented by the archival lists in Samuel and Kings, and the many passages in Kings drawn from the royal histories of both kingdoms. But the popular story still appears, as in the judgement of Solomon, or the visit of the Queen of Sheba, or in the Elijah and Elisha cycles, though the contents of these latter groups vary considerably in character. The biographical and historical interest reappears markedly in them and also in the story of Ahab's campaigns.

Finally, there is the contribution of the Deuteronomist, most obvious in Judges and Kings, least obvious in 2 Samuel. It has been customary to refer to these elements as the work of redactors; and some have even thought of 'pre-Deuteronomic' books of Joshua, Judges, Samuel, and Kings. The analysis offered above suggests that no such works ever existed; but that the precursors of Joshua–Kings were simply the various sources which have been enumerated. We have also noted that there is no clear and coherent evidence for the continuation of the Pentateuchal sources through the Former Prophets. Further, none of these books, except perhaps Joshua, forms anything like a completed story. Not only is Judges the historical sequel to Joshua, but there is also a literary link between Joshua xxiii (and xxiv?) and Judges ii. 6 ff. The age of the Judges ends in 1 Sam. xii. The Court History of David continues into 1 Kings. Thus the present division into books is mainly an artificial partition of a structural unity. Making allowance for later additions, such as have been noted above, it seems clear that this structural unity is the work of the Deuteronomist,[1] who has put together material drawn from his various sources, with his own additions, to form a history of Israel and an interpretation of that history. This view has been strongly argued by Noth in his important work, *Ueberlieferungsgeschichtliche Studien I.* We have already noted (p. 53) his view that there is little evidence of the continuation of J, E, and P after the end of Numbers. He maintains that Deuteronomy–Kings was not originally connected with Genesis–Numbers or with the sources found there, but was the work of a Deuteronomic historian, who incorporated the Deuteronomic code and its hortatory preamble in the framework of his narrative.

Noth appears to make too sharp a distinction between the traditions about the deliverance from Egypt and those about the entry into Canaan. Even if it is difficult to trace J and E in Joshua, the fact remains that, without something like the contents of Joshua, J, E, and P would be incomplete. If Joshua does not contain their conclusion, it must have replaced it.

---

[1] We use the term Deuteronomist, in the singular, for convenience. Evidence may be found of more than one Deuteronomic hand. But the point is that in plan and conception the work is one.

But, even if we do not accept every detail of the literary analysis which Noth offers in support of his thesis, he has made a notable contribution to our understanding of the Former Prophets as a sustained historical work.

The Deuteronomist has selected and arranged the source material at his disposal. The editorial methods vary; but the variation seems to correspond, not simply to the lines of demarcation between the books as we now have them, but to the types of source used. A sustained, coherent source like the Court History, called for little or no addition; whereas the stories of the Judges had to be made into a consecutive history.

The story runs from the entry into the Promised Land to the deportation from it, and beyond, to the dawning of hope, when Jehoiachin was released. At crucial points in the narrative, there are reflections on its meaning, in the form of speeches or of the historian's own comment (Joshua's address in Joshua xxiv; Samuel's in 1 Sam. xii; Solomon's prayer at the dedication of the temple in 1 Kings viii; the comment on the fall of Samaria in 2 Kings xviii). The Deuteronomist is concerned to comment and interpret as well as to record. This distinguishes his intention from that of most of the sources he uses, and helps to explain the nature of the selection. Those who wanted to read of Omri's greatness could consult the Book of the Chronicles of the Kings of Israel (we, unfortunately, cannot); but presumably the facts would not have contributed to the Deuteronomist's purpose. He is not a scientific historian, though he has preserved much that the modern scientific historian can use. His purpose is not to provide a complete narrative, but to apply the religious lessons of history.

Without pressing the comparison too far, we may again find a parallel in the New Testament. There, the Gospels are followed by the Acts, a historical record based on sources, which is highly selective in its account of the life and growth of the Church, leaving us in ignorance of much that we should like to know, but tracing for us certain important lines of

the Church's development, and ending like Kings 'with words
of "good omen" on a note of calm'.[1]

The Deuteronomist applies the principles of Deuteronomy
to his people's history. From the time of the Conquest to the
fall of Jerusalem, obedience to Yahweh's commands is the
test; and it is disobedience and apostasy that finally lead to
disaster. There is a repeated emphasis on the fulfilment of
prophecy, as if to demonstrate that the supreme power which
kings and people encounter in history is the power of
Yahweh's word. Disaster is not misfortune; it is judgement.
If the record is selective, the intention is to make plain God's
purpose and Israel's errors, not to explain away the national
catastrophe or to salvage remnants of the nation's glory.
Perhaps, after all, the selection is not entirely misguided. We
may regret our ignorance about Omri; but since, on the long
view, the cave on Horeb counted for more in Israel's history
than the courts where Omri gloried and drank deep, history
may be said to have justified the Deuteronomist.[2]

[1] B. H. Streeter, *The Four Gospels*, p. 539 n.
[2] For a stimulating account of the theology of history in Kings, see
G. von Rad, *Studies in Deuteronomy*, pp. 74 ff.

# V.—THE LATTER PROPHETS

## I. Introductory

Perhaps no other group of writings in the Bible has been so drastically reinterpreted for us as the books of the Latter Prophets. The reinterpretation is the result, partly of a deeper understanding of the prophetic movement, of which these books are the deposit, and partly of closer study of the nature of the writings themselves. One is tempted to say that critical scholarship has shown first, that the prophetic books are not prophetic, and second, that they are not books. That would be a misleading exaggeration; but it may serve to indicate two of the most important phases in the modern study of these writings.

Whereas, for the Jew, the Hebrew Scriptures were primarily Torah, the early Christian Church, in taking over these same Scriptures, thought of them, in the main, as prophecy; they witnessed beforehand to the coming of Christ. Such predictions were found in all parts of the Old Testament, but chiefly in the prophetic books. The prime task of the prophet was taken to be prediction; and it came to be held that in these books the shape of things to come had been forecast centuries beforehand.

The modern study of Old Testament literature and religion in their historical setting brought about a change. The prophet was seen to be a man of his own time with a message for his own generation. His function was not solely or mainly long-term prediction. It was often said that he was not a *fore*-teller, but a *forth*-teller of the will of Yahweh. This is a misleading statement, if it means that the prophets were more concerned with what men ought to do, than with what Yahweh was doing and purposed to do, or that they did not predict the future at all. They did predict, sometimes the immediate, sometimes the more distant, future. But their function was not to plot the future course of history in detail, but to interpret history in terms of the will of Yahweh. Jeremiah's forecasts of events were often wrong in detail, as he himself tells us; but this does not seriously affect his greatness as a prophet, unless his interpretation of history in terms of the will of Yahweh was unsound. To understand the lasting worth of his teaching, we must try to relate it to the events and circumstances of history. Again, Isaiah's prophecy that Jerusalem would *not* fall, and Ezekiel's recurrent prediction that it *would* fall, cannot be understood unless they are put into their respective settings, the former during Sennacherib's invasion at the end of the 8th century, and the latter at the beginning of the 6th, during the last years of the kingdom of Judah. To relate either prophecy to the wrong situation would involve misunderstanding its message. That is why dating the various parts of the prophetic books is not merely an academic exercise, but often an essential preparation for exegesis.

The historical and literary criticism of the 19th century did much to interpret the prophets' teaching in terms of the events and circumstances of their own times. But there was a tendency to treat the prophetic books as books in the modern sense. The men whose names are associated with these writings were often called 'the Writing Prophets', in distinction from the earlier prophets, such as Nathan, Micaiah ben Imlah, Elijah, and Elisha, who, for all their greatness, had left no comparable memorial. The assumption was that Isaiah, Jeremiah, Ezekiel, and the others had written down, or dictated, their teaching and experiences in something like book form. Not that the books had come down to us exactly as they left their putative authors' hands. Editors and interpolators had been at work; and where, for instance, the original prophet had delivered a message of apparently unmitigated doom, the cheerfulness of the epigoni would keep breaking in, in the form of interpolated predictions of bliss. In their orthodox zeal, they would do their best to eliminate the prophet's theological errors; or, through mere stupidity, they would distort his meaning by what were meant to be illuminating comments. It was one of the tasks of literary criticism to eliminate all such secondary matter, and, as nearly as possible, to reconstruct the 'book' as it left the original author's hand.

Two main kinds of evidence were sought in this process of expurgation. First, there was the prophet's *manner*. Any noteworthy change of style, or peculiarity of vocabulary, or variation of metre, was liable to be regarded as the sign of another hand. Such criteria must, of course, be taken into account. The attentive reader of the book of Isaiah will notice, even in the English versions, the difference between the smooth and ample eloquence of xl–lv and the more nervous and concise style of i. But such tests must be applied with care. We have already noted that change of style and diction need not by themselves indicate change of authorship (p. 25). Metre is a still more uncertain guide, not to be relied on unless supported by other evidence, and to be treated with suspicion, when a critic's metrical theory requires extensive textual emendation.

Secondly, account was taken of the *matter* of the passage in question. If it seemed to be inconsistent with the thought of the prophet as shown in other passages, it might be attributed to an interpolator. Here the danger was that the critic might expect in the prophet an artificial standard of consistency, not allowing for the possibility that he might have had different things to say in different conditions, or changed his emphasis according to the need of the day. An outstanding example of the way in which passages might be regarded, out of hand, as interpolations because of their content is the tendency of some older critics to regard all prophecies of future bliss as post-exilic.

Although consistency of thought is undoubtedly a help towards assigning prophetic passages to a given period or

prophet, it is wrong to expect to find everywhere in the
prophetic literature the ordered progress of thought which
would be appropriate in a modern treatise, and which appears even in a New Testament epistle. For the books of the
prophets are not books in the modern sense. The indications
of date, which often occur in headings to various passages,
show that the arrangement is not strictly chronological (e.g.,
Jer. xxi. 1; xxiv. 1; xxv. 1; xxvi. 1; xxvii. 1; xxviii. 1); and
the frequent change of theme is a sign that the juxtaposition
of sayings or stories is not necessarily a guide to their original
context. The prophetic books are collections of material, or,
more precisely, collections of smaller collections of material.
To analyse and interpret them, it is necessary, in addition to
the methods already mentioned, to recognize and classify the
various types of material which they contain, and, further, so
far as is possible, to distinguish the various subordinate collections of which they are composed.[1]

Three main types of material occur: (A) the actual prophetic utterances, usually in poetical form; (B) narratives
about the prophets, written in the third person; (C) narratives
about the prophets' experiences, written in the first person.

(A) The prophetic oracles are often introduced by the expression 'Thus saith Yahweh', or end with 'saith Yahweh'
($n^{e^,}\bar{u}m$ $YHWH$; lit., 'oracle of Yahweh'); and where such
phrases occur, they serve to indicate the limits of the utterance. But often they are missing; and we must deduce from
the sense of a passage (sometimes, perhaps, with help from
the metre) where the unit of prophetic speech ends. Passages
which have a superficial sequence of thought may prove to
consist of originally separate sayings, later linked together by
a catchword, or because of a general similarity of subject. The
stock example is in Isa. i, where 10 ff is held by many to
begin a passage quite distinct from what precedes, but
artificially linked with $v$. 9 by the catchwords 'Sodom' and

---

[1] This approach to the prophetic books has been lucidly and effectively
expounded by T. H. Robinson. See the introductory chapter on the
prophetic literature in Oesterley and Robinson, *Introduction*.

'Gomorrah'. T. H. Robinson holds that, for the most part, the units of prophetic speech are brief. J. Lindblom, on the other hand, believes that longer consecutive passages often form coherent wholes.

Further application of the methods of form criticism may enable us to recognize among the prophetic utterances various types (e.g., dirges, taunt songs, etc.); but a prophet may well have used more than one literary type in any given utterance; and therefore the end of a literary unit is not necessarily the end of a prophetic speech.

(B) The narratives about the prophets are similar to those which, as mentioned in the previous chapter, have been preserved in Kings. The amount of biographical material varies considerably in the different books. In some, it is entirely absent. In Amos, there is preserved only one brief but illuminating scrap (vii. 10–17). In Jeremiah, there are many such passages.

(C) The autobiographical material includes all those passages in which the prophets tell of their call, and of visions and other extraordinary experiences. The authenticity of many of these passages has often been questioned on inadequate grounds. Unless strong arguments are produced to the contrary, we may regard them as valuable evidence for the nature of prophetic experience. In Jeremiah, we have a particularly interesting group of passages, commonly known as the 'Confessions' in which the prophet records his converse with Yahweh.

It is natural to think of this heterogeneous material as having been preserved (either orally or in written form) in prophetic communities. In them, more than elsewhere, there would be interest in the doings of the prophets; and the prophets themselves would be most likely to transmit their teaching and experiences to their disciples.

Direct evidence of how this was done is, at best, fragmentary. The earliest mention of a prophet's committing part of his message to writing is in Isa. viii. 1 ff, where, in accordance with Yahweh's command, Isaiah writes on a placard

the words, 'FOR MAHER-SHALAL-HASH-BAZ' (speed-spoil-haste-
prey), prophesying invasion. The specific command to write
down these words seems to imply that prophecy was not
usually so recorded. The context makes it clear that the
purpose of the inscription was not so much publication as
attestation: the prophet could make his message known by
word of mouth; but this device would provide sure evidence
after the event that the prophet had delivered this message
(cf. xxx. 8).

Later in the same chapter, the difficult words of *v.* 16 are
taken by many to mean that, when the general public rejected Isaiah's message, he committed it in written form [1] to
his disciples; and this seems to be the most likely interpretation. The prophecies so preserved are, presumably, those connected with the Syro-Ephraimitic invasion.

Over a century later, we find that when Jeremiah was, for
some reason, unable to go into the temple precincts, he was
commanded by Yahweh to dictate to Baruch the substance
of his teaching since his call. Baruch then read in the temple
what he had written. After King Jehoiakim had destroyed
the scroll, its contents were rewritten with additions (Jer.
xxxvi; cf. li. 60). Here, again, we note that Jeremiah's initial
and normal method of reaching his public was by means of
the spoken word, that it was in a special situation, in a time
of crisis, and by express divine command, that he used the
written word, and that writing was used as an aid to the
spoken word, which was still the means by which the prophetic message was conveyed to the people. There is no explicit suggestion here (as in Isa. viii. 1 ff) that the written word
will attest the prophet's message, when it has been fulfilled.
But the fact that the prophecies are written out a second time
suggests that the written record is intended to be a means
of transmitting and preserving them. It also appears that, in
comparison with the evidence, such as it is, in Isa. viii. 1 ff,
16, more was committed to writing, and for a different reason.

---

[1] Some hold that the language is figurative and refers to oral transmission.

In the story of Ezekiel's call, the symbolism of the 'roll of a book', which the prophet is commanded to eat (Ezek. ii. 9–iii. 3), suggests that the association between the written word and the prophetic word is becoming closer. After that, there is no very specific reference to prophecy in literary form, until we come, much later, to the explicit mention of the book of Jeremiah in Dan. ix. 2.

All would agree that the prophets did not normally use the written word as a medium of communication;[1] and most would agree that oral tradition played some part in the preservation and transmission of the materials of which the prophetic books are composed. But there is a difference of opinion about the stage at which, and the extent to which, these materials were committed to writing. During the past half-century the prevailing view has been that the prophetic sayings were written down by the prophets themselves or by their disciples soon after they had been uttered, and that these brief notes were later assembled into collections; that the biographical narratives were told and retold in prophetic circles for a generation or two, and then committed to writing; and that the prophets themselves wrote, or dictated to disciples, those accounts of their experiences which are contained in the autobiographical passages.

During the past twenty years, a far more important part has been claimed for oral tradition. H. S. Nyberg has maintained that the analogy of other ancient oriental literature (and, above all, the memoriter recitation of the Qur'an in Islam) show that oral transmission was predominant in Israel until after the Exile; and that only a very small part of the Old Testament was put into writing in the pre-exilic period. The prophetic material was handed down in the prophetic communities, where it was amplified and modified, so that, although (so Nyberg contended) the text was transmitted with great fidelity, it became impossible to know with

---

[1] A possible exception is Isa. xl–lv, which some have held was circulated in the form of fly-sheets. See Sidney Smith, *Isaiah, Chapters XL–LV. Literary Criticism and History*, p. 21. Cf. also Hab. ii. 2.

certainty what the prophet himself had said and what his disciples had added.

H. Birkeland pursued this line in a study of the composition of the prophetic books, in which (again appealing to the analogy of Islam) he argued that in the living process of oral transmission the prophetic material was not only preserved but arranged in collections or complexes. When it was committed to writing, these complexes were arranged to form something like our present books.

I. Engnell, who also insists on the importance of oral tradition, distinguishes between two types within the prophetic literature: (1) materials formed on the model of liturgy (e.g., Joel, Nahum, Habakkuk, and Isa. xl–lv), which he thinks were committed to writing by individual prophets; and (2) what he calls the *diwan* type (e.g., Amos, Hosea, Isa. i–xxxix, Jeremiah) consisting of prophetic teaching and stories handed down orally in prophetic circles, arranged in complexes, amplified, and then written down. He, too, makes great claims for the fidelity of oral transmission, but says that the attempt to distinguish between the *ipsissima verba* of the prophet and the additions of his disciples is futile.

Some have denied that oral tradition played so important a part. In particular, G. Widengren has pointed out that the extent to which writing was used varied according to general cultural conditions. He adduces evidence from Arabic sources to show that the written record was regarded as more reliable than memory, and argues that, apart from the evidence mentioned above (pp. 101 f), there is a general probability that the Hebrew prophets, and their immediate disciples, who had connexions with priestly circles and with city life, made use of writing.

S. Mowinckel, too, who was one of the first to recognize the importance of the prophetic communities in selecting, pre serving, amplifying, and arranging the contents of our prophetic books, maintains that both methods of transmission must have operated. He also pleads that the attempt to distinguish between the words of the original prophet and the additions of later disciples should not be given up as hopeless, since this means, in effect, abandoning any inquiry into the history of the tradition.

Summing up, then, we may say that, although there is little direct evidence before the time of Jeremiah that pro-phetic teaching was recorded in written form, there is no strong case against it on general grounds. The probability is that both writing and oral repetition were used, and, indeed, that teaching which had already been written down was also still remembered and repeated orally. The analogy of the prophetic narratives in Kings suggests that, though the bio-graphical material may have circulated orally for a time, it may well have been written down at a fairly early stage. By its very nature, it seems likely that some of the autobio-graphical material was originally transmitted to a limited circle of disciples. But here, again, it seems unwise to be dogmatic about the extent to which oral transmission was prolonged. The possibility that the prophets wrote or personally dictated these accounts is certainly not to be ex·cluded.

The varying views just mentioned all presuppose the ex-istence of circles of prophetic disciples who preserved the master's teaching.

We have seen that there may be some evidence of this in Isaiah. The existence of similar religious groups in other parts of the Near East is also often cited in support of this view. These groups had close connexions with the cult; and it has been widely held in recent years that prophetic groups in Israel were also cultic in character. If this were so, it would account for the presence of cultic themes and symbols and of liturgical fragments in the prophetic books. Some think that the alternation of prophecies of doom with promises of salva-tion goes back to cultic pattern of the Enthronement Festival, in which the people's affliction was followed by the enacting of the divine deliverance. But, though this may account for the arrangement of some passages, it seems hazardous to lay too much emphasis on it. The theory that prophetic circles

(whether or not they had direct cultic connexions) transmitted the sayings and stories of the prophets is an illuminating one, enabling us to think of the prophetic books not
simply as scribal compilations, but as the living productions
of religious communities. It was one of the implications of the
idea of corporate personality that the ancestor lived on in the
successive generations of his descendants; and so the prophetic master lived in and still spoke through his disciples.
Even so, this line of thought should be treated with some
reserve. It should not be so pressed as to obscure the great,
individual, prophetic personalities. It has been pertinently
observed that we possess no collection of the sayings of those
prophets (e.g., Elisha) whose connexion with prophetic communities is most evident.

## II. Isaiah

The first of the prophetic books bears the name of Isaiah,
a prophet who lived in the kingdom of Judah during the
reigns of Uzziah, Jotham, Ahaz, and Hezekiah. Of Isaiah
himself we learn that his father's name was Amoz (i. 1), that
he was called to be a prophet in the year of Uzziah's death
(vi. 1), and that he was married (viii. 8) and the father of at
least two sons, who bore the symbolic names Shear-jashub
('a remnant shall return', or 'repent'; vii. 8) and Maher-
shalal-hash-baz ('speed-spoil-haste-prey'; viii. 1–4).

For the Hebrew kingdoms, the period was one of change
and crisis, occasioned principally by the resurgence of Assyria, and by the westward thrust of her armies under
Tiglath-Pileser III, Shalmaneser V, Sargon, and Sennacherib.
In 735 B.C., Syria and Israel tried to coerce Judah into joining
a western alliance against Assyria; but King Ahaz refused,
and became Assyria's vassal in return for support. Assyrian
punitive expeditions reduced Israelite territory and destroyed
Syrian power. Northern Israel continued to give Assyria
trouble; and in 722 B.C., Samaria was taken and many
Israelites were deported. After nearly two decades of unrest, Judah joined with most of her neighbours in a revolt

against Assyria. Sennacherib crushed the rebels and laid
waste the territory of Judah, though Jerusalem remained
inviolate.

Isaiah's public teaching was concerned with these events
and the accompanying international intrigues, and also with
social and religious conditions in Judah during the period.
But it is significant that, from xl onwards, no reference is
made to these matters, and the prophet is not mentioned by
name. For reasons to be stated below, the book should
probably be divided into three main sections: (a) i–xxxix;
(b) xl–lv; (c) lvi–lxvi, of which only the first contains material
directly connected with Isaiah of Jerusalem.

(a) i–xxxix. These chapters are manifestly composite. They
contain smaller collections of varying date, which must once
have had an independent existence. The first dozen chapters
deal almost exclusively with Judah and Jerusalem. xiii–xxiii
are devoted in the main to foreign nations. xxiv–xxvii form
a special section, describing a world-judgement and Israel's
deliverance. xxviii–xxxiii are concerned for the most part
with Judah's foreign policy. xxxiv–xxxv depict the contrast
of Israel's future with that of Edom. xxxvi–xxxix contain
historical narrative, almost identical with 2 Kings xviii. 18,
17–xx. 19. The broad sequence of sections containing judgement on Israel (or Judah), judgement on foreign nations, and
the promise of deliverance, is found elsewhere, notably in
Ezekiel, and in the Greek text of Jeremiah. Closer examination also shows that some of these sections consist of smaller
groups of oracles.

i contains a description of the devastation of Judah
(probably after the invasion of 701 B.C.), followed by a
denunciation of the cult, an appeal for repentance, an elegy
on Jerusalem, and some concluding fragments.

ii–iv begin and end with promises of a new age. The noble
prophecy in ii. 2–4 of a religious confederation of peoples is
also found in Mic. iv. 1–4, and is anonymous. iv. 2–6 (the
Isaianic origin of which is often challenged) describes Zion's
blessedness after the purifying judgement. Between these are

placed a prediction of divine judgement on human pride (ii. 6–19), a description of society disintegrated by sin (iii. 1–15), and a denunciation of the women of Jerusalem (iii. 16–iv. 1).

In v, the Song of the Vineyard (1–7), exposing Israel's unfaithfulness, is followed by a series of 'Woes' on various classes of wrongdoers (8–24). The chapter ends with a passage which may, in part at least, belong to ix. 8–x. 4.

The story of the prophet's call in vi must once have begun an independent collection. It is followed, in vii. 1–ix. 1, by material which seems in the main to belong to the period of the Syro-Ephraimitic coalition, when Isaiah, urging Ahaz to put his trust in Yahweh, promised the Immanuel-sign, and predicted the downfall of the two aggressors. Some of the sayings in these chapters appear to be fragmentary. The promise of the Royal Child in ix. 2–7 was perhaps not originally connected with the same situation. Some scholars (probably wrongly) have denied that it comes from Isaiah. The description of a future ideal king of David's line in xi. 1–9 is also thought to be of later origin. Whether we owe them to Isaiah or not, both passages are of great importance for the early development of the Messianic hope. We may also note that both follow predictions of judgement. ix. 8–x. 4 is a poem with a regularly recurring refrain. Part of it is probably to be found in the closing verses of v. x. 5–34 consists in the main of prophecies about Assyria. The passage is notable for the thought in the opening verses that Yahweh uses the heathen power to chastise His own people, and for the vivid, staccato description near its close (28–32) of the advance of an invader against Jerusalem. xi. 10–16 (usually denied to Isaiah) speaks of the return of dispersed Israelites. xii, which rounds off the opening section of the book, is a psalm (or, possibly, two short psalms) of thanksgiving and praise.

The sequence of prophecies about foreign nations in xiii–xxiii begins with a passage about the fall of Babylon (xiii. 1–xiv. 23). This falls into at least two parts. The first describes the impending destruction of the city by its enemies. The second contains a striking taunt-song over the descent of a tyrant (commonly taken to be the King of Babylon) to the abode of the dead. The entire passage (xiii. 1–xiv. 23) does not come from Isaiah, but belongs to the Babylonian period. The prophecies against Assyria and Philistia in xiv. 24–27, 28–32 presuppose the conditions of Isaiah's lifetime. xv–xvi contain prophecies about Moab, parts of which are also found in Jer. xlviii. These are cryptic and of uncertain date, and probably contain material which has been worked over (see xvi. 13 f). The oracles against Damascus and Ephraim in xvii. 1–11 belong to the time of the Syro-Ephraimitic coalition (cf. vii–viii); and this may well also be true of the sonorous description of international crisis in xvii. 12–14. xviii refers to an Egyptian (Nubian) embassy sent to Judah during the troubled years at the end of the 8th century. It leads on to a group of prophecies about Egypt in xix–xx. The opening passage in xix forecasts disaster for Egypt; but the closing section speaks of the conversion of the Egyptians to Yahweh and of a triple alliance between Egypt, Assyria, and Israel. The historical background of the chapter is difficult to determine, but probably part of it at least is later than Isaiah. By contrast, xx is dated by an Assyrian expedition against Ashdod in 711 B.C. It describes the dramatic symbolism by which Isaiah predicted the subjugation of Egypt and Ethiopia by Assyria. In xxi. 1–10, we are back in the period when the Jews looked for the fall of Babylon. xxi. 11 f and 13–17 are prophecies about Edom and Arabia. xxii seems, at first sight, to be inappropriate in this collection of foreign oracles. *Vv.* 1–14 are obscure and fragmentary, but probably contain Isaiah's denunciation of the light-hearted celebrations after the raising of the siege of Jerusalem in 701 B.C. *Vv.* 15–25 consist of two prophecies about Shebna, an official, and his successor. It may be that the chapter was included here because of the references to foreign contingents in 1–14, and because Shebna was a foreigner. Or perhaps the heading 'The Burden of the Valley of Vision' gained it a place in a collection of oracles, ten of which carry the heading 'Burden'. These ten passages may have been the original contents of the col·lection.

xxiv–xxvii form a quite distinct section. These chapters contain prophecies, with which are interspersed hymns of praise and thanksgiving. There is a description of a catastrophic judgement on the whole world; and, against this general background, there is triumphant satisfaction at the overthrow of a hostile city and the deliverance of the Jews. Although some particular historical situation seems to be presupposed, the references are too vague and indirect to identify it with anything like certainty. The fall of Bab. lon in 485 B.C. (to Xerxes), or in 331 B.C. (to Alexander), the overthrow of Carthage by the Romans in 146 B.C., and the destruction of Samaria by John Hyrcanus towards the end of the 2nd century B.C. have all been suggested. If the Qumran scroll of Isaiah is rightly dated in the 1st or 2nd centuries, these chapters can hardly be later than the 3rd century; and therefore 2nd-century events must be ruled out. The reference to resurrection (xxvi. 19) has been used to show that the passage is late. But it is at least questionable whether individual resurrection is intended; and it may well be that, as in Ezek. xxxvii. 1–14, it is the revival of national life. It has been maintained that a late date is indicated by the general character of these chapters, which, it is alleged, are apocalyptic rather than prophecy.[1] Some of the imagery used, and, above all, the thought of the imminence of a catastrophic world-judgement (as distinct from a historical catastrophe of local import), suggest some connexion with apocalyptic. But the chapters do not display all the characteristics of the apocalypses, and may be taken to represent an intermediate stage between prophecy and apocalyptic (cf. Ezek. xxxviii–xxxix, and the latter part of Zechariah). At all events, they are much later than Isaiah; and although they contain not a few resemblances to his diction and style, the dissimilarities are far more numerous and striking.

---

[1] The section is often referred to as the Isaiah Apocalypse.

xxviii–xxxiii consist of six series of prophecies, each introduced by 'Woe' (xxviii. 1; xxix. 1, 15; xxx. 1; xxxi. 1;
xxxiii. 1). Most of the oracles seem to be Isaiah's, and apply
to the relations of Judah with Assyria shortly before Sennacherib's invasion. In a number, the Egyptian alliance is
denounced. But some, such as the denunciation of Samaria
with which the section opens, come from other periods of
Isaiah's ministry. Others, such as xxix. 16–24; xxx. 18–26;
xxxiii may come from subsequent periods, or may contain
oracles of Isaiah adapted to the needs of later times. The
opening verses of xxxii, which are sometimes classed with
ix. 2–7 and xi. 1–9, are a description of the ideal common-
wealth rather than a prediction of the ideal king. Running
through the whole section there is an emphasis on the importance of faith, which is characteristic of Isaiah's message.
There can be little doubt that it is above all to i–xii and
xxviii–xxxiii that we must go if we would understand the
prophet and his teaching.

xxxiv–xxxv contain contrasted pictures of the future.
xxxiv predicts the divine judgement on all nations, and
supremely on Edom; whereas xxxv depicts in beautiful
imagery the renewal of nature and the ingathering of Israel.
The style is not Isaiah's; the situation presupposed is that of
the exilic or the post-exilic period; and the thought and outlook are those of later prophecy. xxxiv has affinities with
lxiii. 1–6; and xxxv is reminiscent of much in xl ff. It is,
therefore, not surprising that it has been suggested (e.g.,
by Torrey) that the section is of common origin with the
latter part of the book of Isaiah; but the evidence is not conclusive.

As we have seen (p. 87), xxxvi–xxxvii are substantially
identical with 2 Kings xviii. 13–xx. 19, with the important
addition of Hezekiah's psalm of thanksgiving in Isa. xxxviii.
9–20. The chapters may well be a fairly late addition to the
Isaianic corpus; but we cannot be sure whether they were
derived from Kings or from a common source.

From the above it is apparent that the main sections of

which the first part of Isaiah is composed all contain material that is later (some much later) than the prophet's own time. Each section must have had its own literary history. The reconstruction of that process calls for more detailed discussion than is possible here, and must remain partly conjectural. At all events, it must have continued well into the post-exilic age. The dating of the completion of the process depends on the period to which we ascribe xxiv–xxvii.

The authentic prophecies of Isaiah are expressed in a style of great dignity and force, skilfully adapted to varying subjects, yet always displaying the remarkably concentrated energy of which Hebrew is capable. The account of the prophet's call (vi), the Song of the vineyard (v. 1–7), and the moving presentation of sin and calamity with which the book opens, are among the most striking examples of Isaiah's literary power, which is unsurpassed, and probably un-equalled, in the entire range of the prophetic literature.

Like the other pre-exilic prophets, Isaiah attacks the social injustice and religious corruption of his time; but his message has its own distinctive emphasis, which give it both indi-viduality and unity. The thought of the holiness of Yahweh, which dominates the story of the prophet's call, is central in his teaching. Above all forms of sin he denounces pride, the haughtiness of man, which claims independence of God, and which is a denial of the austere majesty of the Holy One of Israel (ii. 6 ff). The antithesis of such pride is faith, the humble dependence on Yahweh, in which Isaiah sees the vital principle of Israel's continued existence (vii. 1–9; xxviii. 16; xxx. 15). Even if Israel is punished for apostasy, those who trust in Yahweh will form a Remnant, whom Yahweh will bless (vii. 3; x. 20 f). This Remnant already exists in the circle of Isaiah's disciples. It is characteristic of Isaiah that the main themes of his thought are related to the community. Sin disrupts community life (iii. 1 ff); faith gives it stability (vii. 9). The promise of the future is, above all, that of an ordered community ruled by an ideal king of David's line (ix. 2–7; xi. 1–9).

(*b*) xl–lv. By contrast with the preceding chapters, this part of the book displays a remarkable measure of unity in content and in style. It is implied or stated throughout that the Jews have been in Exile for a considerable period, and that the time of liberation has come (xl. 2, etc.). The divinely appointed deliverer is Cyrus (xliv. 28; xlv. 1), who will overthrow Babylon and restore the exiles to their homeland. An 8th-century prophet foretelling these events by supernatural inspiration would presumably have predicted both the Exile and the deliverance; but this writer looks *back* on the duration of the Exile and *forward* to its end. He was, therefore, probably living in the closing years of the Exile, *ca.* 546–538.[1]

In spite of some echoes of the language of Isaiah of Jerusalem, the style of xl–lv is distinctive and unlike anything in the first part of the book, other than xxxv. Instead of the terse, vivid, clear-cut speech of the earlier prophet, we find an eloquence which achieves its ends by the cumulative effect of repetition and contrast, and pictures which impress by their colour and content rather than by the sharpness of their contours. It is a studied and self-conscious style, displaying rather than concealing its own artistry. The neat German comment, that the author speaks not 'als ein Prophet' but 'wie ein Prophet', sums up a characteristic which is more apparent in the Hebrew than in the standard English versions. These literary features reinforce the already strong general argument that the chapters are the work of an author other than Isaiah of Jerusalem. He is commonly referred to as the Second Isaiah, or Deutero-Isaiah.

Concerning the extent of this prophet's work two main questions arise. The first is whether all or part of lvi–lxvi

[1] C. C. Torrey (*The Second Isaiah*) has denied that these chapters are the work of a 6th-century prophet. He regards the references to Cyrus and Babylon as interpolations, and dates xxxiv–xxxv; xl–lxvi *ca.* 400 B.C. Though his view has been supported in this country by W. A. L. Elmslie (*How Came Our Faith?*) and U. E. Simon (*A Theology of Salvation*), it has not carried general conviction. It is difficult to accept the argument that, if the work had been produced in the 6th century, it would have been discredited because many of the prophet's predictions were not literally fulfilled.

should be ascribed to him. This will be discussed in our
consideration of these later chapters. The second concerns
the passages known as the Servant Songs: xlii. 1–4; xlix. 1–6;
l. 4–9 (11); lii. 18–liii. 12.[1] It has been argued that the diction
and style of these poems suggest that they come from a
different hand from the rest of the prophecy. But C. R.
North's thorough and dispassionate survey of the evidence
shows that no adequate case has been made for this thesis.[2]

It has also been maintained that the theological outlook of
the Songs differs from Deutero-Isaiah's. They hope for the
conversion of other nations, but he predicts their subjugation to Israel; they speak of an innocent Servant of Yahweh,
whom they describe as the active mediator of salvation, but
he tells of Yahweh's Servant, Israel, who needs and is promised forgiveness and salvation. The supposed contrast has
been taken to indicate either that the Songs are the composition of an earlier prophet, incorporated with the teaching
of Deutero-Isaiah, or that they come from a later author,
who transmitted Deutero-Isaiah's sayings together with his
own poems, or who was a member of the prophetic circle in
which Deutero-Isaiah's teaching was preserved. But it is
probable that the contrast has been exaggerated; and that
there is no greater variety of outlook and emphasis than
might reasonably be expected of an author who had a
message to proclaim rather than a theological system to
formulate. Certainly the thought of the conversion of the
Gentiles is not entirely foreign to the main part of the prophecy (xlv. 22 f). In this connexion, it is perhaps worth noting
that within the prophecy there are two contrasted attitudes
to Israel: the message of consolation, and that of rebuke
(e.g., xliii. 22–28). The severity of some parts of xlviii has led
some critics to regard them as inconsistent with the prophet's
outlook and to treat them as interpolations. But this conclusion, too, is unnecessary.

---

[1] There is disagreement about the delimitation of the Songs; and some
would include among them some other passages.
[2] See *The Suffering Servant in Deutero-Isaiah*, pp. 161 ff.

There has been a good deal of discussion about the literary structure of this prophecy. Some (e.g., Köhler and Mowinckel) hold that it consists of brief units, originally independent of each other, but subsequently assembled and strung together. Others (e.g., Bentzen and Muilenburg) maintain that the literary units are longer, and that there is a sequence of thought which is not of secondary origin, but derives from the prophet himself. It cannot be denied that there is a frequent transition from one brief literary unit or type to another. But these units are not disconnected. They are skilfully woven together into larger wholes; and the patterns of repetition and contrast are not limited to these brief units, but extend over larger passages.

Many passages recall parts of the Psalter, particularly those Psalms which celebrate the kingship of Yahweh. This similarity of form and content has led some scholars to conclude that the prophet's teaching inspired the writing of the Psalms referred to, and that they celebrate the manifestation of Yahweh's kingship in the restoration of the Jews to Palestine. But it has been argued, with at least equal plausibility, that the Psalms came first, and that the prophet is echoing the liturgies of the pre-exilic cult, particularly the hymns used at the autumn festival, at which, according to a widely held view, the kingship of Yahweh was celebrated in pre-exilic times. On literary grounds, it seems probable that the more complicated blend of genres which appears in Isa. xl–lv is later than the simpler forms which we find in the Psalms.

Again, it has been argued that these Psalms reflect a developed belief in God, of which the prophet was the first exponent. But, in fact, the monotheism of Isa. xl–lv is more explicit than that of the Psalms; and it is at least as easy to think that they contain the preparation for the prophet's teaching as that they were composed under its influence.

The chapters consist of poems (with an occasional snatch of prose, or of verse of which the metrical pattern has been obscured) devoted to a few recurring subjects. The dominant themes are the liberation of the Exiles, the renewal of national life in Palestine, and the mission of the Servant of the Lord.

In xl–xlviii, two audiences seem to be addressed: those who worship the true God but have an inadequate trust in His power and goodness, and those who worship false gods and rely on their ability to foretell the future. The message of liberation is driven home in a number of ways. The prophet says simply and directly that God has forgiven His people, and that He will now free them from bondage (xl. 1 ff). Or he describes the power and speed of the conquests of Cyrus, the instrument whom God has prepared to destroy Babylon and set His people free (xli. 1 ff; xliv. 28–xlv. 7). Or again, he speaks in scathing terms of idols and idolaters, and summons the false gods and their worshippers to debate with the God of Israel, who alone can predict events since He alone controls them (xl. 18 ff; xli. 1 ff, 21 ff; xliv. 6 ff; xlv. 18 ff; xlvi. 1 ff). The importance of divination in Babylonian religion, particularly at this period, explains the vigour of the polemic.

In xlix–lv, there are no references to the conquests of Cyrus or the folly of idolatry, and only indirect allusions to the fall of Babylon. The emphasis moves from the liberation of the exiles and their return to the restoration of national life in Palestine. Sometimes it seems that the return has already begun, and that Jews who are still in Babylon are being exhorted to come back to the homeland (e.g., lii. 11 f). It has been claimed that the background of these chapters is Palestinian not Babylonian. Certainly they reveal a concern, not so much with the plight of the Exiles as with the plight of Jerusalem and its environs; and it may be that they belong to a somewhat later phase of the prophet's activity. But this is by no means established.

The message of restoration is effectively presented in passages which describe Jerusalem, in her affliction and hope, as a woman who has been temporarily separated from her husband, but is now to experience again the joys of home and family life (xlix. 14 ff, liv). There is a striking, and probably intentional, contrast between the queenly Babylon, now to be dethroned, enslaved, and humiliated, and the afflicted Zion, raised from degrading slavery and arrayed in fair garments (xlvii; li. 17–lii. 3).

The purpose of Yahweh, not only for Israel but for all nations, is conveyed supremely by another portrait, that of the Servant of Yahweh in the Servant Songs mentioned above. Here, too, there is a striking, and probably intentional, contrast with another figure; for the stirring description of the military conquests of Cyrus (xli. 1–3) is a telling foil to the account in the first Song (xlii. 1–4) of the spiritual methods and triumphs of the Servant. The speaker in the first Song is Yahweh. In the second and third Songs, it is the Servant himself. He describes his sense of vocation and of failure, the enlarged range of his mission, and the opposition he encounters. The last Song is uttered partly by Yahweh and partly by unnamed witnesses of the Servant's humiliation, suffering, and death for the sin of others: it ends with the announcement of the triumph of his purpose.

The identity of the Servant is probably the most vexed question in the whole range of Old Testament study. He has been equated with the real Israel, the ideal Israel, or a part of Israel. Others have identified him with a historical figure of the past, such as Moses, Jeremiah, or Jehoiachin, or of the prophet's own day, such as Zerubbabel or the prophet himself (a view which usually involves the attribution of at least the fourth Song to a disciple), or of the future, such as the Messiah. Three features have been prominent in recent discussion of the problem: (*a*) a combination of communal and individual interpretations by means of the ancient concept of corporate personality; (*b*) the claim that the portrait is dominated by motifs derived from sacral kingship and from the idea of the dying and rising god of fertility; (*c*) a return to the view that the Servant is a future individual, but with significant differences from the traditional, Christian, Messianic interpretation.

It is impossible here to review or appraise even the leading theories. But, although the problem of the Servant's identity must be left in the arena of debate, certain features in the thought of the Songs stand out clearly. First, the fact of innocent suffering, which is so formidable a problem else-where in the Old Testament, is here seen as part of the Servant's vocation and as a means by which he attains his end. Second, this voluntary, unmerited suffering is vicarious and atoning; and thus the Songs make a supremely important contribution to Old Testament thought about sin. Third, the purpose of God and the mission of the Servant are un-mistakably universal. These three features link the thought of the Songs with New Testament teaching; and, in spite of all uncertainties of interpretation, the anticipation in the fourth Song of the Passion of Christ is one of the miracles of Old Testament literature.

The main features in Deutero-Isaiah's teaching have been noted in the course of the above discussion. Two of them are of special importance. The first is his uncompromising mono-theism. If at times he seems to acknowledge the existence of deities other than Yahweh, it is only to demonstrate their utter ineffectiveness. His devastating exposure of idol-worship reminds us of Elijah's sardonic mockery on Mount Carmel. In his message of consolation, belief in Yahweh as sole Lord of history and nature is the ground of his certainty of deliverance.

The second element is his message about the future. It is appropriate to his faith in Yahweh as Lord of history and *nature* that he predicts that Israel's restoration will be ac-companied by the transformation of nature (e.g., lv. 12 f). Whether this is simply poetic eloquence or a genuine eschatology is a matter of debate. But at least it may be claimed that the cosmic framework of later eschatology probably owes much to Deutero-Isaiah.

(c) lvi–lxvi. This section may be summarized as follows:
lvi. 1–8. An appeal for the faithful observance of the Sabbath and loyalty to the covenant. On these terms,

eunuchs and foreigners will be admitted to the worship of
the temple.

lvi. 9–lvii. 2. Criticism of bad rulers.

lvii. 3–13. A bitter attack on those who practise pagan
worship.

lvii. 14–21. A promise of mercy for the humble.

lviii. A denunciation of unreality in worship, particularly
in fasting, and an appeal for right dealing and Sabbath
observance.

lix. 1–15a. A denunciation and confession of Israel's sin.

lix. 15b–21. A promise of deliverance.

lx–lxii. A description of the future blessedness of Zion.

lxiii. 1–6. Yahweh returns from His vengeance on Edom.

lxiii. 7–lxiv. 12. A confession of Yahweh's past goodness,
and a prayer for deliverance from enemies.

lxv–lxvi. A description of the apostates and the faithful.
The latter will inherit the land; the former will be destroyed.

Among those who do not accept the unity of the whole of
Isaiah, there are three main views about these chapters. Some
hold that they are by Deutero-Isaiah. But Duhm, in his
commentary on Isaiah (1st edition, 1892), separated them
from xl–lv, and attributed them to another prophet (Trito-
Isaiah), whom he dated shortly before Nehemiah's arrival in
Jerusalem. *Ca.* 520 B.C. has also been suggested as the *floruit*
of this prophet. The third view is that in lvi–lxvi we have a
collection of prophecies from different hands and different
periods.

There are, undoubtedly, several links between xl–lv and
lvi–lxvi. The distinctive style and temper of Deutero-Isaiah
appears, not only in passages like lvii. 14–21 and lx–lxii,
but also in brief phrases and clauses (e.g., lvi. 1b, 8; lviii. 8,
9a, 10b, 12). In other passages, however, both the literary
characteristics and the outlook are different. This is true, for
example, of almost the whole of lvi. 1–8 or lviii. Even in
English the style is unmistakably different. The interest in
outward religious practice, such as Sabbath observance, has
no parallel in xl–lv. Even passages which denounce idolatrous

or pagan worship (e.g., lvii. 1–6; lxv. 8 ff) have little in common with the debates in which Deutero-Isaiah attacks false gods and their worshippers.

The provenance of lvi–lxvi is Palestine, not Babylon. There are no precise political references to help us to date the chapters. Indeed, the general situation which they presuppose does not seem to be the same throughout. lvi. 5 f suggests that the restored temple is in use. lxiii. 7–lxiv. 12 (see especially lxiv. 11) implies that the temple has been destroyed. This latter passage is strikingly similar to parts of Lamentations, and may well date from shortly after the fall of Jerusalem.

This variety of style, subject matter, and situation suggests that the closing section of Isaiah is neither the work of Deutero-Isaiah nor of a single Trito-Isaiah. It is a collection of prophecies, possibly spanning the period 586–400, affording us varied glimpses of the Jewish community in Palestine in its struggle with apostasy, its sense of sin, its longing for deliverance, and its thrilling hope. Now and then, as in lviii, we seem to hear an echo of the authentic voice of pre-exilic prophecy.

The passages which resemble xl–lv may be from Deutero-Isaiah, or, more probably, from an imitator or disciple, or group of disciples. Perhaps such a group, which may be labelled Deutero-Isaianic or Trito-Isaianic, gathered these prophecies together, including a number from other sources, and added them to the teaching of Deutero-Isaiah. The suggestion has been made that an Isaianic circle, brought into existence by Isaiah of Jerusalem, survived for centuries after his death, and preserved and arranged the book which bears his name; but, though it stirs the imagination, the theory is unproved.

## III. JEREMIAH

It is a striking fact, and one of considerable significance for the nature of prophetic piety, that the prophet who is the greatest exemplar in the Old Testament of personal communion with God was no recluse, but was intimately involved in public events during one of the most disturbed periods of his people's history.

Jeremiah was born, probably soon after 650 B.C., towards the end of the long reign of Manasseh, when pagan influence had corrupted the religion of Judah. He was of a priestly family from Anathoth, a village near Jerusalem. His call to be a prophet came in 626 B.C., the year of the death of Ashurbanipal, the last great king of Assyria. The decline of Assyrian power restored independence to Judah, so that, when the Book of the Law was found in the temple in 621, King Josiah was able, without outside interference, to make this code the basis of a national reform of religion. Whether as an opponent of pagan practices, or as connected with one of the suppressed high places, Jeremiah can hardly have been unmoved by the reform.

Josiah was killed in 608 B.C., when an Egyptian army passed through Palestine in order to bolster up the last remnants of Assyrian power. Thus began a period of recurring crises, which ended with the fall of Jerusalem, and a time of conflict and persecution for Jeremiah. The Egyptians deposed Jehoahaz, Josiah's successor, and installed as king his brother Eliakim (Jehoiakim), a harsh ruler, who reversed his father's religious policy. The Babylonian victory at Carchemish in 605 B.C. ended Egyptian domination in Palestine. It was shortly afterwards that Jeremiah dictated to Baruch his earlier prophecies and had them read in the temple (xxxvi). The king destroyed the document; but it was rewritten and expanded, and presumably forms part of our book of Jeremiah. A year or two later, Jehoiakim withdrew his allegiance from Babylon, but died before the arrival of Nebuchadrezzar's army. His successor, Jehoiachin, capitulated and was deported together with many of the leading persons in his kingdom, and replaced by Josiah's son Mattaniah (Zedekiah). During the decade before the fall of Jerusalem and the second deportation, there was conflict between the pro-Babylonian and pro-Egyptian parties in

Judah, in which Jeremiah, as an advocate of submission to
Babylon, was inevitably involved. He had to face bitter opposition and hatred, was accused of treason, imprisoned, and
in danger of death. After the fall of Jerusalem, the Babylon
ians allowed him to join the community set up at Mizpah
under Gedaliah. But, when Gedaliah was assassinatcd, the
panic-stricken company of Jews fled to Egypt, taking
Jeremiah with them; and there he seems to have died.

Jeremiah's ministry may be divided into four periods:

(a) from his call till the reform (626–621);
(b) from the reform till the death of Josiah (621–608);
(c) from the death of Josiah till the second deportation
(608–586);
(d) from the second deportation till his death.

A certain rough chronological order, corresponding to the first
(i–vi), third (vii–xxxix), and fourth (xl–xlv) of these periods,
may be traced in the arrangement of the book. The closing
chapters contain collected oracles against foreign nations
(xlvi–li) and a historical narrative (lii). It is an interesting
fact that in the whole book there is little that can be attributed with any probability to the years between the reform
and the death of Josiah.

i–vi comes almost entirely from the period 626–621. The
opening chapter describes Jeremiah's call and two visions,
and ends with a prediction of danger from the north. ii. 1–
iii. 5 is an indictment of Judah's sin, which is continued in
iii. 19–iv. 4. iii. 6–18, depicting Judah as less righteous than
Israel, interrupts the sequence. iv. 5–31 foretells invasion and
its aftermath in a series of vivid pictures. v is a condemnation
of the corruption of all classes in Jerusalem; and vi returns to
the theme of invasion.

The material in vii–xx seems to come, in the main, from
the time of Jehoiakim. vii. 1–viii. 8 contains denunciations
of false trust in the temple and of the sacrificial system.
viii. 4–ix. 26 consists of renewed laments over the national
sin and the coming doom. x. 1–16, an exposure of idolatry,

rather in the manner of Deutero-Isaiah, is usually regarded as inappropriate to Jeremiah's situation and attributed to a later period.

x. 17–25 returns to the theme of impending disaster. xi. 1–8 records a call to Jeremiah to recall Israel to the covenant; it may well belong to the early days of the reform. By contrast, xi. 9–17 deplores the nation's subsequent lapse, presumably in Jehoiakim's reign. xi. 18–xii. 6 refers to a plot at Anathoth against Jeremiah's life, and raises the problem of the prosperity of the wicked.

xii. 7–17 seems to refer to the Babylonian invasion of 597. xiii, which begins with a piece of dramatic symbolism, contains further indictments of the nation's sin. The moving description of a drought in xiv. 1–6 introduces a varied group of prophecies (xiv–xvii), among which are interspersed some of those passionately outspoken prayers and soliloquies (xv. 10–12; xvii. 9 f, 14–18), which are commonly referred to as the Confessions of Jeremiah. Further examples are found in xviii (*vv.* 18–23) and xx (*vv.* 7–18), together with sections which are linked by reference to pottery: in xviii. 1–17, the potter's work illustrates the divine action; and in xix. 1–xx. 6, the breaking of a potter's vessel is an acted prophecy of judgement, for which message Jeremiah is put in the stocks.

xxi–xxiv belongs mostly to a slightly later period. xxi. 1–10 contains a prediction of the fall of Jerusalem, in answer to an inquiry from King Zedekiah. xxi. 11–xxiii. 8 deals with the royal house, includes prophecies about Shallum (Jehoahaz) and Jehoiakim, and ends with a prediction of the coming scion of David. In xxiii. 9–40, Jeremiah denounces the prophets. xxiv contains the comparison of those who accompanied Jehoiachin into exile to good figs and of those who remained behind to bad figs.

xxv brings us back to the reign of Jehoiakim, with a prophecy in 1–14 of the subjugation of Judah by Babylon; this is followed in 15–38 by a list of nations whom God will punish.

xxvi tells what happened when Jeremiah uttered the prophecy contained in vii. 1–15: it belongs to the beginning of Jehoiakim's reign. xxvii–xxix shows Jeremiah, in Zedekiah's reign (in xxvii. 1, 'Jehoiakim' is a scribal slip), combating his countrymen's false hopes of a speedy end of Babylonian power. xxx–xxxiii contains prophecies of the restoration of Jerusalem and the Davidic line, and of Ephraim and Judah, and includes the prophecy of the New Covenant (xxxi. 31–34) and the story of how Jeremiah, while in prison, bought from a kinsman land occupied by the besieging Babylonian army (xxxii). Some parts of these four chapters (e.g., xxxi. 7–14; xxxiii. 14–26) have been attributed to a later period.

xxxiv–xxxix consists of narratives, chiefly of the time of the siege. In xxxiv Jeremiah predicts to Zedekiah the fall of the city, and denounces the treacherous treatment of Hebrew slaves. xxxv, which belongs to Jehoiakim's reign, presents the fidelity of the Rechabites as an example to Judah. The story of the writing, reading, and destruction of Baruch's roll (also from Jehoiakim's reign) is contained in xxxvi. xxxvii–xxxviii. 28a tells of Jeremiah's tribulations during the siege. xxxviii. 28b–xxxix. 14 describes the fall of the city, and is followed by a message to Ebed-Melech (xxxix. 15–18).

xl–xliv recounts the fortunes of the community at Mizpah; the assassination of Gedaliah, the Governor; the flight of a company of Jews to Egypt, taking the unwilling Jeremiah with them; a prophecy against Egypt; and a denunciation of the idolatry of the Egyptian Jews. xlv is a personal message to Baruch after the dictation of the roll.

xlvi–li is a sequence of prophecies against foreign nations, closely resembling the list in xxv. 19–26.

lii is an account of the fall of Jerusalem, agreeing (apart from *vv.* 28–30) with 2 Kings xxiv. 18–xxv. 21, 27–30.

There are interesting differences in the Greek text of the book. It is 2,700 words shorter than the Hebrew text. Many of the omissions are of words and phrases which contribute nothing essential to the sense, but others are more substantial. There is also an important difference in arrangement. In the Greek text, the prophecies against foreign nations (xlvi–li) are inserted, in a somewhat different order, between xxv. 13 and 15, *v.* 14 being omitted. Thus these foreign oracles are prefixed to the short passage about foreign nations in xxv. 15–38. This points to an arrangement of the material according to subject matter:

(*a*) prophecies of doom on Jerusalem and Judah (i–xxv. 13);

(*b*) prophecies of doom on foreign nations (xlvi–li + xxv. 15–38);

(*c*) prophecies in the main of deliverance for Israel and Judah (xxvi–xxxv);

(*d*) stories of Jeremiah's sufferings (xxxvi–xlv).

The arrangement of (*a*), (*b*), and (*c*) corresponds to that of Isaiah i–xxxix and of Ezekiel. This difference of structure between the Greek and Hebrew forms of the book points to a stage at which the elements of which it is composed were still in a fluid state.

Yet another aspect of the arrangement of the contents is the relationship to each other of the several types of material. In the first half of the book, prophetic oracles and autobiographical material predominate; but, in the second half, we find many narratives in the third person, and some autobiographical sections, but little oracular material, apart from the prophecies of consolation and the main block of prophecies against foreign nations.

It seems reasonable to suppose that the prophecies dictated to Baruch form a substantial part of the poetical oracles in the book; but there have been widely differing views about their extent. Some have attributed to Baruch's roll all the oracles which may reasonably be dated before 605 B.C., or the bulk of the material in i–xxv. But it needs to be remembered that, when the roll was rewritten, sections were added to it; and we have even less evidence of the identity of these additions than of the original document. Further, the varied arrangement of the oracular material in Jeremiah makes it improbable that a document such as Baruch's roll was included without modification. It is more likely to have been a *source* from which material was derived than a *section* in the present book of Jeremiah. The prophecies of restoration in xxx and xxxi doubtless belong to a separate collection. Those against foreign nations raise difficult problems. That they include some non-Jeremianic material is generally conceded. But opinions differ whether they contain an authentic kernel which has been expanded, or form a unity to be attributed to a 'Deutero-Jeremiah'.

The biographical narratives range from the beginning of the reign of Jehoiakim to the sojourn in Egypt. Though no proof can be offered, it is probable that they come from Baruch, whose association with the prophet appears to belong to that period. Reference is sometimes made to a supposed biography of Jeremiah written by Baruch. But the scope of the material suggests that what Baruch wrote was an account of the sufferings of Jeremiah in his later years rather than a biography.

The autobiographical material belongs in the main to the earlier part of Jeremiah's ministry, though sections of this type range from the prophet's call (i. 4 ff) to the siege of Jerusalem (xxxii; xxxv). It seems unnecessary to deny that most of this material goes back to the prophet. T. H. Robinson and others have suggested that much of it was contained in Baruch's roll. Some of these passages describe special auditory and visual experiences or prophetic actions (i. 4 ff; xiii. 1–11; xxiv. 1–10; xxv. 15 ff). Others (e.g., vii. 1–viii. 8; xi. 1–14; xviii. 1–12; xxii. 1–5) include prophetic utterances in a prose style which resembles that of Deuteronomy. It has, accordingly, been argued that these latter passages are the work of a Deuteronomistic writer in the 6th century, though their substance may, in part at least, go back to Jeremiah. But T. H. Robinson has claimed that the presence of the Deuteronomic style is not conclusive evidence that we owe a given passage to a later Deuteronomic writer, for 'the so-called "Deuteronomic style" is simply the form which Hebrew rhetorical prose took in the latter part of the seventh century and the first part of the sixth'.[1] Further, G. Widengren has drawn attention to the presence in the Qur'an both of vivid, terse sayings, and also of longer passages in more tedious and prosaic language, sometimes repeating or amending previous revelations. He therefore holds that neither the contrast between the lyrical and the prosaic style in Jeremiah, nor the presence of prose doublets to poetical oracles, necessarily justifies us in attributing the prose passages to a later writer.[2]

The process by which the various collections of material were combined cannot be traced with accuracy; but the different arrangement of the Greek text suggests that it was a protracted one. We have seen that a considerable part of the book had been committed to writing during the lifetime of Jeremiah; and it may well be that the two processes of oral and literary transmission continued for several generations. If we accept the view that many of the prose passages are of Deuteronomic origin, we must conclude that there was considerable expansion and reshaping of the material, in the middle or later part of the 6th century.

It is to the poetical oracles that we must look for the distinctive literary characteristics of the book. They are couched in a simple, direct, passionate style, differing as much from the prose homilies as the lyrics of Burns differ from his prose letters. We miss the controlled energy of Isaiah and Amos. But, both in lament and appeal, Jeremiah reveals a singular power of expressing emotion. That emotional quality appears, too, in his denunciation of Israel's sin (ii. 10 ff), and in his description of invasion and its aftermath (iv. 5 ff).

Jeremiah is usually thought of as the great individualist. But it is well to remember that his 'individualism' arose in large measure from two factors in his experience: a profound conviction of divine appointment, and the seeming failure of

---

[1] Oesterley and Robinson, *Introduction*, p. 298; cf. p. 304.
[2] G. Widengren, *Literary and Psychological Aspects of the Hebrew Prophets*, pp. 48 ff; 80 ff. Cf. O. Eissfeldt, *Introduction*, p. 352.

his mission to Israel. His prophecies seemed to gain little response from his countrymen except hatred and persecution. Thus thwarted and isolated, he was driven back on the God who had commanded him to prophesy. The confessions, which record his violent protests, are very different in character from conventional devotional literature; but they give an unforgettably vivid picture of Jeremiah's inner conflict and of his personal communion with God.

An emphasis on the inward and individual elements in religion runs through much of his teaching. He denounces superstitious trust in the temple (vii. 1 ff). More violently than any other prophet, he attacks the sacrificial worship of his day (vii. 21 ff). Though, like his prophetic predecessors, he condemns social evils, he also emphasizes the subtle, personal character of sin (xiii. 23; xvii. 9; xxxi. 30). It is supremely characteristic of his message that his teaching about the future includes the prophecy of the New Covenant, with its promise of an individual knowledge of God. But it is also typical that this covenant is 'with the house of Israel', and thus preserves the corporate element.

There has been much discussion about Jeremiah's attitude to the most important public event in the religious life of his day, the Josianic Reform. At first sight, xi. 1 ff seems to show that Jeremiah felt called to advocate the principles of the Reform. Against this, however, it has been argued that the passage bears strong marks of Deuteronomic style and therefore is unreliable as evidence of Jeremiah's thought, that Jeremiah's attitude to the outward forms of religion makes it impossible or unlikely that he supported measures which were so intimately concerned with cultic practice, and that viii. 8 is a forthright condemnation of the Law Book on which the reform was based. But, even if it be conceded that the Deuteronomic phraseology in xi. 1 ff points to editorial revision, it is improbable that the entire substance of the passage is fictitious. Further, if Jeremiah was an advocate of the Reform, we can the more readily understand the bitter hostility which he met from his kinsmen at Anathoth

(xi. 18 ff), whose sanctuary had been suppressed. The view that Jeremiah thought that religion could exist without any outward forms probably misrepresents him.[1] Finally, it is by no means evident that viii. 8 refers to the Law Book of the Reform. It may be, as many have held, that Jeremiah at first supported the Reform and later recognized its short-comings, and that the prophecy of the New Covenant reflects that recognition. But, at all events, his eulogy of Josiah betrays no disapproval of the most prominent feature in that king's policy (xxii. 5 f).

At least as important as any record of Jeremiah's teaching is the picture which the book gives of the prophet himself, of what he was and of how he suffered. It is here that the affinity between Jeremiah and the Suffering Servant is most evident. In both, the prophetic message is summed up in a person.

## IV. Ezekiel

The book of Ezekiel bears the appearance of unity and orderliness. Of its forty-eight chapters, the first twenty-four contain the account of the prophet's call (i–iii) and prophecies of doom on Israel (iv–xxiv). It has been aptly said that the theme of this part of the book is: 'Jerusalem must be destroyed'. The message of the remaining twenty-four chapters is the contrasted one of deliverance and renewal. They consist of prophecies of judgement on foreign nations (xxv–xxxii), promises of the restoration of Israel (xxxiii–xxxix), and a detailed description of the temple and its ministers, the land and its boundaries, in the new age.

This massive simplicity of structure is accompanied by the precise dating of a number of the oracles and a chronological arrangement of them, which contrasts markedly with the lack of such sequence in other prophetic books. The dates are given at fourteen points: i. 1 f; iii. 16; viii. 1; xx. 1; xxiv. 1; xxvi. 1; xxix. 1; xxix. 17; xxx. 20; xxxi. 1; xxxii. 1; xxxii.

---

[1] On this highly controversial theme and its wider context, see especially, H. H. Rowley, *The Unity of the Bible* (reprinted from *Bulletin of the John Rylands Library*, xxix, 1945–46).

17; xxxiii. 21; xl. 1. Apart from the fact that xxix. 17 gives the latest date in the whole book, these chronological notices are substantially in the right order. The variation from it is probably the result of an arrangement of oracles according to nations in xxv–xxxii.

Although it does not follow that all the material which comes between any two dates is to be assigned to the former of them, the system of dating suggests that the prophet was active between 593 and 571 B.C.; and the literary structure seems to represent faithfully the outline of a prophetic ministry which was divided between judgement and consolation.

Ezekiel was a Jerusalemite priest, who was among those deported with Jehoiachin to Babylonia in 597. In 593, he had a vision of a chariot bearing a throne on which God was seated, and heard God's voice calling him to be a prophet. Seven days later it was revealed to him that this ministry laid on him a special responsibility for individuals (i–iii).

In a series of symbolic actions, he portrayed the siege of Jerusalem and the fate of its inhabitants as God's punishment for the national idolatry (iv–v. 4). These are followed by sweeping denunciations of religious corruption and predictions of swift and severe punishment (v. 5–vii. 27).

The following year, while in the presence of the Jewish elders, Ezekiel fell into a trance, in which he felt himself transported to Jerusalem and there witnessed the pagan worship in the temple, and God's condemnation of the city and departure from it (viii–xi). As before, the account of a visionary experience is followed by acted prophecies: in these he represented the coming deportation of Zedekiah and his subjects, and the hardships of the siege (xii. 1–20). The absence of precise dating at xii. 1 suggests that the sequence is not necessarily strictly chronological. The revelations which follow are also probably connected by subject matter rather than by date. They deal with prophecy (xii. 21–28), false prophets (xiii. 1–16), false prophetesses and sorceresses (xiii. 17–23), and idolatrous inquirers (xiv. 1–11), and assert the certainty and absolute justice of the punishment of Jerusalem

(xiv. 12–23). In a series of allegories, Jerusalem is described as the useless wood of the vine (xv) and as a foundling child who became an adulteress (xvi), and Nebuchadrezzar as a vulture which carried off the top branch of a cedar (Jehoiachin) and planted in good soil a vine (Zedekiah), which inclined to another vulture (Egypt) (xvii). The people's complaint that God's acts are unjust is answered by a statement of the moral responsibility of each generation and each individual, and of the possibility of repentance now (xviii). Then follow two allegorical laments, describing the fate of the lioness's whelps (Jehoahaz and Jehoiachin), and of the vine (Judah).

In 591 B.C., when consulted by the elders, Ezekiel received from God as reply a survey of Israel's unbroken apostasy from the sojourn in Egypt up to the present, and of the deliverances and chastisements which God had wrought and would work for His name's sake (xx. 1–44). There follow prophecies about the fire of punishment (xx. 45–49), and the sword of God (xxi). Jerusalem's sins are enumerated (xxii. 1–16); her punishment is described under the figure of dross in a furnace (xxii. 17–22); and all sections of the community are indicted (xxii. 23–31). In the allegory of the two sisters, Oholah and Oholibah, the unfaithfulness of Samaria and Jerusalem are depicted (xxiii).

Then came the long-awaited blow, described in the figure of the boiling and rusted caldron (xxiv. 1–14). The death of Ezekiel's wife was foretold and he was forbidden to mourn her, as a sign to the people, who would be unable to express their dismay when the city fell. A new stage in Ezekiel's ministry was now begun (xxiv. 15–27).

The blow having fallen, Ezekiel's message became one of restoration. Of this the first phase was the judgement on Israel's enemies. These prophecies (xxv–xxxii) are directed against Ammon, Moab, Edom, and Philistia (xxv), Tyre and Sidon (xxvi–xxviii), and Egypt (xxix–xxxii). As we have noted, the departure from the chronological sequence here is probably the result of grouping according to nations, xxix. 17–21 (571 B.C.) being brought forward to follow the other

prophecy on Egypt in xxix. 1–16 (587 B.C.), and xxvi. 1–
xxviii. 19 (586 B.C.), on Tyre, being put earlier because of the
allusion to the siege of Tyre in xxix. 18.

In one sense, this block of oracles interrupts the story of
Ezekiel's ministry. For the new phase in his work begins in
xxxiii. There the prophet's pastoral function as watchman is
again described; and the arrival of news of Jerusalem's fall
unlooses Ezekiel's tongue (xxxiii. 21 f; cf. xxiv. 26 f). In xxxiv
God promises that He will care for His flock, Israel, whom
their rulers have neglected and oppressed, and will raise up
a new David. Mount Seir, the home of Edom, the most-hated
enemy in this period, will be destroyed (xxxv); but the
mountains of Israel will be freed from foreign occupation and
blessed (xxxvi. 1–15). For His name's sake, God will give the
people of Israel a new heart (xxxvi. 16–38). In symbolic
vision, Ezekiel saw the nation raised from the dead (xxxvii.
1–14); and in symbolic act, he represented the future reunion
of Ephraim and Judah (xxxvii. 15–28).

The promise at the end of xxxvii, that God's sanctuary
would be in the midst of Israel forever, provides an excellent
transition to the last nine chapters of the book. But first there
is a prophecy of the distant future, when Gog of Magog will
attack Israel with a great army from the north, but will be
utterly defeated. So God's glory will be manifested to all
nations (xxxviii–xxxix).

Some thirteen years after receiving the news of the fate of
Jerusalem, Ezekiel was transported in visionary experience
to a mountain in Palestine, from whose summit he beheld the
temple and the home of the restored Israel. First, there is a
detailed description of the temple court and buildings, as
displayed to Ezekiel by a man who acts as his guide (xl–xlii).
Then the glory of God returns from the east to fill the vacant
sanctuary (xliii. 1–12; cf. x. 19). Ezekiel is then initiated into
the religious ordinances of the new age: the exclusion of
foreigners from the temple, the restriction of the priestly
office to Zadokites, and the assigning of inferior duties to
other Levites; the provision made for priests, the allocation

of territory to priests, Levites, city, and prince, the dues and duties of the prince, the six-monthly atonement for the sanctuary, and other regulations for worship (xliv–xlvi). Finally, Ezekiel is shown a stream from under the temple, which brings fertility to the Dead Sea region and sweetness to the Sea itself (xlvii. 1–12); and God announces the new divisions of the country, with seven tribes north of the sanctuary and five south of it, the portions of the Levites, the prince, and the city around the priests' portion, and the priests' portion round the temple (xlvii. 13–xlviii. 35). This detailed description of temple, ordinances, and land ends with the announcement of the new name of the city: Yahweh is there.

Until the end of the 19th century, few critics questioned the integrity and authenticity of the book. But, since then, it has become one of the storm centres of criticism. The main questions under debate are: (a) unity and composition; (b) the place or places in which the prophet exercised his ministry; (c) chronology.

(a) In spite of the impressive unity of its structure, the book reflects a diversity of interest and outlook, which points at least to an author of extraordinary character and, it might be thought, to multiple authorship. Prophet, priest, moralist, ecstatic, legalist, apocalyptist; all seem to make some contribution to its contents. Does the detailed cultic legislation of the last nine chapters come from the prophet of judgement and consolation who speaks in the earlier part of the book? Can chapters xxxviii and xxxix, with their marked affinities with the later apocalyptic literature, be attributed to a 6th-century prophet?

Moreover, many features in the text point at least to editorial revision. There are evident doublets, of which the most notable is iii. 16–21 = xxxiii. 1–9 (cf. xviii. 21–25 = xxxiii. 10–20). Some have thought that the opening account of the vision and of the prophet's call and commission conflates two quite separate experiences. The last nine chapters have been analysed into sections which describe how a

heavenly man acted as Ezekiel's guide in his vision, and
others which may be subsequent additions to the narrative
of the vision (xliii. 18–27; xliv. 25–27, 31; xlv; xlvi. 1–18;
xlviii. 35). The denunciations in the earlier part of the book
sometimes include words of promise which seem out of place.

Features such as these have led some to hold that Ezekiel
revised the records of his teaching at a late stage in his
ministry, or that our present book is a combination of two
earlier drafts, one in the first person and the other in the
third, or that many short oracles, originally independent,
were assembled by Ezekiel himself and given their present
semblance of structural unity. The contrast in character
between the original prophecy and later additions is presented
in an extreme form by G. Hölscher (*Hesekiel, der Dichter und
das Buch*), who attributes to the prophet only some of the
poems and a few brief prose passages, and traces the remainder (some six-sevenths of the whole) to a 5th-century
editor (or editors). The former was a real prophet, in the old
pre-exilic tradition. The latter was a writer, influenced by the
later parts of the Pentateuchal legislation, whose additions to
the book included promises of restoration and the last nine
chapters: his purpose was to present the policy of the Za-
dokite party in Jerusalem. Before Hölscher, Mowinckel had
ascribed the bulk of the book to later hands; and, more
recently, W. A. Irwin has attributed to Ezekiel only about
one-fifth of the whole.

(*b*) Literary analysis may suggest that prophecies uttered
by Ezekiel in Babylonia were expanded elsewhere; but some
features have been taken to indicate that Ezekiel exercised
only part of his ministry in Babylonia, or even that he was
never there at all, and that the entire Babylonian setting is
an editorial fiction.

To most modern readers it must seem strange to find a
prophet in exile addressing denunciations to his countrymen
in Palestine hundreds of miles away. One would expect, too,
that the symbolic acts would be performed in the presence
of those whose fate they portrayed. The vision of events in

Jerusalem, and Ezekiel's knowledge of conditions there, seem to some to be best explained on the theory that he was still in the doomed capital. It was not a heavenly hand that brought Ezekiel to Jerusalem (viii. 1 ff), but a literary device that transferred him to Babylonia.

Thus, V. Herntrich (*Ezechielprobleme*) has argued that Ezekiel was in Palestine from the time of his call in 593 until the second deportation, that Jerusalem was the scene of his prophecies and symbolic acts, and that he was actually present in the body to see the things which he is reported to have witnessed by supernormal means, but that, during the Exile, an editor added to Ezekiel's oracles, adapted them to exilic conditions, and supplied the descriptions of supernormal experiences, and probably the last nine chapters.

In his second commentary on Ezekiel,[1] A. Bertholet advanced the view that Ezekiel's ministry began in Jerusalem in 593 with the experience which is described in ii. 3–iii. 9, and was carried on there until he moved outside the city (xii. 3). After hearing the news of the fall of Jerusalem (xxxiii. 21), he went to Babylonia, and there received a second call to prophesy (i. 4–ii. 2). The Babylonian background was supplied for the first phase of Ezekiel's ministry by a later editor, who expanded and arranged his teaching.

Other scholars would change the date as well as the setting of Ezekiel. Their views will be considered below.

(c) The reliability of the seemingly orderly chronology has been questioned. We have already seen that the dated passages are not in unbroken chronological order, and that probably each date refers only to the passage which immediately follows it. This raises no really serious problem. But the opening words of the book, with their reference to

---

[1] The first was published in 1897, in the *Kurzer Hand-Commentar zum Alten Testament*, and represented no striking change from the critical opinion then prevalent. The second, in the *Handbuch zum Alten Testament*, appeared in 1936. It has now been replaced by the commentary by G. Fohrer (1955), which, the author observes, differs as much from Bertholet's second commentary as the latter did from the work of 1897.

'the thirtieth year', present a tantalizing riddle. The number has been variously explained as referring to (*a*) Ezekiel's age, (*b*) the period since the discovery of the Law Book, (*c*) the year of the current jubilee period, (*d*) the year of Jehoiachin's age (reckoning from 615 B.C., and thus making the date 586 instead of 593), (*e*) the year of Jehoiachin's exile (altering 'thirtieth' to 'fifth'), (*f*) the year of Nebuchadrezzar's reign (altering 'thirtieth' to 'thirteenth'), (*g*) the year of the new Babylonian empire, (*h*) the year of the Exile (referring to the completion of the book, 567 B.C.). No solution has won general acceptance; but some of these interpretations, combined with doubts about the authenticity of some or all of the dates in the book, have led some scholars to hold that Ezekiel's ministry began at an earlier point in the period to which the dates assign him, or that he belongs to a quite different period.

In Oesterley and Robinson's *Introduction*, the call of Ezekiel is dated in the reign of Jehoiakim. On such a view, Ezekiel's ministry began in Palestine.

Among the more drastic changes of date, that proposed by Torrey (*Pseudo-Ezekiel and the Original Prophecy*) is perhaps the most striking. He holds that the 'thirtieth year' in i. 1 refers to the regnal year of a king, and that the king is Manasseh, the religious corruption of whose reign is described in the prophecy. In its original form the book purported to record the work of a prophet among the people of Palestine at that period, though in fact it was a pseudepigraph, written about 230 B.C., but edited later in such a way as to transfer it to a Babylonian setting.

On the other hand, James Smith (*The Book of the Prophet Ezekiel*) has argued that Ezekiel really prophesied in the reign of Manasseh, that he belonged to Northern Israel, and that he condemned cultic practices at Jerusalem and sought to encourage his fellow-countrymen (to whom, so Smith contends, the expression 'House of Israel' refers). The 'thirtieth year' (i. 1) was reckoned from the fall of Samaria, and thus was 692 B.C., the fifth year (i. 2) of Manasseh's reign. The twelfth year of the captivity (xxxiii. 21) was 722 (twelve years after the deportation of 734); and the news brought in that year was of the fall of Samaria, not Jerusalem. Ezekiel prophesied in Palestine and also among the North Israelite exiles.[1] But a later editor gave a Babylonian setting to the entire prophecy.

For the most part, however those who would remove Ezekiel from the exilic period transfer him to the time after the return, *ca.* 400 B.C., or to the time of Alexander, or even later. To examine, or even enumerate, all the varieties of theory is impossible here; but we may note that the older critical view (or something like it) is not without new defenders.[2]

The discussion of Ezekiel during the past generation has not led to generally agreed answers to any of the three main questions raised. We may recognize the importance of these questions and the need for further discussion of them, and yet hold that the evidence is not sufficient to support the more drastic theories which have been advanced.

(*a*) When all is said, the impressive unity of the book remains. Skinner's assertion, that the book bears 'the stamp of a single mind in its phraseology, its imagery, and its mode of thought',[3] needs little, if any, qualification. The diversity of interest, to which reference has been made above (p. 133) bears witness to a remarkable, but not an incredible, personality.[4]

The parts of the book in which the strongest case can be made for the presence of later material are xxxviii–xxxix and xl–xlviii. Elsewhere, the existence of doublets, and the juxtaposition of passages on similar themes, suggest that the book

---

[1] Smith suggests that this twofold ministry may be confirmed by the statement of Josephus (*Antt.* X, v, 1) that Ezekiel wrote two books.

[2] Note especially the work of C. G. Howie (*The Date and Composition of Ezekiel*) and G. Fohrer (*Die Hauptprobleme des Buches Ezekiel*, and his commentary on Ezekiel in the *Handbuch zum Alten Testament*).

[3] J. Hastings, *Dictionary of the Bible* i, p. 817a.

[4] In spite of all differences of time and place, it is, perhaps, not entirely misleading to suggest a parallel in John Wesley: evangelist, organizer, and sacramentalist, who, for all his calm logic, was associated with abnormal psychological phenomena.

was compiled by a process roughly similar to that assumed
for earlier prophets. But the bulk of the material may well go
back to Ezekiel himself, although the process of compiling
and arranging continued later. Widengren has argued that
the descriptions of visionary experiences, such as we find in
Ezekiel, impressive and rich in detail, yet vague in outline
and fantastic in character, are the result of conscious literary
effort.[1]

It may well be that Ezekiel had more of the writer about
him than his predecessors.

(*b*) The various theories that all or part of Ezekiel's
ministry took place in Palestine have serious difficulties to
face. The Babylonian setting is not obtruded, as one would
expect, if it had been deliberately foisted on the material in
the process of editing. But both in language and in background there is considerable indirect evidence of Babylonian
origin. It may, of course, be held that Ezekiel himself gave
a Babylonian setting and colour to prophecies originally
uttered in Palestine. But that assumption is unnecessary.
Spoken and acted prophecies about the Jews in Palestine did
not require a Palestinian audience and spectators; for elsewhere we find prophecies spoken and acted in Palestine which
applied to, or were addressed to, distant foreign nations.
Ezekiel's knowledge of conditions and events in Jerusalem
would be derived partly from experience, and partly from
reports brought to Babylonia. That he sometimes had, in
addition, abnormal knowledge of events taking place elsewhere, or visionary experience in which he felt himself to be
transported to Jerusalem, need not be denied on *a priori*
grounds.

(*c*) The chronology of the book raises problems; but it is
questionable whether any of them are eased by changes in
the dating of Ezekiel's ministry. If the Babylonian setting is
retained, no serious change in the dating is at all likely. The
early dating proposed by Smith is unacceptable because his
arguments for a North-Israelite origin are inadequate. The

[1] *Literary and Psychological Aspects of the Hebrew Prophets,* pp. 117 ff.

various post-exilic dates proposed are inherently improbable. The historical allusions in Ezekiel are best explained in terms of the early exilic period; and there are no convincing references to subsequent history. Further, the cultic regulations in the closing chapters are more easily accounted for as an exilic programme coming between the Deuteronomic and Priestly legislation than on any other hypothesis.[1]

If, then, we accept the bulk of the book as coming from a prophet who lived and worked among the Jewish exiles in Babylonia between 593 and *ca.* 570 B.C., we have in Ezekiel a figure of cardinal importance in the life of ancient Israel. In his person and teaching he gathers up the traditions of pre-exilic religion. He was a priest; and his concern for the right ordering of ritual doubtless reflects the highest traditions of the Jerusalemite priesthood. He was a prophet. His abnormal psychological experiences exemplify in a striking way one feature of the prophetic movement. He is also the prophet of judgement, condemning the apostasy of his people and the corruption of their worship and announcing the impending acts of God in history. But he also represents a transition to a new emphasis in prophecy and to new developments in Israel's religion. Although the message of restoration is by no means absent from the teaching of his predecessors, he presents it with a fullness of detail which is new. In this he heralds the post-exilic prophecies of restoration. He is also the morning star of apocalyptic, even if we hold that xxxviii and xxxix are from a later writer. His imagery, which is often artificial and bizarre, is more akin to the symbolism of apocalyptic than the simpler and more natural symbolism of earlier prophets. In his prophecies of restoration, he heightens the element of sheer miracle; and here, too, he is nearer to the apocalyptists than to the pre-exilic prophets. Again, much of his teaching about the future is presented in a form which points forward to the detailed legislation of post-exilic Judaism.

[1] The relation of these chapters to the Holiness Code is an involved problem, too complex for discussion here.

Ezekiel has often been likened to Calvin, because of his emphasis on the majesty of God. This is evident, not only in the mysterious visions, but in the recurring formula by which the prophet is addressed: 'Son of man' (mere man, mortal man). It also appears in his account of God's dealings with Israel. Israel's record is one of unbroken apostasy. God's goodness to them is, therefore, not prompted by their virtue or merit; He has acted, and will act, for His name's sake.[1]

P. T. Forsyth observes somewhere that, in the 17th century, those who contended most valiantly for human rights were those who believed most firmly in the sovereignty of God. Similarly, Ezekiel's exalted conception of the Godhead, which may at times seem rather cold and impersonal, is accompanied by a concern for the individual. On Ezekiel himself God lays the obligation to warn, not only the nation, but individuals: the prophet thus becomes, in some sort, a pastor (iii. 16–21; xxxiii. 1–9). The responsibility of the individual before God is memorably expressed in xviii: neither his father's virtue nor his own past good deeds can avail the backslider; nor do his father's or his own past sins tell against one who repents. This passage is to be understood not as a theoretical discussion of a moral question, but as a prophetic message, addressed to the querulous despondency of Ezekiel's contemporaries. It is significant that it includes a statement of God's active desire to reclaim and forgive the sinner (xviii. 23).

This element of compassion also appears in Ezekiel's teaching about national restoration, notably in the beautiful passage in xxxiv, in which God promises to seek out His scattered sheep and to give them the care which their leaders have denied them.

Thus, within its ordered unity, the book is a book of striking contrasts: laboured prose and brilliant poetry, fantastic vision and reasoned argument, prophetic eloquence and detailed cultic threat and promise, austerity and compassion.

---

[1] This may be both compared and contrasted with the Deuteronomic statement that God chose Israel because He loved them (Deut. iv. 37; vii. 7 f; x. 15).

## V. The Book of the Twelve

The fourth book of the Latter Prophets may be regarded
as an anthology of prophetic material, even more varied
than the Isaianic corpus and spanning at least as great a
period of time. It is divided into short books, each of which
is associated with the name of a prophet. The name
Minor Prophets was applied to these books because of their
brevity.

The order in the Greek Bible (Hosea, Amos, Micah, Joel,
Obadiah, Jonah) differs slightly from that in the Hebrew. It
is thought that this is an attempt to arrange the books in
order of length, Jonah being put later because it is a prophetic
narrative rather than a record of prophetic teaching. In
general, the order in the Hebrew Bible is roughly chronological, with the post-exilic prophets at the end. Although,
as we shall see, the book of Jonah is in all probability post-
exilic, it is included among the pre-exilic prophets, because
of the reference to the pre-exilic prophet Jonah in 2 Kings
xiv. 25. Other factors besides chronology seem to have
affected the grouping. There are certain verbal links between
Joel and Amos (Amos i. 2 and Joel iii. 16 ff; Amos vii. 1 ff
and Joel i–ii). The phrase 'the day of Yahweh' recurs in Joel,
Amos, and Obadiah. In Zech. ix. 1; xii. 1; Mal. i. 1, the word
'burden' appears, introducing prophetic pronouncements:
this suggests that the catchword principle was applied, and
that it overlapped the boundaries of what we now know as
books.

Ecclus. xlix. 10 refers to the twelve prophets, after men-
tioning Isaiah, Jeremiah, and Ezekiel. The collection was
therefore probably complete by the end of the 3rd century
B.C.

### (a) Hosea

The book of Hosea has with some justice been called the
most obscure book in the Old Testament. In many passages,
the text seems to have been badly preserved; the exegetical

problems are often perplexing; and the details of the prophet's personal experience, which is intimately connected
with his message, are difficult to reconstruct.

Yet the general structure of the book is plain. It falls into
two main parts: (a) i–iii, containing narratives about the
prophet's family life (i, in the third person, and iii, in the first
person) and oracles of judgement and promise (ii); (b) iv–xiv,
containing varied oracles, mainly denouncing the Northern
Kingdom, but also promising restoration. The oracles do not
appear to be grouped according to any clear plan; but some
are linked by catchwords, or by the association of subject
matter.

Although there are some references to Judah, the bulk of
the book deals with Northern Israel; and Hosea himself was
doubtless from that kingdom. The superscription (i. 1) dates
his activity in the days of Uzziah, Jotham, Ahaz, and
Hezekiah of Judah, and Jeroboam II of Israel. The book
itself reflects the conditions of the troubled period in Northern Israel in the third quarter of the 8th century, when kings
were assassinated, intrigue was rife in court circles, and
society was corrupt (iv. 1 ff; vii. 1 ff; viii. 4). The prediction,
in i. 4, of the fall of Jehu's dynasty, shows that Hosea's
ministry had begun before the end of the reign of Jeroboam
II. Allusions to Gilead as part of Israel (vi. 8; xii. 11) belong
to the period before the Assyrian annexation of that region
(2 Kings xv. 29). But there is no clear reference to the alliance
of Syria and Israel against Judah during the reign of Ahaz
(2 Kings xvi. 5; Isa. vii. 1 ff), or to the fall of Samaria. The
length of Hosea's ministry must, therefore, remain uncertain.

According to i. 2, the prophet was commanded to take
'a wife of whoredom and children of whoredom'. He married
Gomer, daughter of Diblaim, who bore three children, to
whom symbolic names were given: Jezreel, Lo-ruhamah, and
Lo-ammi, expressing God's judgement on the royal house
and His rejection of the people. iii records a further divine
command to love an immoral woman as God loved his
apostate people, and tells how Hosea bought her and kept

her secluded from her former associates, symbolizing Israel's future loss of political leaders and religious institutions.

These short narratives are very variously interpreted. The view that they are allegorical fiction is quite improbable. Granted that they record actual events, is iii the sequel to i, or does it tell in the first person what has already been told in the third? If the latter, perhaps the book should be divided into i + ii and iii + iv–xiv, the duplicate narratives each introducing a collection of sayings.[1]

Of those who think that iii does not narrate the same events as i, some hold that Gomer is not the adulteress mentioned in iii, but that she was a pure and faithful wife, and was called 'a wife of whoredom' simply because of the apostasy (commonly called 'whoredom') of Israel. If, however, both chapters refer to Gomer, presumably iii means that she had been living apart from Hosea, had fallen into slavery, and had to be bought back.[2] There is much to be said for a rearrangement of passages, inserting iii between i. 9 and 10: the last verses of ii then make a fitting climax to the whole story.

It appears from i. 2 that Hosea believed that God had commanded him to marry an immoral woman, and, therefore, that he was aware of Gomer's character from the outset. Repugnant as the idea may be to the modern reader, it has been said that Hosea's action was a piece of dramatic symbolism, akin to, though more extreme than, some of the prophecies enacted in bizarre fashion by other prophets.

On the other hand, it is at least possible that Hosea did not become aware of Gomer's character until they had been married for some time, and that i. 2 represents the prophet's subsequent conviction that he had acted under divine guidance (cf. Jer. xxxii. 6–8, though the parallel is not exact). If Gomer's immorality did not, in fact, begin until after the marriage, this would offer a better analogy to the relationship

---

[1] If the narratives are regarded as duplicates, the word 'yet' must be deleted from iii. 1.

[2] The view has been advanced that she was a temple prostitute.

between Israel and Yahweh, which began happily (ii. 15b), but was marred by Israel's apostasy.

On balance, then, it seems best to conclude that Hosea married Gomer in ignorance of her character, that after she had been unfaithful to him they were separated, but that he still loved her, and later took her back into his home. It is not surprising that the story is difficult to reconstruct; for Hosea's aim was not to give a complete account of his domestic tragedy, but to tell as much of it as was necessary to convey his message about God and Israel. Detailed reconstructions of the events, which go beyond the evidence, are, therefore, beside the mark.

As in some other parts of the Old Testament (notably the last of the Servant Songs), uncertainty about details of interpretation does not obscure the main elements in the prophet's teaching. Hosea's marriage to Gomer, her infidelity, and his enduring love for her, were counterparts of the bond between God and Israel, Israel's lapses into Baal worship, and God's loving purpose to win her back to Himself. This use of marriage symbolism is the more striking because of the association which it had with elements in Canaanite religion to which the prophets were opposed. The symbol continued to be used, and reappears in the thought of the Bride of Christ in the New Testament and later Christian literature. This figure is appropriate to that blend of duty and affection which is summed up in the Hebrew word *ḥeseḏ*. *Ḥeseḏ* is the unwavering constancy which God shows to His people. It is also the response which He requires of them in their relations with Him and with each other.

The love of God for Israel is also expressed in terms of the care of a father for his child (xi. 1 ff), the verb used being *'āhēḇ*, which denotes ordinary human affection.

The indictment against Israel is that she has forsaken Yahweh for Baal, and contaminated the worship of Yahweh by pagan usage (ii. *passim*; viii. 5 f; x. 5). Foreign alliances are condemned (v. 13; vii. 11; xii. 1). Though the emphasis on social evils is perhaps less obvious than in Amos, we are given a vivid, and at times lurid, picture of society in Northern Israel. But behind specific evils the prophet sees the fundamental lack of *ḥeseḏ*, trustworthiness, and knowledge of God (iv. 1 f).

The great affirmation, 'I desire *ḥeseḏ* and not sacrifice' (vi. 6), is an austere reminder that superficial penitence will not lead to an inevitable restoration. But Hosea does prophesy restoration, not only in xiv, parts of which have often been regarded as late, but supremely in ii. 14 ff, where discipline and renewal are both depicted as the work of God's love.

It is quite unnecessary to assume that these and other hopeful passages do not come from Hosea; though some parts of xiv may, on other grounds, be so treated. i. 10–ii. 1; iii. 4 f; and other passages which refer to Judah are also commonly regarded as additions. After the fall of the Northern Kingdom, the record of Hosea's teaching was no doubt preserved in the south and it would be natural to add to it references to Judah. If the prophecy had already been written down, these would be textual interpolations. But if it was still in the stage of oral transmission in some prophetic community, the recognition of these additions belongs to tradition history rather than to literary or textual criticism. Where the evidence is so tenuous, it is unwise to dogmatize. At all events, the book of Jeremiah makes it clear that, whether by written or oral transmission, the teaching of Hosea was still a vital force in prophetic circles at the end of the following century.

## (b) *Joel*

The book of Joel falls into two parts: (*a*) i. 1–ii. 27; (*b*) ii. 28–iii. 21.[1]

(*a*) contains a description of a devastating plague of locusts

[1] Here, as elsewhere in the present work, the references are to the chapter and verse divisions of the standard English versions. These, however, are not everywhere identical with the arrangement in the Hebrew Bible. In Joel, the following variations should be noted: E. VV. ii. 28 = Heb. iii. 1; E. VV. iii. 1 = Heb. iv. 1.

accompanied by a severe drought. There is an exhortation to
fasting and prayer: the Day of the Lord is at hand, heralded
by another and more severe visitation. But calamity may be
averted by penitence. Then comes a description of the divine
deliverance and promises of plenty and of God's presence with
His people.

(b) begins with a prophecy of the outpouring of the Spirit
in the Day of the Lord. The Jews will be delivered; other
nations will be assembled in the Valley of Jehoshaphat to be
judged and punished.

The position of the book in the collection suggests that it
was regarded as pre-exilic. But we know nothing about the
prophet Joel from other sources; the superscription gives no
information about the period in which he lived; and, in
determining the date, we are dependent on internal evidence.

It has been argued that the minority of King Joash of
Judah is the most appropriate period. The time of Jeremiah
has also been suggested; and, in a recent work, the Norwegian
scholar, A. S. Kapelrud has argued that the prophecy dates
from about 600 B.C., though it was not written down until the
4th or 3rd century.

The balance of evidence seems to favour a post-exilic date,
though some of it is not entirely cogent. It is probably unwise
to lay much stress on diction and style, which are not
markedly late, though the presence of Aramaisms has been
taken as a post-exilic feature. The absence of references to
Northern Israel and to the royal house, and the apparent
implication that priests and elders are the leaders in the
community (i. 2, 13 f; ii. 16 f), are not in themselves strong
evidence of a post-exilic date. The association of meal-offering
and drink-offering (i. 9, 13) is in line with post-exilic cultic
usage. The phrase in iii. 1 commonly translated 'bring again
the captivity' probably means 'restore the fortunes', and
therefore does not imply Exile or Dispersion; but iii. 2
clearly does. From i. 14; ii. 7 ff, 17, it appears that Jerusalem
and its temple have been restored. Although a pre-exilic
reference to the Ionians is perhaps not entirely out of the

question,[1] the statement that the Phoenicians have sold Jews
to the Ionians best fits the post-exilic period; but, since the
Greeks are not referred to as powerful enemies who are close
at hand, the book can hardly be brought down into the
Hellenistic epoch.

These arguments are reinforced by general considerations.
There are many verbal parallels to other prophetic books.
These need not, in themselves, prove that Joel is the
borrower; but, taken together with the other signs of post-
exilic date, they suggest that he is. There are no denunciations
of the religious, moral, and social abuses attacked by the pre-
exilic prophets; and the general recall to loyal observance of
the cult is typical of the post-exilic period. The description
of the coming Day of Yahweh, and of the judgement of
the nations is also in keeping with later prophecy. Taken
as a whole, the atmosphere and ideas of the book are typical
of the stage of transition from prophecy to apocalyptic.
Probably the latter half of the 5th century B.C. is the most
likely date.

But it has been doubted whether we *can* take the work as
a whole. The contrast between the narrative portion in i. 1–
ii. 27 and the apocalyptic predictions of ii. 28–iii. 21 is considerable. It is argued that the two sections are independent,
and that the references to the Day of Yahweh in the narrative
are later additions. But this theory is unnecessary. Specific
events, which the prophet witnessed and interpreted in terms
of God's will, might well have led his thought to the final
divine intervention. This transition of thought may be
paralleled elsewhere (e.g., Isa. xxiv–xxvii).

The first section of the book is held by some to be a
liturgy; but there is no adequate ground for thinking that it
is other than it appears to be, a blend of oracular narrative
and exhortation.

The style of Joel is lively, and does not show the marks of
literary decline which appear in some post-exilic prophets.
The descriptions are highly coloured, yet not as bizarre as in

[1] See W. F. Albright, *From the Stone Age to Christianity*, p. 259.

later apocalyptic writing. In thought, as we have seen, the book illustrates the transition to apocalyptic; the account which it gives of the Day of Yahweh is an interesting sample of the development of that theme in Biblical thought. The supremely memorable passage is ii. 28–32, which, in the New Testament, is given a universal reference and applied to Pentecost.

## (c) *Amos*

The superscription to the book of Amos dates the prophet's ministry in the reigns of Uzziah of Judah and Jeroboam of Israel, in what has aptly been called 'the Victorian Age of the Hebrew kingdoms'. It was a time of prosperity, of success-ful irredentism (2 Kings xiv. 25), and of renewed national confidence. The official religion was a going concern: the festivals were popular, and the sanctuaries were thronged. But the old social order had disintegrated; and the contrast between the arrogant luxury of the rich and the misery of the poor made the old Israelite ideal of brotherhood seem an anachronism.

The book falls into three parts. The first (i–ii) consists of a series of prophecies against neighbouring nations (Damascus, Gaza, Tyre, Edom, Ammon, Moab, Judah), reaching its climax in a denunciation of Northern Israel. All of these prophecies follow the same pattern, except the last, which is much more detailed. The second part (iii–vi) is a collection of oracles denouncing the corruption of society and religion in Northern Israel. The third (vii–ix) contains five visions (vii. 1–8, 4–6, 7–9; viii. 1–3; ix. 1–4), combined with the story of a clash between Amos and Amaziah, priest of Bethel (vii. 10–17), and with other groups of oracles (viii. 4–14; ix. 5–15).

Thus the book contains all three main types of prophetic material. The bulk of it consists of poetic oracles; vii. 10–17 is narrative in the third person; and the visions are auto-biographical.

In all probability, the series of oracles on the nations (i–ii) is not an artificial collection, but a connected speech. The element of surprise in the denunciation of Israel is a climax prepared for in the preceding oracles: to disintegrate the passage would ruin the rhetorical effect. In iii–vi, the recurrence of 'Hear this word' (iii. 1; iv. 1; v. 1), and of 'Woe' (v. 18; vi. 1) probably indicates that smaller groups of oracles have been linked together on the catchword principle. Presumably the five visions originally formed a unity; but the sequence has been broken at vii. 9, where the closing words provided an obvious link with the beginning of a piece of biographical narrative (vii. 10–17), and again at viii. 3, by a series of oracles.

The text of the book is remarkably sound. There are also few oracles which can plausibly be regarded as not coming from Amos. The denunciations of Tyre, Edom, and Judah (i. 9 f, 11 f; ii. 4 f) are thought by some to be later insertions. The strongest arguments can be levelled against the third of these, since the language is Deuteronomic, the condemnation is general rather than specific, and (though this perhaps begs the question) Israel, not Judah, was the field of Amos' activity. The so-called doxologies in iv. 13; v. 8 f; ix. 5 f are also widely regarded as secondary on grounds of diction, thought, and lack of connexion with context; but these arguments are probably not conclusive. Nor is the hymnic character of these verses sufficient ground for denying that Amos composed or quoted them. The strongest case can be made against ix. 11–15, which appears to presuppose the destruction of the monarchy and the fact of the Exile. But some would retain the passage, holding that Amos is referring to the disruption of the kingdom and to a restoration after the affliction which he elsewhere predicts.

Like Hosea, Amos foresees the catastrophe by which the Northern Kingdom was threatened; but he does not actually name the Assyrians as the hostile power. Like Hosea, too, he predicts disaster for the dynasty of Jehu (Hosea i. 4; Amos vii. 9, 11); but, unlike Hosea, he does not allude to the subsequent dynastic troubles. Accordingly, it is customary to

date Amos slightly earlier than Hosea.[1] The suggestion that
viii. 9 shows that the prophet had witnessed the solar eclipse
of 763 B.C. does not greatly help towards dating Amos more
precisely. Nor does the reference to the earthquake (i. 1),
which may be the one alluded to in Zech. xiv. 5. The widely
accepted view that Amos prophesied *ca.* 760–750 B.C. need
not be discarded, in spite of the attempt of R. S. Cripps to
establish a later date.

The oracles are directed, in the main, against the Northern
Kingdom. Amos himself 'was among the shepherds of Tekoa',
(i. 1), a village in the hills south of Bethlehem in the kingdom
of Judah. He may well have been a Judahite by birth. The
word used here for 'shepherd' (*nôḵēḏ*) is applied to Mesha,
King of Moab (2 Kings iii. 4), and thus need not indicate a
man of humble station. Though there is Ugaritic evidence
that the term could have cultic connexions, recent attempts
to show that Amos was a cultic functionary are not convincing. He was called from his work as a shepherd and a dresser
of sycamore trees to speak God's word to Israel (vii. 14 f).
There has been much argument whether we should translate,
in vii. 14, 'I *was* not a prophet' or 'I *am* not a prophet'. But,
whether or not Amos is repudiating the name of prophet, he
contrasts a particular religious function, to which he has been
called, with his normal way of life. To regard the latter as
having been specifically cultic is unnatural.

Still more unjustified is the idea, commonly found in
popular works, that Amos was an uneducated rustic. The
powerful effect of his words is the result not only of profound
conviction but also of literary skill. His language is classical,
and his style regular. Even in translation the carefully
balanced structure of the oracles is evident (e.g., iii. 3–8;
iv. 6–11).

The superb sequence of denunciations in the first two
chapters implies the conception of Yahweh as Lord of nations.

---

[1] The order of the books in the collection of the Twelve reflects an old
tradition that Hosea preceded Amos, and was, in fact, the earliest of the
canonical prophets.

Its climax emphasizes the special bond between Yahweh and Israel as shown in deliverance and direction. This bond, which does not involve favouritism on Yahweh's part (ix. 7), lays on Israel a special responsibility (iii. 1 f). The wanton luxury of the rich and their heartless oppression of the poor, the venality of judges, the corruption of religion, and the failure to read the signs of the times are the objects of the prophet's scathing denunciation. He is a herald of doom; and it is sometimes said that he predicts nothing else. But, even if we reject ix. 11–15 as of later origin, there still remains at least a gleam of hope in the possibility of repentance and renewal (v. 4, 6, 14); and even the prophet's sternest words are redeemed from blank pessimism by his unshaken confidence that the God who is Lord of all is utterly righteous.

## (d) Obadiah

The shortest book in the Old Testament is ascribed to Obadiah. The name was a common one; and nothing is known of the prophet who bore it. The book contains (a) a prediction of the punishment of Edom (1–9), (b) a description of the hostility of Edom towards Judah at the time of the fall of Jerusalem (10–14), (c) a prediction that the Day of Yahweh is coming on all nations, that Judah and Israel will be united, and that Edom will be destroyed (15–21).

The close similarity of vv. 1–8 to parts of Jer. xlix. 7–16 raises the problem of the possible dependence of either book on the other, or of both on a common source. The verses in question seem to be in a more original form in Obadiah. If it could be shown that Jeremiah had borrowed or quoted them, then Obadiah, or this part of the prophecy, would be preexilic. But the Jeremianic origin of xlix is open to question; and therefore no secure conclusion about the date of Obadiah can be drawn from the relation of the two passages. Indeed, it may well be that we should think here not of the inclusion of material from one document in another, or of the dependence of two documents on a lost original, but of prophetic

material preserved orally in varying form in different tradition circles.

It has been argued that 1–10 is pre-exilic, and refers to the
relations between Edom and Judah in the middle of the
9th century (2 Kings viii. 20–22), and that the remainder
comes from a later period or later periods. But there seems
to be no adequate reason for discarding the view that the
book is a prophecy from the exilic period. It fits the historical
situation. There had, indeed, been recurrent hostility between
Judah and Edom during the period of the monarchy. But the
vindictive advantage which the Edomites took of the plight
of Judah when Jerusalem fell is answered by the intense
hatred of Edom in several exilic and post-exilic passages
elsewhere in the Old Testament. The prediction of Edom's
discomfiture may refer to the invasion of Edomite territory
by Arab tribes, *ca.* 500 B.C. Further, the presentation of the
Day of Yahweh as a day of judgement on all nations accords
with the post-exilic development of that concept.

### (e) Jonah

With the exception of the poem in ii. 2–9, the book of
Jonah consists of a story about a prophet. Having been sent
by God to prophesy to the Ninevites, Jonah tried to evade
the divine call by taking ship from Joppa. A great storm
arose; and lots were cast to discover who among those on
board was the cause of it. The lot indicated Jonah, who was
then thrown into the sea, but was swallowed by a great fish,
which, after three days, vomited him up on dry land. He
then received again the charge to prophesy, and this time
carried it out. But the destruction of the city was averted by
nation-wide repentance; and Jonah, distressed that his prediction had not been fulfilled, prayed that he might die. A
plant, which had quickly grown up and afforded him shelter,
was as speedily destroyed by a worm. From Jonah's concern
at the loss of the plant, God justified His own concern that
Nineveh and its inhabitants should not be destroyed.

The poem in ii. 2–9 is a psalm of thanksgiving for deliverance from dire affliction. The references to the deep, the seas, the flood, the waters, and the like, are such as are commonly found in the Psalter. They belong to the phraseology (some would say the mythology) of ancient Hebrew worship, and denote suffering and distress. They should not be taken to refer literally to Jonah's situation. The poem contains no reference to the fish. Further, it is strange that this thanksgiving for deliverance should come before Jonah has actually been delivered. It therefore seems probable that the poem was originally independent of the book, and was introduced here because it was felt to be generally appropriate.

In the remainder of the book, the message lies in the story, and in what God said to Jonah, rather than in what Jonah was commanded to say to the Ninevites. There is here a general contrast with the bulk of the prophetic literature; but parallels may be found, e.g., in 1 Kings xix, or, in apocalyptic, in the stories at the beginning of the book of Daniel.

The prophet who is the central figure in the book is meant to be identified with the eighth century Jonah of 2 Kings xiv. 25. But there can be little doubt that the book comes from a much later period, possibly late Persian or early Hellenistic. Several features in the diction point to this. Other considerations arise from the substance of the story. The historical Nineveh was considerably smaller than the city described here (iii. 3; iv. 11); and therefore the narrative probably belongs to a period long after the age of Nineveh's greatness. This is further suggested by the fact that the title, 'King of Nineveh', is not otherwise known to have been applied to Assyrian monarchs. Nor is the writer concerned to give an accurate record of past events. The conversion of the Ninevites is not recorded elsewhere; and it is difficult to believe that it could have taken place so swiftly and on such a scale, and yet have left no other trace.

In short, here, as in other parts of the Bible, notably the Gospel parables, we have fiction used to convey a religious message. Arguments about the possibility or otherwise of

Jonah's survival in the belly of the fish are beside the point. Parallels to this theme have been sought in folk lore. But, however interesting they may be, they scarcely serve to illuminate the message of the book, which can best be understood in the context of Old Testament thought. It is a protest against the narrowness of a certain type of religiosity, which, out of a concern to preserve the purity of a particular tradition, forgets the breadth of the divine mercy. More positively, it is a missionary appeal, inspired, not by the spirit of fanatical proselytization, but by compassion for men in their need. Thus, Jonah has something in common with the message of Deutero-Isaiah, though probably from a later period. At a time when Judaism was subject to the pressure of surrounding paganism, this book pleads that loyalty to God requires more than waiting for the fulfilment of God's judgement on the heathen.

Jonah has been described above as fiction. Some regard it as a parable; others as an allegory. If we think of a parable as symbolic in its main points or in its broad outline, and of an allegory as symbolic in its details, then Jonah is more appropriately classed with the former. The prophet may be equated with the Jews. The fish may represent Babylon (cf. Jer. li. 34, 44), by which Israel was swallowed up in the Exile; though some have maintained that this is inappropriate, since the fish in fact saved Jonah. But it is difficult to attribute allegorical significance to many details in the story, and probably pointless to attempt to do so.

### (f) Micah

We do not often find in the prophetic literature references by one prophet, or by his disciples, to another. A striking exception occurs in the story of Jeremiah's temple prophecy, where elders from the provinces offer a defence of Jeremiah's action by citing the case and the words of Micah, who prophesied against Jerusalem and the temple in Hezekiah's reign, but was not executed (Jer. xxvi. 18). This agrees with the superscription of the book of Micah in dating the prophet's activity towards the end of the eighth century (according to the superscription, in the reigns of Jotham, Ahaz, and Hezekiah), and indicates that, nearly a century after his lifetime, Micah was still commonly remembered as a prophet of judgement. The vexed and inconclusive critical debate about the composition of the book has been concerned mainly with two questions: how much of the material may reasonably be assigned to that period, and whether Micah's message was solely one of punitive judgement.

The book is commonly divided into three sections:

(*a*) i–iii. The punishment of Samaria and Jerusalem is foretold; the oppression of the poor by the rich is denounced; the prophet's opponents, the rulers, and the mercenary prophets are rebuked; and the destruction of Jerusalem is prophesied. The only gleam of hope in these sombre chapters is ii. 12–13.

(*b*) iv–v. By contrast, these chapters contain a series of prophecies of hope and restoration: the establishment of Zion as the religious centre of the world, the ingathering of the dispersed Israelites, the destruction of their enemies, the coming of a second David, the influence of the remnant, the purification of Israel's religion.

(*c*) vi–vii. This is a blend of rebuke and promise. The divine arraignment of Israel leads up to the classic statement of prophetic religion in vi. 8. This is followed by a condemnation of dishonesty, a lament over the state of the nation, and a final prayer of hope and confidence.

It is possible that we should divide the book into two un-equal parts (i–v; vi–vii), each displaying the same alternating pattern of judgement and hope, a pattern which, as we have seen, is common in the prophetic collections. This division serves merely to indicate the way in which the material has been grouped. It does not necessarily reflect diversity of origin.

There has been a general tendency to attribute i–iii (with the exception of ii. 12, 13) to Micah, and to regard the rest of the book as of later origin. But the variety of theory about these other chapters is so great that a survey of it might well serve as an object lesson in the need to scrutinize the assumptions of literary critics.

Two arguments commonly advanced for denying certain passages to Micah must be considered. The first is that he was exclusively a prophet of divine retribution, and, therefore, that any expression of hope or promise of renewal cannot come from him. The fact that in Jeremiah's day Micah was remembered as having predicted the destruction of Jerusalem might seem to support this, but is slender evidence on which to base so sweeping a negation. When we consider the variety of denunciation and promise found in the teaching of other prophets, such as Micah's contemporaries, Hosea and Isaiah, it is unrealistic to claim that a prophet could not predict severe punishment (even in the drastic terms of iii. 12), and also, at some other stage in his ministry, promise restoration.

The second argument is that there are allusions in some of the oracles to later conditions than those of Micah's lifetime. Thus, though it is possible that Micah predicted restoration as well as chastisement, sayings which seem to presuppose the fall of Jerusalem and the experience of exile and dispersion may be held to be of later date (e.g., ii. 13; iv. 6 ff; vii. 11). An allusion to Babylon (iv. 10) may indicate a later accretion. The reference to human sacrifice (vi. 7) has been taken to show that vi. 1–8 originated in the 7th century, when that practice was rife. Even if that be granted, there is no reason why Micah should not have survived into the reign of Manasseh, though it must be admitted that Manasseh is not mentioned in the superscription to the book.

On the whole, then, it is well to treat with caution those theories by which the putative literary remains of Micah are scattered across the centuries. Later touches there may be; but a later touch does not commit us to a judgement about the entire passage in which it occurs. Two passages merit particular attention. One is the anonymous prophecy in iv. 1–5, which also appears in briefer and slightly different form in Isa. ii. 2–4. It was probably included here to provide a contrast with the grim conclusion of iii. The other is vii.

(7) 8–20, one of the passages most frequently and plausibly
assigned to the post-exilic period, though it is at least possible
that the affliction which it presupposes is not that of Judah
in the 6th century but that of Northern Israel in the 8th. The
passage is commonly regarded as liturgical in character.

Some of those scholars who emphasize the part played by
groups of disciples in the transmission of prophetic teaching
claim that the book is a unity in the sense that it comes from
one man and his circle, and deprecate attempts to decide
what Micah did, and did not, say. But, at all events, the book
contains sufficient teaching directed to the situation at the
close of the 8th century to enable us to form some idea of
the prophet, his message, and his relation to his prophetic
contemporaries.

Micah came from Moresheth-Gath, a small country town
near the Philistine plain. His country origin gives special
point to his passionate denunciation of the oppression of
the small farmer by the rich (ii. 1–5), an evil which Isaiah
also attacks (v. 8 ff). Like Isaiah, too, he is scathing in his
denunciation of political leaders and mercenary prophets (cf.
iii with Isa. iii. 1–15; x. 1–4; xxviii. 7; xxix. 10); and, like
both Isaiah and Amos, he rebukes those who would silence
the authentic word of prophecy (ii. 6–11; Isa. xxviii. 7–18;
xxx. 9–11; Amos ii. 11 f). The description of invasion in
i. 10–16 is in some ways reminiscent of Isa. x. 28 ff; and
the prediction in v. 10–15, that the things in which the people
trust will be destroyed, recalls Isa. ii. 6 ff. The Immanuel
prophecy in Isa. vii. 14 is probably echoed in v. 2 ff, with its
cryptic expression 'she who travails'. These close similarities
make it not altogether fanciful to suppose that there was
some link between Micah and Isaiah or the Isaianic circle.
The inclusion of the same oracle in both collections (Micah
iv. 1–5; Isa. ii. 2–4) may not be entirely fortuitous.

On the other hand, we miss in Micah the incisive comments
on foreign policy which are so striking a feature in Isaiah.
Thus there is little to help us to date his utterances precisely.
There is nothing which must be as early as Jotham, and no

reference to the events arising from the Syro-Ephraimitic coalition. But vi. 9–16, with its reference to the statutes of Omri and the works of the house of Ahab, may well be a denunciation of Northern Israel before its fall. i. 2–7, which predicts the destruction of Samaria, must be earlier than 722. As we have seen, vii. (7) 8–20 may have as its background the subjugation of the north by Assyria. Those passages which predict the punishment of Jerusalem may well come from the troubled decade, 711–701.

One is perhaps tempted to think of Micah as a book characterized by its intensity rather than its range. But a work which uses oracle, lament, and dialogue so effectively, and which includes the trenchant invective of i–iii, the sublime picture of world peace in iv. 1–5, the haunting prediction of a new David in v. 2 ff, the classic formulation of prophetic religion in vi. 1–8, and the moving conclusion of vii, must have an honoured place in the prophetic corpus.

### (g) Nahum

The book of Nahum begins with a description of the coming of Yahweh to overthrow His enemies (i. 2 ff). This is in the form of an incomplete acrostic poem, which breaks off about halfway through the Hebrew alphabet. Included in it is a word of comfort to Judah (12, 13, 15). In ii there is a vivid picture of the fall of Nineveh, and of its subsequent plight. The attack on the city is again described in brilliant poetry (iii. 1–17). A brief dirge ends the book (iii. 18, 19).

The reference to No-Amon (the Egyptian Thebes), which fell to the Assyrians in 663 B.C., indicates that the book must be later than that date. It probably cannot be later than 612 B.C., the year in which Nineveh fell. The sense of immediately impending catastrophe on the tyrant city makes it likely that the prophecy is no more than a year or two earlier than the events predicted. It has been held that it is a liturgical composition, celebrating, and therefore slightly later than, the fall of Nineveh. But it is more natural to take the descriptions as predictive; and presumably such a liturgy would have included a psalm of thanksgiving to Yahweh.

The fragmentary acrostic is evidently part of an independent poem, and is usually regarded as a later addition to the prophecy. But it may be that the prophet used part of an older hymn, describing a theophany, to introduce his message.

Nothing is known of Nahum apart from what may be gathered from the prophecy. He is described as an Elkoshite. A site near Nineveh, another in Galilee, and another in the south of Palestine have been claimed as his home.

Nahum's brilliant descriptive poetry is almost without equal in the Old Testament. As a nationalistic prophet, he presents a striking contrast to his contemporary, Jeremiah. His exultation over the fall of an enemy may seem savage; but the fall was that of a tyrant as well as an enemy; and, like other prophets, Nahum saw the tyrant as under the judgement of God.

## (h) Habakkuk

The book of Habakkuk begins with a twofold sequence of complaint and answering oracle. i. 2–4 is an appeal to God against the ruthless conduct of the wicked. In i. 5–11, God answers that He is raising up the powerful Chaldean nation to punish the oppressor. There is a renewed complaint, in i. 12–17, that God does not intervene to end the cruelty of the wicked. Then the prophet takes up his stand, awaiting an answering revelation from God, and is given the assurance that the vision, though delayed, will be granted him, and that, by contrast with the wicked, the righteous will live by his faithfulness (ii. 1–4). Then come five 'woes' on the wicked (ii. 5–20). iii. 1 describes what follows as 'a prayer of Habakkuk the prophet upon Shigionoth'. It consists of a description of God's coming in judgement (vv. 2–16), and an assertion of utter faith in God's goodness in spite of adversity (17–19). It is rounded off by a musical or liturgical rubric.

The problem of dating is closely linked with that of interpretation. The reference to the Chaldeans as a people whom

God is raising up indicates that the prophecy belongs, in all probability, to the last quarter of the 7th century B.C., when Babylonia reasserted her independence and then replaced Assyria as the dominant power in Western Asia. But the precise point in that period to which the prophecy is to be referred depends on the identification of the oppressor, or oppressors, in i. 2–4 and 12–17.

If the wicked in i. 2–4 are the Assyrians, who have oppressed Judah, then the Chaldeans are represented in 5–11 as deliverers; and in 12–17 the prophet is again perplexed because the Chaldeans themselves now act ruthlessly. This would put the beginning of the prophecy in the earlier part of the period, before Assyrian power was finally destroyed. But it may be doubted whether, even then, Assyria was in a position to act strongly in Palestine. The wicked of i. 2–4 might, however, be identified with the Egyptians, who, after defeating Josiah at Megiddo in 608 B.C., controlled Palestine until they were overthrown by the Chaldeans. But are the wicked of i. 2–4 necessarily foreigners? By contrast with i. 12–17, which appears to describe the policy of a great power (e.g., *v*. 17), i. 2–4 may well depict the misconduct of wrongdoers within Judah during the reign of Jehoiakim, whose tyrannous arrogance was criticized by Jeremiah (xxii. 13 ff).

The bold suggestion of Duhm that the book refers to the conquests of Alexander the Great, and that *Kaśdîm* (Chaldeans) in i. 6 should be emended to *Kittîm* (Cypriots, meaning Greeks) would scarcely merit mention here, were it not that the ancient commentary on Habakkuk discovered near the Dead Sea in 1947 says of *Kaśdîm*, 'this means the *Kittîm*'. The fact that *Kaśdîm* is thus interpreted tells against Duhm's otherwise improbable theory by emphasizing that *Kaśdîm* is, after all, in the text used for the commentary.

The third chapter is often regarded as an addition to the prophecy, taken from some liturgical collection. The word 'Shigionoth' in the superscription is the plural of 'Shiggaion', a term of uncertain meaning, which appears in the title of Psalm vii. The liturgical or musical note, 'Selah', which is

frequent in the Psalms, occurs here in vv. 8, 9, 18. The rubric
with which the book closes looks like the heading of a Psalm,
and, if this chapter is an extract from some liturgical collection, may have been the heading of the poem which followed.
The Dead Sea Commentary on Habakkuk makes no allusion
to the chapter; but this is not necessarily in itself evidence
that it did not originally form part of the book. Its place as
an integral part of the prophecy has been defended on the
ground that it contains the vision promised in ii. 8. The unity of
the book has also been supported by the claim that its various
elements are combined to form a liturgical composition.

This last theory should be treated with reserve. But there
is a reasonable unity of thought in the book. It raises the
question of the demonstration of the divine justice in the
outward course of events. A comparison with the teaching of
Habakkuk's great contemporary, Jeremiah (e.g., Jer. xii.
1 ff), is natural. Common to both prophets is not only the
problem, but the form of a dialogue with God (Hab. i. 2, 5,
12; ii. 2; Jer. xi. 20 ff; xii. 1 ff; xiv. 11 ff; xv. 15 ff; etc.).

Whether or not the closing chapter comes from Habakkuk
himself, it is in line with the central theme just noted. Like
descriptions of a theophany elsewhere in the Old Testament,
it depicts the coming of God in judgement, to succour His
people and to overthrow their enemies. The concluding verses
express the steadfastness of those who trust in Yahweh when
His justice is not outwardly manifested; and thus this passage
echoes the thought of ii. 4, 'the righteous shall live by his
faithfulness'. While it may be admitted that, in quoting these
words, St. Paul adds to their meaning (Rom. i. 17; Gal. iii.
11), the contrast should not be exaggerated. The 'faithfulness'
of which Habakkuk speaks could not exist in the situation
which he describes apart from the faith which is personal
trust.

## (i) Zephaniah

Brief as it is, the book of Zephaniah illustrates aptly a
pattern of arrangement which we have already seen in the

larger prophetic collections: judgement on Israel; judgement
on the nations; the promise of restoration. The first chapter
announces a Day of the Lord in which punishment will fall
in Judah on idolaters, apostates, imitators of foreign ways,
and the indifferent. In ii, an exhortation to the meek to seek
Yahweh and His righteousness is followed by a prediction
of disaster on Philistines, Moabites, Ammonites, Ethiopians,
and Assyrians. iii begins with a rebuke to Jerusalem and its
leaders, and predicts a judgement on the nations and the
survival of a remnant in Israel: it ends with a thanksgiving
for the divine deliverance.

The superscription traces the prophet's ancestry through
four generations to a Hezekiah. Both the name and the
genealogical detail (unparalleled in a prophetic book) have
been taken as evidence that Zephaniah was of royal descent;
but, if this is so, it is surprising that Hezekiah is not called
'king'. Cushi (the Ethiopian), the name of the prophet's
father, is the only one in the list which does not include the
name of the God of Israel (-iah = Yahweh). It may reflect
a pro-Egyptian interest. The prophet's own name means
'Yahweh has hidden' (cf. ii. 3).

Zephaniah is said (i. 1) to have received his message during
the reign of Josiah. His condemnation of prevalent pagan
practice in Judah (i. 4–6, 8, 9), and of princes and other
leaders as specially blameworthy (i. 8; iii. 3, 4), points to a
date before 621 B.C., when Josiah carried through his reform
in accordance with the law book found in the temple. The
descriptions of punitive judgement, though allusive rather
than precise in their detail, suggest the destruction wrought
by an invading army (e.g., i. 16; iii. 6). Herodotus (i. 103–106)
tells of the havoc caused in Western Asia at this time (ca. 625)
by marauding hosts of Scythians; and both Zephaniah's predictions and Jeremiah's oracles about the foe from the north
may allude to this invasion. It has, however, been denied
that Palestine ever suffered from the Scythian hordes, and
that the oracles in Jeremiah and Zephaniah should be so
interpreted.

Various parts of the book have been treated as interpolations; but there is little or nothing which is inappropriate to the period just mentioned. There is a looseness of connexion about the book, which suggests that it contains utterances from a number of different occasions.

In his description of the Day of the Lord, Zephaniah is the heir of Amos (v. 18 ff) and Isaiah (ii. 7 ff), and links their teaching with later developments of this theme. In contrast with this sombre picture, yet still in the tradition of his 8th-century predecessors, particularly Isaiah, he sees in the humble poor the true core of God's people, the remnant to whom His promises will be fulfilled (ii. 3; iii. 12 f).

## (j) Haggai

In pointed contrast to Deutero-Isaiah's glowing prophecies of a restored Zion, Haggai shows the depressing conditions with which the returned community had to contend: drought, bad harvests, and consequent poverty. The time was the second year of Darius I of Persia (520 B.C.). At the beginning of the new reign there had been widespread revolt throughout the empire. In and around Jerusalem, the little community of returned exiles seems to have lapsed into religious indifference under the stress of economic difficulties. Haggai's mission was to persuade them to rebuild the Temple with all speed, and to predict the restoration of the lost glory of Israel.

His prophecies are recorded in five short passages, set in a framework of third-person narrative, and all precisely dated. In the first (i. 1–14 (15); August–September, 520 B.C.), he upbraids the people for neglecting the rebuilding of the temple in order to build their own houses, and asserts that, if they will put first things first, prosperity will be restored. Haggai's words roused Zerubbabel and Joshua, the civil and religious leaders of the community, to get the work started.

Seven weeks later, Haggai addressed a word (ii. 1–9) to those who felt that the temple was far inferior to the glorious building which they remembered before the Exile. He foretold that political convulsions would lead to a new world order, in which all nations would bring their tribute to the temple.

The third passage (ii. 10–14) applies a priestly ruling about the contagious power of holiness and uncleanness to the effect of the uncleanness of the people on their service and offering.

The fourth (ii. 15–19) promises a time of prosperity. It is commonly held to be misplaced, since ii. 18 puts the foundation of the temple on the twenty-fourth day of the *ninth* month. This contrasts with the statement in i. 15 that it took place on the twenty-fourth day of the *sixth* month. It has, therefore, been suggested that 'ninth' in ii. 18 should be changed to 'sixth', and the passage transferred to follow i. 15, which would then serve to introduce it.

The fifth section (ii. 20–23) is a further prophecy of the overthrow of the nations, and an assurance of special divine power to Zerubbabel, who was of David's line.

The book is written in the form of third-person narrative; and if it records the substance of poetical oracles, these have been reduced to prose. Haggai's message is also commonly dismissed as prosaic and pedestrian. But the historical importance of the book is unmistakable. Together with Zech. i–viii, it provides valuable contemporary evidence about events and conditions in the restored Jewish community, evidence which must be considered in any treatment of the early chapters of Ezra. The plea for the restoration of the temple is in harmony with the positive attitude to the cult found in other post-exilic prophets and in the post-exilic period generally. Pre-exilic prophets had said, 'Your worship is an offence to God'; but their post-exilic successors said, 'Your neglect of worship is an offence to God'. Finally, both here and in Zech. i–viii, the prophecies about Zerubbabel form an important stage in the development of the Messianic hope.

### (k) Zechariah

For reasons which will be considered later, only the first eight chapters of the book of Zechariah contain the teaching of the prophet of that name. ix–xiv will, therefore, be discussed separately.

i–viii falls into three main parts: a call to repentance (i. 1–6); eight dream visions (i. 7–vi. 8) followed by a command to crown Joshua the high priest (vi. 9–15); various prophecies of restoration (vii–viii).

Zechariah is described in i. 1, 7 as the son of Berechiah and the grandson of Iddo. But in Ezra v. 1; vi. 14, he is said to be the son of Iddo. It is probable that 'the son of Berechiah' has been wrongly inserted in i. 1 under the influence of Isa. viii. 2, where there is mention of a Zechariah, son of Jeberechiah. Iddo is included in Neh. xii. 4, 16, in a list of priestly houses; and thus Zechariah, like more than one of his prophetic predecessors, was of priestly descent.

His activity overlapped that of Haggai. The first revelation to him is dated in the eighth month of the second year of Darius (i. 1), i.e., October–November, 520 B.C., a month before the last recorded utterance of Haggai. The dream visions are dated (i. 7) the twenty-fourth day of the eleventh month of the second year of Darius, i.e., February–March, 519 B.C. The last date in the book, the fourth day of the ninth month of the fourth year of Darius (vii. 1), which is probably intended to cover vii and viii, brings us down to the end of 518 B.C.

The situation is the same as that presupposed in Haggai. The disturbances in the Persian Empire have now been suppressed (i. 11). The restored Jewish community in Palestine is still facing discouraging difficulties (viii. 10). Zechariah's message is concerned with the purification and strengthening of the life of that community, with its future government, and with the restoration of the temple and of worship.

The substance of his teaching is chiefly contained in the remarkable series of eight dream visions, of which the first and last stand by themselves, while the second and third, fourth and fifth, sixth and seventh, are in pairs. (a) i. 7–17 is a vision of four horsemen who bring news of the quelling of revolts in the Empire; but God promises to intervene on behalf of his people. (*b*) i. 18-21, the vision of the smiths striking down the horns which scattered Judah, is a prediction of deliverance from enemies. (*c*) ii. 1-5, the man with the measuring line, signifies the rebuilding of a spacious and secure Jerusalem. (*d*) iii. 1-9 (10) tells of the accusation by the Satan of the high priest, Joshua (the representative of the community), and his acquittal and cleansing. (*e*) The extent and meaning of the fifth vision are disputed; but, if we take iv. 1-6a with 10b-14, the point is probably that the lampstand with its seven lamps (the eyes of Yahweh) represents God and His constant vigilance, and that the two olive trees represent Joshua and Zerubbabel. (*f*) v. 1-4, the vision of the flying scroll, symbolizes the purging of evildoers from Israel. (*g*) v. 5-11, the woman carried in an ephah measure to Babylon signifies the removal of wickedness from the land. (*h*) vi. 1-8, tells how four chariots are sent out to different parts of the earth, to suppress Israel's enemies and to punish the north country (Babylon).

These visions are a narrative in the first person (Type C; see p. 101, above; and cf. Amos vii. 1-9; viii. 1 ff; ix. 1 ff). They are preceded (i. 1-6) and followed (vi. 9-15; vii; viii) by prophetic oracles. Other prophetic oracles (ii. 6-13; iv. 6b-10a) are inserted within the sequence of visions.

The call to repentance in i. 1-6 is interesting because of its backward look to an earlier prophetic tradition. ii. 6-13 is an appeal to exiles to return and a promise of God's advent. iv. 6b-10a predicts the completion of the temple by Zerubbabel. vi. 9-15, was probably originally a command to crown Zerubbabel (not Joshua) as is shown by the use of the messianic title 'the Branch' (Zerubbabel = branch from Babel). vii and viii contain an inquiry from Bethel about fasting and the reply that God requires righteousness and love, to which are added seven prophecies about the glorious future.

These colourful chapters form an interesting contrast to the more prosaic and pedestrian book of Haggai. They also show the development of prophecy towards apocalyptic. The dream vision is used as a medium of revelation; the symbolism is artificial, and even bizarre; there are frequent references to angelic beings, and, in particular, to an interpreting angel. The emphasis on the transcendence of God, and the reference to the Satan as a malevolent accuser are further marks of the later phases of Old Testament religion.

The remaining chapters of the book of Zechariah contain two collections of prophecies (ix–xi; xii–xiv) each introduced by the expression (not found elsewhere) 'the burden of the word of Yahweh'. The same phrase is found at the beginning of Malachi; and it therefore seems likely that three anonymous collections have been placed here at the end of the Book of the Twelve.

The interpretation, analysis, dating, and literary relations of these chapters all present difficult problems. ix describes the overthrow of foreign nations including the Greeks, the coming of an ideal king, and the ingathering of Israel. x. 1–2 enjoins prayer to Yahweh in time of drought. x. 3–12 predicts the downfall of foreign tyrants, a thought which is continued in xi. 1–3. xi. 4–17, with which xiii. 7–9 is commonly associated, tells in symbolic language of the relations of Israel with its rulers. xii. 1–xiii. 6 describes the siege, deliverance, and purification of Jerusalem. xiv contains another description of the siege and deliverance of Jerusalem, leading to the universal dominion of Yahweh in the new age.

Unlike i–viii, these chapters contain no allusions to 6th-century conditions or to Joshua and Zerubbabel. The reference to Greece (ix. 13) points to a later period; and in content and expression this part of the book is further removed from prophecy and nearer to apocalyptic. It is, indeed, questionable whether the whole of ix–xiv comes from one source. Some would divide it into Deutero-Zechariah (ix–xi) and Trito-Zechariah (xii–xiv). It may well be that the authorship of the chapters is still more diverse. But the indefiniteness and obscurity of the references to historical events complicate the problem and make dating difficult.

Some have referred the material to the Maccabean period.
But this is, in itself, improbable, and would involve the
assumption that these chapters were added after the completion of the prophetic collection. It is more likely that the
references to foreign rule allude to the earlier Ptolemies, and
even possible that the background of ix. 1–12 is the conquests
of Alexander.

Daunting as these chapters are to the exegete, they provide
valuable material for the study of the Jewish national hope
in the later Old Testament period. Most modern Christians
find much here that is unattractive; but the echoes and
quotations in the Gospel narratives of the Passion (cf. ix. 9
with Matt. xxi. 4 f and John xii. 12–15; xi. 12 f with Matt.
xxvii. 3–10; xii. 10 with John xix. 37; xiii. 7 with Matt. xxvi.
31 and Mark xiv. 27) show that the early Church was greatly
influenced by these predictions.

## (l) Malachi

The book of Malachi is the last of the three collections, each
headed 'the burden of the word of Yahweh', with which the
Book of the Twelve Prophets ends. It is probable that it was
separated from the others in order to bring the number of the
Minor Prophets to twelve. In all likelihood it is anonymous.
'Malachi' means 'my messenger'; and may well have been
inserted in i. 1 under the influence of iii. 1.

There are seven sections in the book. In all but the last of
them the prophet's teaching is driven home by a series of
questions and answers in poetic form.

1. i. 2–5. An argument for the love of God towards Israel as
shown in the contrasted experiences of Edom and Israel.

2. i. 6–ii. 9. A protest against the negligence of the priests
in worship.

3. ii. 10–16. Condemnation of those who divorce their wives
and marry foreign women.

4. ii. 17–iii. 6. An answer to those who complain that God
is indifferent to injustice: a day of judgement is at hand.

5. iii. 7–12. A rebuke of niggardliness in tithes and offerings.

6. iii. 13–iv. 3. A reply to doubters, and a promise to the faithful.

7. iv. 4–6. A recall to the Law, and a prophecy of the coming of Elijah.

Some rearrangement of these sections has been suggested, in order to produce a more orderly sequence, viz., 1, 5, 3—Prophecies to the nation; 2—Prophecy to the priests; 4, 6—Prophecy to doubters. The closing section is commonly regarded as a later addition, not only to this collection, but to the Book of the Twelve, recalling men to the written Law at a time when the age of prophecy was thought to be past. But the book presents no serious literary problems It reflects a single mind and the circumstances of a single situation at a date which can be determined with reasonable accuracy.

The references to the temple (iii. 1, 10) and the governor (i. 8) point to the Persian period in the time after the re building. If the Nabatean invasion of Edom could be dated with certainty, the probable reference to it in i. 3, 4 would provide a more precise clue; but this is not possible. However, the general conditions which the book describes suggest the end of the period between Haggai and Zechariah on the one hand and Ezra and Nehemiah on the other. As in Haggai's day, there is a casual attitude to worship; and, as in the later period, the problem of divorce and of marriages with foreign women has arisen. Nehemiah forbade marriage with foreign women. Ezra urged that such marriages should be dissolved. Malachi condemns the practice of divorcing Jewesses to marry foreigners. The description of the priests as sons of Levi (iii. 3; cf. ii. 4) agrees with Deuteronomy, rather than with the Priestly Code, where they are called sons of Aaron, and suggests that the Priestly Code had not yet been introduced into the life of the restored community. On the other hand, the command to bring tithes into the storehouse (iii. 10) agrees with Num. xviii. 21–24 (P) as against Deut. xiv. 22–29, where tithes are to be used for a sacred meal, and every third year to be given to the needy. This suggests a time of transition to the usage of the Priestly Code. There is no indication that a vigorous policy of reform has yet begun; and the book may therefore be put somewhere between 470 and 450 B.C., on the eve of the coming of Ezra (457 B.C.) or, if the later dating of Ezra (397 B.C.) be accepted, of Nehemiah.

The most interesting feature in the form of the book is the use of rhetorical question and answer, which anticipates the later catechetical method of teacher and pupil. Yet something of the authentic prophetic fire is still present in Malachi. 'Prophecy within the Law' (George Adam Smith) is an appropriate title for his teaching.

His attitude to Edom, which is typical of so much post-exilic literature, has been condemned as narrow and vindictive. It has been pointed out that the words, 'Have we not all one Father? Has not one God created us?' refer to Israel, and not to all mankind. But the noble saying about the worship which the Gentiles offer to God (i. 11; cf. 14) is in the line which links the words of Amos about God's providence for Philistines and Syrians with St. Paul's about the law written in the hearts of the Gentiles. Malachi's plea against divorce has all the old prophetic compassion for the oppressed. Like Haggai, he pleads for fidelity and whole-heartedness in ritual observance; and, like other post-exilic prophets, he looks forward to a day of judgement, purification, and renewal. The unforgettable glimpse he gives us of the company of those who received his message and waited in hope (iii. 16–18) is a reminder of the link between the prophetic word and the fellowship of believers.

# VI.—THE WRITINGS

## I. THE FORMS OF HEBREW POETRY

THE first three books in the Hagiographa (Psalms, Proverbs, and Job) are traditionally known as the Poetical Books; and there is applied to them in the Hebrew Bible a system of accentuation different from that in the rest of the Old Testament. These are by no means the only books which contain poetry; for, as we have seen, considerable parts of the prophetic literature are in poetical form, and a few poems and snatches of verse are included in the narrative books. There are also other poetical books among the Hagiographa (e.g., the Song of Songs and Lamentations). But it is appropriate at this point to say something about the structure and characteristics of Hebrew poetry.[1]

The most important structural feature of Hebrew verse is *parallelism*. In its simplest form this means that the poetical line is divided into two members, the second of which repeats the thought of the first, e.g.,

> 'Who shall ascend into the hill of Yahweh?
> And who shall stand in His holy place?'
>
> (Ps. xxiv. 8)

This is called *synonymous* parallelism. In *antithetical* parallelism, the sense of the two members is contrasted (e.g., Ps. i. 6). In synthetic or *formal* parallelism, the balance is one of form rather than of thought (e.g., Ps. ii. 6), which, as Buchanan Gray observed, is really the absence of parallelism.

---

[1] This section is designedly brief, since there is an admirable treatment of the subject, at greater length, in another volume in this series, *The Poetry of the Old Testament*, by T. H. Robinson.

In *emblematic* parallelism, the thought of one member is expressed in the other by metaphor or simile (e.g., Ps. ciii. 13). *Stair-like* parallelism repeats part of the first member in the second, and then adds to it (e.g., Ps. xxix. 1, 2). *Introverted* parallelism is exemplified by at least four members in the pattern *a, b, b, a* (e.g., Prov. xxiii. 15, 16). Buchanan Gray distinguished between *complete* parallelism, in which every element in one member corresponds to an element in the second, and *incomplete* parallelism, in which this is not so. Incomplete parallelism may occur *with compensation*, in which a new element appears in the second member which is not a true counterpart to the corresponding element in the first.

The second important feature in Hebrew poetry is the *rhythm*. Theories about this have varied considerably. According to the most widely accepted view, the metre is reckoned in terms of the accented syllables. The most common pattern is 3 + 3 (i.e., 3 accented syllables in each member of the line). The *Qinah* or elegiac metre (so called because it was first identified in Lamentations) is 3 + 2. Another fairly common rhythm is 2 + 2. The forms 2 + 3, 4 + 3, and 4 + 4 are considerably less frequent. Occasionally the poetic line consists of three members, which may be 3 + 3 + 3 or 2 + 2 + 2. It has sometimes been assumed that a particular metrical pattern was adhered to throughout any given poem. Accordingly, textual emendations have often been suggested in order to remove irregularities in rhythm. But there is no ground for the assumption; and textual emendations should not be advanced purely on metrical grounds.

It is very doubtful whether we can claim that a third feature, *strophic structure*, occurs in Hebrew poetry. There are, it is true, passages like Isa. ix. 8–x. 4, which is divided into sections by a recurring refrain; but genuine strophic structure involves a correspondence in the number of lines and in their metrical form; and of this there is little or no convincing evidence in the Old Testament.

In a few poems, an acrostic pattern is found, in which

successive lines or groups of lines begin with the letters of the alphabet in the appropriate order. Examples of this are found in Ps. xxxiv and cxix, and in Lam. i–iv.

Our knowledge of the relationship between Hebrew poetic form and the poetry of other ancient Near Eastern literatures has been considerably enriched in recent years by our increasing knowledge of Ugaritic literature.[1] The close dependence in form emphasizes the contrast in content.

## II. THE PSALMS

The Psalter (Hebrew, *Tᵉhillîm*, Praises) in its present form in the Hebrew Bible consists of 150 psalms arranged in five books: I, i–xli; II, xlii–lxxii; III, lxxiii–lxxxix; IV, xc–cvi; V, cvii–cl.[2] This five-fold arrangement was no doubt suggested by the number of the books attributed to Moses. But, independently of this formal arrangement, there are other groupings of psalms within the Psalter, which point to the process of its growth from smaller, earlier collections.

With the exception of i, ii, and xxxiii, all the psalms in Book I have 'of David' in their titles, and generally use the divine name Yahweh. It seems likely that xxxiii is a later addition, that i was added as an introduction to the entire Psalter, and that ii originally had 'of David' as its title. ii–xxxii + xxxiv–xli would then form a Yahwistic Davidic collection.

In xlii–lxxxiii, *'Elōhîm* is, on the whole, used instead of Yahweh; and that this is deliberate can be seen from liii and lxx, which repeat xiv and xl. 13–17 with this and other minor changes. xlii–xlix are 'of the sons of Korah'; l and lxxiii–lxxxiii are 'of Asaph'; and li–lxxii are 'of David'. It is possible that an earlier arrangement was: li–lxxii; xlii–xlix; l + lxxiii–lxxxiii. This would bring together the Asaphite psalms, link the Elohistic Davidic psalms with the Yahwistic collection

---

[1] W. F. Albright, *Archaeology and the Religion of Israel*, pp. 14–16.

[2] It should be noted that in the Greek and Latin Bibles, and in Roman Catholic versions, there are differences of numbering, because ix and x are treated as one Psalm, as are cxiv and cxv, while cxvi and cxlvii are each treated as two.

in Book I, and give point to lxxii. 20 ('the prayers of David, the son of Jesse, are ended'). lxxxiv–lxxxix, a miscellaneous collection in which Yahweh is used, is probably an appendix added after the Yahwistic and Elohistic collections had been combined.

Smaller groups are also to be found in xc–cl; but they are more varied and sporadic: e.g., Hallelujah psalms in cxi–cxiii; cxv; cxxxv; cxlvi–cl; and the songs of ascents or degrees in cxx–cxxxiv.

There is insufficient evidence to trace in any detail the process by which these various groups were combined; but that there was such a process is sufficiently clear. As the prophetic books were compiled from smaller collections of varied material, so the Psalter was built up out of smaller collections of religious poems.

The wish to date individual psalms and to refer them to specific historical and personal situations is natural. It is reflected already in some of the headings, which relate certain Psalms to incidents in the life of David (e.g., iii; xviii; xxxiv; li; lii; liv; lvi; lvii; lix; lx). But these headings are not part of the original text, and usually correspond only in a general and superficial way to the content of the psalms which they introduce. Scholars who have rejected the Davidic authorship of most or all of the psalms have often tried to link certain of them with specific incidents in later history; e.g., xlvi with the deliverance of Jerusalem from the Assyrians in 701 B.C., or lxxiv with the fall of Jerusalem in 586 B.C. or with some later disaster. But it remains, in general, true that the poetry of devotion is related to recurring situations in congregational worship and in the life of the believer, rather than to specific incidents in history. A few psalms may reflect particular historical situations; but these are by no means easy to determine in the light of internal evidence. Linguistic features may sometimes suggest a late rather than an early date. The religious ideas contained in a given psalm have sometimes been taken as an indication of date; but there is nowadays less confidence in our ability to trace the historical development of religious ideas in Israel; and this criterion can be applied only in a general way. But the great majority of the psalms cannot be dated with anything approaching precision; and, because they are devotional rather than historical documents, this does not greatly matter. To understand them we must ask rather what was their function in worship.

It was the chief contribution of Hermann Gunkel to the study of the Psalter that he essayed a classification of the psalms according to literary types (*Gattungen*), each with its setting in life (*Sitz im Leben*). Among the various types which he recognized, five are of special importance.

The first of these is the *Hymn*, which celebrates the greatness and goodness of Yahweh; e.g., cxlv–cl.

The second is the *Individual Song of Thanksgiving* (*Danklied des Einzelnen*), in which a worshipper, who has experienced some deliverance, describes his former distress, his appeal to God, and God's response, and makes an act of thanksgiving which would normally be accompanied by an offering (see cxvi. 12–14). Examples of this type are xxx; xcii; cxvi; cxviii; cxxxviii; cf. Isa. xxxviii. 10–20; Jonah ii. 2–9.

The third type is the *Communal Lament* (*Klagelied des Volkes*), which is appropriate to times of distress affecting the whole community, and would be used on days of fasting and penitence. The plight of the community is described; God's past mercies are recalled; and He is implored to succour His people. Examples are xliv; lxxiv; lxxix; lxxx; lxxxiii.

The fourth type is the *Individual Lament* (*Klagelied des Einzelnen*), which occurs in the Psalter more frequently than any other. Some description of the affliction of the worshipper is a constant element in this class; but a distinction may be made between penitential psalms, which acknowledge that the suffering is a punishment for sin, and others in which the worshipper protests his innocence. A common feature is the conviction that God will hear the appeal (*Gewissheit der Erhörung*); and this is sometimes accompanied by a vow of some kind. Examples of this type of Psalm are iii; v; vi; vii;

xiii; xxii; xxxi; xlii–xliii; li; lxiv; lxix; lxxi; cxx; cxxx; cxl; cxli; cxlii; cxliii.

The above are the types to which Gunkel assigned special importance in his original classification; but to them must be added a fifth, the *Royal Psalms* (*Königspsalmen*), which refer, so Gunkel held, to kings of Israel and Judah in the pre-exilic period, and not, as had sometimes been argued, either to the king as an idealization of the people or to the rulers of the Greek period. In recent decades, increasing attention has been devoted to these psalms as evidence for the important cultic functions which kings are held to have exercised in pre-exilic Israel; and parallels have been drawn with the religious status of kings elsewhere in the ancient Near East. In the class of Royal Psalms may be included ii; xviii; xx; xxi; xlv; ci; cx; cxxxii. But it should be noted that these psalms are linked by their subject and not by any formal pattern which they all share.

The lesser types include *Pilgrimage Songs* (*Wallfahrtslieder*; e.g., lxxxiv), *Torah Liturgies* (*Thoraliturgien*; e.g., xv), and *Wisdom Poetry* (*Weisheitsdichtung*; e.g., lxxiii).

In making this classification, Gunkel moved the problem of dating away from the individual psalm to the types, and sought to trace their literary history. He maintained that the simplest and shortest forms were the oldest, and put communal psalms earlier than those of the individual, and thanksgivings earlier than laments. But these are not safe criteria. Though he was not himself one of the exponents of the very early dating of the psalms, the stimulus which he gave to the study of the relation of the Old Testament to other ancient oriental literatures has favoured the modern tendency to date many or most of the psalms in the pre-exilic age. In particular, Babylonian and Ugaritic poetry provide parallels of considerable antiquity. This suggests that Hebrew psalmody is not, in its origins, a late growth, though it continued well into the post-exilic period. The Psalms of Solomon, which may be dated about the middle of the 1st century B.C., are a striking instance of later psalmody.

The distinction made between communal and individual psalms has an important bearing on the meaning of 'I' in the Psalter. The once-prevalent view that 'I' normally denotes the community is now generally discarded. It seems more likely that, with few exceptions (e.g., cxxix. 1 ff), 'I' represents the individual worshipper. But sometimes the 'I' may be a king or other leading person who represents the congregation.

The setting in life of most of the types is in the cult. But Gunkel held that the examples of these types which are contained in the Psalter come, in the main, from a later stage, at which the connexion with the cult had been broken, and express the spirituality of pietistic circles. Against this, Sigmund Mowinckel has maintained that most of the psalms were composed for use in the cult. Three of his contentions have aroused much discussion.

The first and most important of these is the view that in pre-exilic Israel there was an annual celebration of the enthronement of Yahweh at the New Year festival in the autumn, at which He renewed His victory over chaos at the creation, overthrew His enemies, vindicated His people's cause, and renewed His covenant with them and with the Davidic dynasty. He associates many psalms with this festival as parts of its liturgy. Of these, the most important are xlvii; xciii; xcv–c. These psalms of the kingship of Yahweh have, however, also been interpreted, not as celebrating the cultic enthronement of Yahweh, but in two other ways. (a) They have been taken to refer to a historical manifestation of God's power, viz., the overthrow of Babylon and the restoration of the exiles. On this view, the psalms are dated in the latter part of the 6th century, and regarded as dependent on Deutero-Isaiah (see above, p. 115). (b) They have been interpreted eschatologically, as looking forward to the final manifestation of God's kingship. This may be combined with the cultic interpretation, on the view that the cult expressed an eschatological hope.[1]

[1] See the important work by A. R. Johnson: *Sacral Kingship in Ancient Israel.*

Mowinckel's theory has been widely accepted; and some other scholars have modified and amplified it. In particular, it has been claimed that some of the psalms provide evidence of the part played by the king in the cult. While it would be rash to deny that such evidence exists, it should be scrutinized with caution. To interpret it solely in the light of analogies in the worship of Israel's neighbours is hazardous, since in this field we must probably allow for distinctive variations in Israelite practice.

Of the criticisms which have been made of Mowinckel's theory, it must suffice here to mention the work of N. H. Snaith, who has argued that there is no evidence for the connexion of the New Year Festival with the kingdom of God before the 2nd century A.D., and that practically all the Enthronement psalms are Sabbath psalms.

The second of Mowinckel's views to be noticed is that in the individual laments the 'workers of iniquity' who are often mentioned are sorcerers who by their arts brought suffering on the 'humble' or 'afflicted', and that these psalms invoked the divine power to break the spells. In spite of the learning with which the view has been advanced, it is probable that the expression 'workers of iniquity' is usually to be taken in its general sense. The 'enemies' in these laments have also been taken to be foreigners (H. Birkeland) and as false accusers (H. Schmidt).

Thirdly, Mowinckel has argued that the prophetic or oracular passages in the psalms are the work of cultic prophets rather than evidence of the influence of the canonical prophets.

Whatever reserves we may have concerning some theories about the cultic significance of the Psalter, there can be little doubt that this general approach has made a real contribution to our understanding of many of the psalms. The Psalter has often been called the hymn-book of the second temple; but parts of it come from the liturgies of Solomon's temple, and parts from the sanctuaries of the Northern Kingdom, relics of a ritual in which word and action linked the worshippers

with the unseen. These ancient hymns and prayers continued
to be used in the later period; and the altered setting must
sometimes have meant that psalms were reinterpreted and
even modified.

Only scraps of information have survived about the early
history of the liturgical use of the Psalter. The Mishnah gives
a list of the special psalms used in the temple for each day of
the week (*Tamid* vii. 4); and the tractate *Sopherim* provides
data about the psalms appropriate for festivals. It may be
that the titles of the psalms contain indications of liturgical
and cultic use at an earlier period; but unfortunately there is
considerable doubt about the meaning of the terms used.

We have already (p. 174) referred to the historical allusions
prefixed to some of the psalms. The rest of the material found
in the titles varies in character and may be classified as
follows:

(*a*) Words which describe the poem: *mizmôr* (psalm), *šîr*
(song), *tehillâh* (praise), *tepillâh* (prayer), *maśkîl* (from a root
meaning 'to have insight', hence variously understood as
'meditation', 'didactic poem', 'skilful song', but of uncertain
meaning and prefixed to psalms of different kinds), *šiggāyôn*
(apparently from a root meaning 'to err', 'to go astray', and
taken by some to refer to the irregular rhythm of the music
and by others to indicate a connexion with sin-offering, but
of uncertain meaning), *miktām* (sometimes connected with
*ketem*, 'gold'; but possibly from a root meaning 'to cover', and
referring to covering sins).

(*b*) Terms which may be meant to indicate the authorship
or source of the psalm. The most familiar is 'of David',
traditionally taken to indicate Davidic authorship. But many
psalms so ascribed are, on internal evidence, unlikely to have
been written by David; and the fact that the Greek Bible
ascribes additional psalms (including cxxxvii) to David shows
that on this matter ancient tradition was neither constant
nor reliable. The expression may indicate the existence of
a collection or collections which in some loose sense were
'Davidic'. Some hold that the preposition should not be

rendered 'of' but 'for', that David is a royal title rather than
a personal name, and that these psalms were intended for use
by the king.

The terms 'of Asaph' and 'of the sons of Korah' seem to
point to collections associated with Levitical singers. 'For
(or of) Jeduthun' (xxxix) may be a similar reference (see
1 Chron. xvi. 41), though 'Jeduthun' occurs elsewhere (lxii;
lxxvii) in a different sense. xc is ascribed to Moses, lxxii and
cxxvii to Solomon, lxxxviii to Heman the Ezrahite (also to
the sons of Korah), and lxxxix to Ethan the Ezrahite
(1 Kings iv. 31).

Fifty-five psalms (the majority of which are 'of David') are
headed *lammᵉnaṣṣēᵃḥ*, which is commonly taken to mean 'for
(to, of) the chief musician', referring to another special
collection. But it has been suggested that the term (with a
change of vowels) refers to a special musical rendering, or that
it indicates the cultic propitiation of God.

(c) Expressions which seem to refer to the musical accompaniment: *binᵉgînôt* (iv; vi; liv; lv; lxvii; lxxvi; cf.
Hab. iii. 19; on stringed instruments), *'el-hannᵉḥîlôt* (v),
*'al-haššᵉmînît* (vi; xii), *'al-haggittît* (viii; lxxxi; lxxxiv),
*'al-ᶜᵃlāmôt* (xlvi), *'al-maḥᵃlat* (liii). All of these terms, except
the first, are obscure.

(d) Phrases which appear to be titles of tunes: *'al-mût
labbēn* (ix), *'al-šōšannîm* (xlv; lxix), *šûšan ᶜēdût* (lx), *'el-
šōšannîm ᶜēdût* (lxxx), *'al-'ayyelet haššaḥar* (xxii), *'al-yônat
'ēlem rᵉḥōkîm* (lvi), *'al-tašḥet* (lvii–lix, lxxv; cf. Isa. lxv. 8). It
may be that some of these had cultic significance; but of this
we cannot be sure.

(e) Terms which indicate some special use: *lᵉtôdâh* (for
thanksgiving, or, for the thankoffering, c; cf. Lev. vii. 11–15),
*lᵉᶜannôt* (for antiphonal singing? or, for humble submission?
lxxxviii), *lᵉhazkîr* (for making a memorial, possibly in connexion with the *'azkārâh* or memorial offering; xxxviii; lxx;
cf. Lev. ii. 2, 9, 16; vi. 15; xxiv. 7), a song at the dedication
of the house (i.e., the temple; xxx), a song for the Sabbath
day (xcii).

Several interpretations have been offered of the term *selâh*, which occurs seventy-one times in the Psalter and thrice in Hab. iii. By derivation from the verb *sālal*, 'to lift up', it has been taken to mean the lifting up of the voices or of the musical accompaniment. The rendering in the Septuagint (διάψαλμα) may indicate an interlude of some kind. Again, it has been thought that the three consonants are abbreviations of three words which expressed some instruction about the rendering. Possibly the word indicated the point at which a refrain should be sung.

It is unfortunate that our understanding of these technical terms is so sketchy. More precise information about them would illuminate the use of the Psalter in early times, and would enrich our knowledge of the content of the psalms. But, in spite of the gaps in our knowledge, the spiritual greatness of the Psalter is manifest; and the new evidence of the links between Hebrew psalmody and that of neighbouring peoples does not impair its distinctive quality. In its range and depth it has enriched the worship of Judaism and Christianity immeasurably. It should also be remembered that it reflects the ways of the worshipping community in Old Testament times. The prophetic literature records the message of exceptional men. In the Psalter we have the poems in which the worship and devotion of the ordinary man were expressed.

## III. The Wisdom Literature

Of the canonical books of the Old Testament, Job, Proverbs, Ecclesiastes, and certain psalms belong to the Wisdom Literature. The Song of Songs is often also included in this class, but for no adequate reason. Outside the Canon, outstanding examples of this type of book are Wisdom and Ecclesiasticus.

The Wisdom books have been described as the literature of Hebrew humanism, and as containing the nearest thing to philosophical speculation which the Old Testament can offer. They devote much attention to the right conduct of human life, and to the problem of retribution. Except in the later period, they do not appeal to the specifically Hebraic religious tradition, to the events of the Exodus, the covenant, and the giving of the *Tôrâh*; and often their ideal of character and conduct appears to be the wise man, irrespective of race.[1]

The Wisdom (*Ḥokmâh*) which is in different ways the subject of these books is not merely speculative and intellectual, but practical, ethical, and religious. Its foundation and source is the divine Wisdom, which was the agent in creation, and is the guide of human action. The Wisdom writers combine a concern for the problems of conduct with an interest in the natural world and in creation. In a few outstanding passages, the divine Wisdom is described in personal terms which seem almost to go beyond the limits of literary personification towards hypostatization (Prov. viii; Job xxviii; cf. Wisdom vii. 22–80; Ecclus. xxiv).

The wise (*ḥᵃkāmîm*), to whom we owe this literature, are mentioned in Jer. xviii. 18 as a class comparable with the priests and the prophets; and in Jer. viii. 8 the wise and the scribes seem to be identified. Elsewhere (e.g., Isa. v. 21; xxix. 14) there are signs that the prophets were critical of the wise. There is, certainly, a marked difference between prophecy and the Wisdom books, not least in ethics, where the teaching of the wise often seems pedestrian and prudential. But the religious basis of Wisdom teaching is evident: 'The fear of Yahweh is the beginning of wisdom'.

The Old Testament itself shows that Wisdom was a feature of the culture of Israel's neighbours (Egypt: Gen. xli. 8; Exod. vii. 11; 1 Kings iv. 80; Isa. xix. 11. Babylon: Isa. xliv. 25; Jer. l. 85; li. 57. Edom: Jer. xlix. 7; Obad. 8; Job ii. 11). The extant specimens of Egyptian and Babylonian didactic literature show the affinities of Hebrew Wisdom to this cosmopolitan literature, which we are now able to trace back to Sumerian times; and the evidence of the Ras Shamra texts

---

[1] Later, however, the Jewish inheritance is emphasized. This is seen clearly in Ecclesiasticus, where wisdom is identified with the *Tôrâh*, and the wise man is he who studies and obeys it.

presents many linguistic parallels to the Wisdom literature of the Old Testament. There is, therefore, no reason for regarding Hebrew Wisdom as a late development; and even if the extant literary form of the Wisdom books is late, much of the material may well be quite early. Solomon, the wise man *par excellence*, is traditionally credited with the authorship of some of the Wisdom books. He was, no doubt, a patron as well as a practitioner of Wisdom; and the conditions of his reign, when communications with neighbouring countries were easy, may well have fostered cosmopolitan literary influence.

## IV. JOB

The book of Job is a long poetic work, with a prologue (i–ii) and epilogue (xlii. 7–17) in prose. The prologue contains a sequence of scenes on earth and in the heavenly court. Job is a man of surpassing wealth and unblemished piety. The Satan, a member of the heavenly court, alleges that Job serves God for reward, and is allowed to afflict him by the loss of his possessions and his children. But Job's piety remains constant. The Satan is then allowed to lay on Job a painful and loathsome disease. This, too, fails to turn Job against God. Three friends, Eliphaz, Bildad, and Zophar, come to comfort him.

In the poem which follows, after a bitter complaint by Job (iii), there are three cycles of debate (iv–xiv; xv–xxi; xxii–xxvii), in which the friends try to convince Job that his suffering should be accepted as punishment from the hand of God, and Job protests that he has done nothing to deserve such punishment. xxviii, a poem on Wisdom, is followed by Job's final assertion of innocence (xxix–xxxi). A young man called Elihu then tries to improve on the friends' arguments against Job in a further series of speeches (xxxii–xxxvii). No reply is made to these, but in two speeches God answers Job, showing him the wonder and variety of creation, and rebuking him for his presumption in questioning the divine ordering of events (xxxviii. 1–xl. 2; xl. 6–xli. 34). Job's answers (xl. 3–5; xlii. 1–6) express submission and repentance.

The epilogue tells how God rebuked the three friends and restored Job's prosperity (xlii. 7–17).

Certain parts of the book are commonly regarded as later additions to the original work. (*a*) xxviii is held to be an independent poem about Wisdom, inappropriate in its present setting, because in it Job anticipates what God says to him in xxxviii. 1–xl. 2. But, if treated as separate from the dialogue, it has something of the character of a chorus in a Greek tragedy, commenting on the theme of the debate which has just ended. (*b*) The Elihu speeches read like an intrusion into the original structure. Elihu appears nowhere else in the book, and is not included in God's rebuke to Job's friends. No reference is made elsewhere to his views. The beginning of the first divine speech implies (xxxviii. 2) that Job, not Elihu, was the last speaker, although the Elihu speeches immediately precede. It is maintained that Elihu adds little to the arguments of the friends, though he does emphasize particularly the purifying effect of suffering, and to some extent anticipates (xxxvii) the divine speech. There are also linguistic differences between these speeches and the rest of the dialogue. (*c*) The descriptions of Behemoth and Leviathan in the second divine speech are held to be out of keeping with the brilliant verbal economy of xxxviii. 39–xxxix. 30 and out of place in a context which answers Job's challenge to the righteousness of God.

Somewhat larger questions are raised by the claim that the prologue and epilogue are not by the author of the poem. None of the arguments for this is decisive. (i) The Satan appears in the prologue, but not in the poem. But it is part of the point of the story that the events in the heavenly court are not known by the human characters. (ii) The Job of the prologue is submissive, whereas the Job of the dialogue is rebellious. But the initial submission contributes to the nobility of Job's protests. (iii) The restoration of Job's fortunes in the epilogue is said to be at variance with the spiritual greatness of the poem and the lesson of the divine speeches. But the restoration is presented as the conclusion of the book rather than as a solution to Job's problem. (iv) The name Yahweh is used in the prose: El, Eloah, and Shaddai occur in the poetry (Yahweh occurs in xxxviii. 1, xlii. 6). But this need point to no more than deliberate varia-tion by the author, in keeping with the different character of the various parts of his work.

Even if the author is responsible for the present text of the prose as well as the poetry, many think that the substance of the prose portions is derived from an old traditional story (not necessarily Israelite, and possibly Edomite) about Job, and that in the poetry the author adapted it to his own purposes. This view has been advanced in several different forms which need not be recounted here. That Job was a traditional paragon of piety is clear from Ezek. xiv. 14, 20. On the other hand, it is less clear that ancient tradition told of his suffering. It may well be that the author was the first to associate Job with unmerited affliction, and that he deliber-ately chose a traditional character of unassailable uprightness in order to challenge the more successfully the accepted doctrine of retribution. But, whatever the extent of the author's indebtedness to tradition, the prose framework is an essential part of the book as we have it.

The third cycle of speeches appears to be incomplete and disarranged. Only five verses are attributed to Bildad; Zophar says nothing; and Job is made to say things which resemble Bildad's other speeches (xxvi. 5–14). The following suggested reconstruction seems plausible. Bildad: xxv. 2–3 + xxvi. 5–14; Zophar: xxvii. 13–23 (? + 7–10); Job: xxvi. 2–4 + xxvii. 2–6, 11–12. But, since part of the poem may have been lost, we cannot even approach certainty on this point.

The book deals with the problem of innocent suffering, which is also the problem of God's righteousness as expressed in His ordering of the world and of human life. In the Deuteronomic literature we find the view that national righteousness brings material reward and unrighteousness and apostasy bring suffering. Job and his friends held this view and applied it rigidly to individual experience in such a way that prosperity implied piety and affliction implied grievous sin. But when misfortune befell Job himself, he knew of nothing that he had done to deserve it, and refused to repent of what he had not committed. His experience is presented as a challenge to the accepted doctrine of retribution.

In one sense it is true to say that the book fails to solve the problem which it raises; for it offers no complete explanation of the suffering of the innocent. But it is, after all, not a treatise, leading by rational argument to a conclusion, but a great work of literature, which enlarges our understanding of the problem by the ways in which it presents it and even by partial answers to it. It may well be that the book reflects the writer's own experience of suffering, and that Job sometimes speaks for him. Though Job is humbled at the end of the poem, his innocence is not repudiated; and thus the view that suffering always implies sin is rejected. Even Job's most violent outbursts express a deeper and more discerning concern for God's honour than the friends show. But it would be a mistake to think that everything that Job says represents the writer's own view or that he would reject everything that the friends say.

It may seem that even the divine speech does not really answer Job's protest. But Job's greatest problem is not the intensity of his suffering but the sense of estrangement from God which it brings. 'Oh that I knew where I might find Him' expresses his deepest need, which is met when God answers him, even in rebuke for his presumption.

The book contains no references to historical events which might help us to date it. Nor do links with other parts of the Old Testament provide very precise evidence. vii. 17, 18 presupposes Psalm viii. 4; and iii is strikingly similar to Jer. xx. 14–18. Probably the religious content of the book is the safest guide to its age. The nature of the problem raised and the way in which it is treated are usually held to point to the exilic or post-exilic period. This seems more likely than the suggestion that the book comes from the time of Jeremiah,

in spite of the similarities between the two books. The figure
of the Satan in the prologue resembles that in Zech. iii, but
is slightly nearer to the later conception of the Tempter, since
he is not content to scrutinize Job's conduct but tries to incite
him to impiety.

A Babylonian poem which has come to be known as 'the
Babylonian Job' has often been compared with the Hebrew
poem; but it is, at best, a remote parallel, lacking the depth
and insight of the biblical Job; and there can be no question
of literary dependence. The geographical references to places
east and south-east of Palestine have suggested to some
scholars that the story comes from an Edomite source. Again,
from the mention of papyrus (viii. 11), ships of reed (ix. 26),
mines (xxviii. 1–11), the ostrich (xxx. 29), the hippopotamus
(xl. 15 ff), and the crocodile (xli. 1 ff), some have deduced that
the book has an Egyptian background. Apart from the fact
that some of these passages may be later additions, the
evidence need indicate no more than that the writer was well-
informed. The psychology of the book, as Pedersen has
shown, is essentially Israelite; and there is no strong reason
for denying it a Palestinian origin. In some ways, questions
of date and provenance matter less for the understanding
of Job than of any other book in the Old Testament; for
its greatness and truth are timeless and universal. Yet,
as literature and as a religious document it is essentially
Hebraic, even in its protest against an Israelite orthodoxy.

## V. Proverbs

The title 'The Proverbs of Solomon', which has become the
name of the entire book, is in fact part of the superscription
of the first of seven collections, of which the book is composed.

The first of these is i–ix, which consists of a series of poems
of varying length, advocating the life of wisdom and virtue,
and warning against folly and vice. In viii; ix (cf. i. 20 ff),
wisdom is personified as a woman. It is, perhaps, going too
far to say that wisdom is hypostatized; but the passage resembles others (Job xxviii; Ecclus. xxiv; Wisdom vii. 22–

viii. 1) in which wisdom is described in terms which at least approach hypostatization. This feature, and the presence of fairly long connected passages, suggest that this collection is quite late. It is usually assigned to the 4th or 3rd century B.C.

A marked contrast is offered by the second collection (x. 1–xxii. 16), which is headed 'The Proverbs of Solomon'. It consists of short, pithy sayings (some 375 in all), which do not reveal any logical sequence and were doubtless originally independent of each other. For the most part they present the contrast in character, action, and lot between the wise and the foolish. The brevity of these sayings and their lack of connexion probably point to an early stage in the literary history of the Hebrew proverb (*māšāl*). The section is usually reckoned to be the oldest in the book and to date from the pre-exilic period. The reference to kings in xvi. 10 ff is not necessarily cogent evidence of this; for it might apply to Gentile rulers in the post-exilic age.

The third section (xxii. 17–xxiv. 22) has no heading; but the phrase 'the words of the wise' in the opening verse appears to have been the original title. The first part of the section (xxii. 17–xxiii. 14) closely resembles the Egyptian Wisdom text, *The Teaching of Amenemope*, which has been assigned to various dates between 900 and 600 B.C. There are close verbal parallels, the most striking of which is the clause in xxii. 20, formerly translated 'Have I not written unto thee *excellent things*'. The Egyptian text has the clause, 'Consider these *thirty chapters*'; and it is now generally recognized that the Hebrew should read '*thirty (sayings)*'. There are, in fact, some thirty sayings in xxii. 17–xxiv. 22, about a third of which have been adapted from the Egyptian text.

'These also are (sayings) of the wise' introduces the fourth section (xxiv. 23–34), a short series of maxims against partiality and laziness, which contains no indication of its date.

The fifth section (xxv–xxix) has the superscription, 'These also are proverbs of Solomon, which the men of Hezekiah king of Judah copied'. Nothing in the contents of the collec-

tion makes this statement unlikely. The individual proverbs
have the brevity of form which is probably characteristic of
the earlier period. The references to kings (e.g., xxv. 2 ff) are
in keeping with this, though they would not by themselves
necessarily demonstrate a pre-exilic date.

The sixth section (xxx) is attributed to Agur, son of Jakeh,
of the Ishmaelite tribe of Massa (Gen. xxv. 14). Several of the
sayings have a numerical character; but nothing in their
contents gives a clue to their date. Some think that this
collection ends at *v.* 6, others at *v.* 14.

The seventh section (xxxi. 1–9) is described as 'The words
of Lemuel, king of Massa, which his mother taught him'. It
contains warnings against women and wine, and an exhortation to care for the needy. The date is quite uncertain.

The book closes with an acrostic poem in praise of the
ideal wife (xxxi. 10–31).

The material in the closing chapters of the book is arranged
in the Septuagint in the following order: xxii. 17–xxiv. 22;
xxx. 1–14; xxiv. 23–34; xxx. 15–33; xxxi. 1–9; xxv–xxix;
xxxi. 10–31. Only xxv–xxix has a title. This difference in
order may indicate that these closing sections were added
after the rest of the book had been compiled. At all events, it
emphasizes the fact that the book is a compilation of collections which were originally independent.

The analysis given above shows that the book cannot well
be, and, indeed, does not claim to be, entirely the work of
Solomon, though parts of it may go back to his time. It
covers a span of several centuries, and thus represents more
than one phase in the development of Wisdom. It also illustrates several aspects of the Hebrew Wisdom literature: its
intense concern with character and conduct; its interest in
the mundane affairs of daily life; its seemingly prudential
ethics; its emphasis on the religious character of Wisdom.
Though material rewards often seem to be the aim of the
virtue which it inculcates, its dominant teaching is fairly
summed up in the words, 'The fear of Yahweh is the beginning
of wisdom'.

## VI. THE FIVE SCROLLS

As indicated above (p. 12), the five short books, Ruth, the Song of Songs, Ecclesiastes, Lamentations, and Esther, form a group known as the five Scrolls, and are traditionally associated with five religious festivals.

### (a) Ruth

The story of Ruth is set in the period of the judges. A Bethlehemite named Elimelech migrated to Moab with his wife and their two sons in time of famine. While there, the sons married Moabite wives, Ruth and Orpah. Father and sons died; and when the famine was over, Naomi returned to Bethlehem, accompanied by Ruth, who steadfastly refused to leave her. To help to maintain the home, Ruth went gleaning in the fields, and was kindly treated by the owner, Boaz, a kinsman of Elimelech. On Naomi's advice, Ruth visited Boaz by night at his threshing-floor and appealed to him to play the part of next-of-kin by purchasing Elimelech's estate and marrying her. Having skilfully dealt with another kinsman, who had a prior claim, Boaz accepted both responsibilities. The son whom Ruth bore to him was Obed, father of Jesse and grandfather of David.

This story, told with great artistry, and yet with memorable simplicity, raises a number of problems for the student, most of which arise in a consideration of its aim.

The fact that David's ancestress is portrayed as a Moabitess has suggested that the book is propaganda against the policies by which Ezra and Nehemiah tried to prevent marriages with foreign women. This view is open to two objections. (a) Though a foreigner, Ruth had adopted the religion of Israel, and therefore does not really provide a parallel to the foreign wives to whom the reformers took exception. (b) The story does not read like propaganda.

The obligation incumbent on a relative to take a dead man's widow and ensure the continuance of his house plays an important part in the climax of the story. The action of drawing off the shoe (iv. 7 f) resembles the custom described in Deuteronomy xxv. 9 as part of the levirate law, requiring the brother of a childless dead man to marry his widow (xxv. 5–10). But there is a difference both in the act and also in the fact that neither Boaz nor the other kinsman was brother to Ruth's former husband, Mahlon. The same passage in Ruth also contains a reference (iv. 12) to the story of Judah and Tamar (Gen. xxxviii), which presupposes the duty of levirate marriage and describes the union of a childless widow with a relative other than a brother-in-law. iv. 7 implies that the author is describing a custom no longer practised. It may well be that the levirate law as contained in Deuteronomy limited and made more precise ancient obligations incumbent on the male kin of a dead man.[1] The very lack of precision on this point makes it unlikely that Ruth was written to revive or enforce the levirate duty.

Attempts have been made to interpret the book in terms of the fertility cult and divine kingship: Elimelech (= my God is king) is equated with the dying god, Naomi with the mother goddess, and Ruth with a sacred prostitute; the name Boaz is linked with the pillar at the entrance to the temple, and Bethlehem with the god Lachmu. But this is to depart from the plain sense of the story on inadequate evidence.

The writer's purpose may have been to tell something about David's ancestors. Against this it has been argued that both the concluding genealogy (iv. 18–22; cf. 1 Chron. ii. 4 ff) and even the reference to David in iv. 17 are later additions. But it is highly improbable that at a late date any writer or interpolator would invent for David a partly Moabite ancestry. It is safest to seek the writer's main interest in the connexion with David and also in the examples of piety and fidelity which the book provides.

Ruth is best classified as a historical novel, provided that we do not allow the noun to empty the adjective of meaning.

---

[1] On this whole question see H. H. Rowley's study, 'The Marriage of Ruth', in *The Servant of the Lord*, pp. 163–186.

The language is, with occasional exceptions, pure and classical. But the writer may be consciously assuming the Hebrew of a period earlier than his own. At all events, he appears to look back to the age of the Judges as long past; and i. 1, with its implication that the Judges ruled all Israel, indicates knowledge of the Deuteronomic history of the Judges. A post-exilic date (5th century?) seems most likely, though not absolutely demonstrable.

## (b) The Song of Songs

The title of the book means 'the best of songs'; but it is easier to recognize its rare poetic quality than to reach firm conclusions about its meaning and character. Debate about the Song has been mainly concerned with its interpretation, to which questions of date and authorship are secondary. This debate is ancient; for Akiba's plea for the sacred character of the book was based on an allegorical interpretation which not all his contemporaries shared. No doubt it was included in the Canon because it was so interpreted and also because it was attributed to Solomon.

On the face of it, the Song is an expression, in sensuous language and highly wrought imagery, of passionate love. It is evident that there are frequent changes of speaker or singer; but it is not always clear who is speaking.

Traditional Jewish interpretation has understood the book as an allegorical expression of the love between God and Israel. Traditional Christian interpretation has also understood it allegorically, usually in terms of the love of Christ for His bride, the Church, or the believing soul, but sometimes also of God's love for Israel. Although this type of interpretation has so long a history, and has been so widely adopted, it provides no clear guide to the understanding of the text, since its application in detail has often been fantastic and, being necessarily arbitrary, varies considerably.[1]

[1] The arbitrary nature of this type of interpretation is aptly illustrated by Denney's account of a sermon preached by Spurgeon on 'Return, return, O Shulammite' (vi. 13). 'He said he did not know whether the voice was that of Christ calling to a backsliding Church, or that of the

If the book is understood at its face value as an expression of human love, there remain important differences of interpretation according to the view taken of its form.

1. It has been regarded as a drama. But the absence of stage directions and the frequent uncertainty about the identity of the speakers make dramatic reconstruction difficult; and this line of interpretation rivals the allegorical in arbitrariness and variety. Two main types of theory may be recognized. According to the first, the structure of the drama is relatively simple, and the main characters only two, Solomon and the Shulammite shepherdess, whom he made his bride. The second type proposes a more complex plot (the details of which vary in different forms of the theory), with three main characters, Solomon, the Shulammite, and her rustic lover, to whom she remains true in spite of Solomon's attempts to win her love. Parts of the book have sometimes been assigned to male and female choruses.

2. Some who reject the dramatic interpretation regard the book as a single poem describing the progress of erotic love from the first expressions of affection through courtship and betrothal to the married state. This may be combined with the allegorical interpretation. But the episodic character of the book and the lack of any evident progress of thought present difficulties for this view.

3. If, then, the book is neither a drama nor a single lyric, it must presumably be a collection of poems. This view of its structure appears in three main forms.

(a) Parallels to the Song have been adduced from modern Syrian wedding ceremonies lasting seven days, during which the bride and bridegroom are enthroned as king and queen and their beauty is extolled in a type of song known as a *wasf*. It is claimed that the book contains a cycle of songs derived from similar ceremonies in ancient Israel. Against

---

old companions of the Church calling her away from Christ: but to be sure of getting the truth, he preached on it quite earnestly first in the one sense, and then in the other!' (*Letters of Principal James Denney to W. Robertson Nicoll, 1893–1917*, p. 215).

this view it has been pointed out that, although 'Solomon' may be a royal name applied to the male lover in the Song, the Shulammite is nowhere called queen; that parts of the book are love songs but not wedding songs; and that the argument for the view would be more cogent if the modern parallels came not from Syria, but from Palestine.

(*b*) It would be surprising if the ritual of the fertility cult, which has been offered as the key to so many parts of the Old Testament, had not been suggested as the explanation of the erotic poetry of the Song. The suggestion has taken a number of forms, in most of which the book is regarded as a collection of liturgical poems connected with the Adonis-Tammuz cult of the dying and rising god, in which the sacred marriage played an important part. This ritual was associated with New Year festivities, its aim being to ensure fertility in the ensuing year. It is held that the references to springtime in the Song suggest a connexion with a vernal New Year festival, the feast of Unleavened Bread, and that this is further supported by the use of the book at Passover in later times. Parts of the Song are also held to belong to the ritual of the autumnal New Year, associated with the feast of Tabernacles.

This view is in keeping with the dramatic and choral elements in the Song; and even some scholars who do not accept it admit that the symbolism of the fertility cult may well have influenced the Song. Influence of this kind is evident elsewhere in the Old Testament. Even those prophets who were hostile to the fertility cult sometimes borrowed its imagery. This may be fully recognized; and it may be agreed that the cult was widely practised in Israel. But it is difficult to suppose that part of its liturgy was accepted into the Canon without drastic modification. Some exponents of this theory do indeed claim that the Song has been revised in the interests of orthodoxy. But deliberate modification of this sort would surely have been apparent; and the forced fantasies of allegorical interpretation would have been unnecessary if it had been.

(c) It has been held that the book is a collection of love
songs, composed simply as an expression of erotic love. On
this view it is possible to admit the influence of the language
and symbolism of the fertility cult while rejecting the con-
tention that the book is a liturgical text. Some adherents
of this theory attribute the book to several authors; but,
though it does not display a coherent structure, the unity of
style and atmosphere points to unity of authorship.

The attribution of the Song to Solomon probably arose
from the tradition that he wrote songs (1.Kings iv. 82) and
from the occurrence of his name in the text (i. 5; iii. 7 ff;
viii. 11 f). The Song is not a Wisdom book; but if, as has
been suggested, it was arranged and transmitted among the
Wise, this, too, may help to explain the attribution. The name
of the other character in the book, the Shulammite, has been
variously explained as 'the perfect one', 'the female Solomon',
and 'the woman from Shunem'.

The general argument against Solomonic authorship is that
the language points to a late date. The vocabulary used is
highly individual. There are frequent Aramaisms. The form
of the relative particle which is used throughout the book
except in the superscription is dialectal or late; and the
occurrence of a Persian loan word in iv. 18 and a Greek loan
word in iii. 9 seems to rule out an early date. But if the
poems are ancient, they may well have acquired, in the course
of popular use, later linguistic elements; and therefore the
sporadic occurrence of late words does not prove that the
book as a whole is late. It is usually dated in the 3rd or 2nd
century b.c.; but, on the cultic interpretation, the original
form of the Song is pre-exilic.

The peculiar linguistic features have sometimes been said
to be northern; and the references to Tirzah (vi. 4), once
capital of the Northern Kingdom, and to other places in
the north, have been used to support both an early date
and northern origin. But these are balanced by allusions to
Jerusalem and other places in the south.

Rabbi Akiba struggled hard to justify the inclusion of the

Song in the Canon. Those who reject the allegorical interpretation have often been hard put to it to know what to do
with it now that it is in the Canon. Most argue that its
presence in the Bible is a witness to the sacredness of passionate love. To this view no exception need be taken, provided that we do not attribute such a didactic purpose to
the writer.

### (c) *Ecclesiastes*

In both ancient and modern times, the melancholy scepticism of Ecclesiastes has caused as much difficulty as the lush
eroticism of the Song of Songs.   The Solomonic origin implied by i. 1, and the presence of pious sentiments which
offset the scepticism, prevented the exclusion of the book
from the Canon. According to a frequently quoted Talmudic
saying (Shabbath 30b), it was retained, 'because its beginning is religious teaching and its end is religious teaching'.
But the moderns almost without exception deny that
Solomon wrote the book. Many of them regard the sceptical
and pious parts as having come from different hands; and,
irrespective of questions of authorship and integrity, the
modern justification of its place in the Canon is usually that
the scepticism offsets the pious sentiments by preparing the
way for a deeper faith.

Ecclesiastes is a Wisdom book. It resembles Job in that it
contradicts accepted beliefs, but differs from it in its lack of
clearly marked structure and progress of thought. Yet it has
greater coherence than the collections of aphorisms which
form a considerable part of Proverbs. Though it has often
been described as philosophical, it contains no sustained
logical argument, but rather a series of reflections on the
problem of existence. These are, in the main, pessimistic:
the natural order (which, elsewhere in the Wisdom literature,
is regarded as a witness to God's creative Wisdom) is presented as a constantly repeated cycle of processes (e.g., i.
2-11); life on earth appears to be purposeless (e.g., ii. 11,
17, 20, 22, 23); there is no adequate apportioning of reward

VI] **ECCLESIASTES** 197

and punishment (e.g., ii. 15, 16); and beyond death there is no prospect of satisfaction or fulfilment (e.g., iii. 20, 21). In some passages, the reader is advised to enjoy life while he may (e.g., ii. 24; iii. 13, 22); in others, we find the traditional Wisdom teaching that God is judge of human life, and that He rewards the righteous and punishes the wicked (e.g., iii. 17).

Attempts have been made to account for the sharp contrast between sceptical pessimism and traditional orthodoxy by the suggestion that the book was originally entirely sceptical in its outlook, and that the conventionally pious passages were added in order to correct it. This, it should be noted, is a theory of editorial revision rather than of source analysis. In its more moderate forms, it is held that only brief insertions, similar in tone and tendency to the conclusion (xii. 13, 14), have been made. According to the more drastic forms of the theory, the book has been extensively revised more than once; e.g., an original treatise, sceptical in outlook, was expanded, first by a Wisdom writer (ḥākām) who was responsible for passages such as vii. 1–12, and then by a pious orthodox Jew (ḥāsîḏ), who added statements asserting the righteousness of God's judgements (e.g., iii. 14).

Again, it has been argued that the lack of coherence in the thought of the book is the result, not of revision by editors other than the original author, but of the literary form in which the author expressed his teaching. This was the aphorism, a literary unit varying in length but always relatively brief. The teaching of Ecclesiastes on various subjects was expressed in these aphorisms, which were originally independent of each other. Later he collected them; but their occasional and unsystematic character is evident in the discursiveness and inconsistencies of the book.

This literary approach to the problem of Ecclesiastes has been carefully worked out by K. Galling. But, while it may explain the loose structure of the book, it will scarcely account for the sharp internal contradictions. Galling has, indeed, suggested that, where a contradiction appears within a given aphorism, the author may be quoting a dictum

current in Wisdom circles and setting it alongside his own
observation (iv. 4 and 5, 6). Apart from the fact that the
text gives no hint that the author is quoting, this kind of
explanation does not account for the occurrence of contra-
dictory statements in different contexts.

Yet another suggestion is that the contradictions arise
neither from extensive interpolation nor from the way in
which the author produced the book, but rather from his
approach to life and religion. The autobiographical element
in his reflections reveals a candid inquirer who tests the accepted religious teaching of his time by what he has seen and
experienced. He puts the case against traditional orthodoxy,
yet has not entirely discarded it, and, on occasion, asserts
parts of its teaching. For him, to travel despairingly is better
than to arrive at any haven of orthodoxy; but he is not un-
mindful of that country from which he went out. On this
view, though there may be some editorial touches, Ecclesiastes is essentially a unity.

It is, then, not as an outsider, but as one who is within the
Jewish tradition that the author makes his protest against
elements in that tradition. Was he influenced by non-Jewish
thought? Attempts have been made to trace Greek influence
of various kinds. H. Ranston has suggested that Ecclesiastes
is indirectly dependent on Theognis, the 6th-century gnomic
elegist. Other scholars have found in his teaching elements
of Epicureanism or Stoicism. But no clear and convincing case can be made for any of these claims. At the late
period to which the book is commonly assigned (see below)
it would not be surprising if so open-minded a writer owed
something to Greek thought. But any such influence was
probably quite general.

Affinities have also been claimed with Accadian, Aramaic,
and, more recently, with Ugaritic literature. But there is
stronger evidence of dependence on Egyptian Wisdom. The
advice to enjoy life while it lasts (ii. 24; iii, 12; ix. 7–9), contrasts such as those expressed in ix. 11 and x. 7, and the description of old age in xii. 1–7, all have close parallels in

Egyptian texts. This is in keeping with the evidence elsewhere (e.g., in Proverbs) of the links between Hebrew and Egyptian Wisdom.

It need not, however, be concluded that the book originated in Egypt, though the allusion to seaborne merchandise in xi. 1 has been held to indicate Alexandria. On the other hand, Palestinian weather conditions are said to be reflected in xi. 4 and xii. 2. The evidence is not really strong either way. Such foreign evidence as can be detected in Ecclesiastes is, on the whole, in keeping with a Palestinian setting in the late Persian or Greek period.

This is the date to which the book is commonly assigned. In i. 1, the author appears to be identified with Solomon. But this is no guide to the age of the work; for the Solomonic authorship cannot be adequately defended. iii. 16; iv. 1; x. 4, 5, are the critical comments of a subject, not of a reigning monarch. Again, in i. 16; ii. 9, the author refers to generations of his predecessors in Jerusalem; but Solomon was preceded only by David. No help is given by the word *Kōhelet* (i. 1, 12; cf. xii. 8-10), which is applied to the author and is the Hebrew title of the book. The Greek rendering of it gives us 'Ecclesiastes'. *Kōhelet* is the singular of a feminine participle, which probably means 'one who assembles', or, 'one who addresses an assembly'.[1] The word may be intended either to describe the author as a Wisdom teacher or simply as a *nom de plume*.

Such references as the book contains to contemporary conditions suggest the disturbed régimes of the late Persian and Greek periods (iv. 13-16; x. 16-20). More specific allusions to actual events have been sought in iv. 13-16 and x. 16 (the accession of the young Ptolemy V in 204 B.C.) and in ix. 13-16 (the part played by Archimedes in the defence of Syracuse against the Romans in 212 B.C.). But these are very doubtful.

The language of Ecclesiastes represents a very late phase of

---

[1] The feminine is explained as indicating an office or function, and then the holder of the office or function. As parallels, the words *sōperet* (Ezra ii. 55) and *pōkeret* (Ezra ii. 57) are cited.

Biblical Hebrew, with affinities to Mishnaic Hebrew, many
Aramaisms, and perhaps a few Grecisms. Attempts have been
made to prove that the book is a Hebrew rendering of an
Aramaic original; but this is unlikely. In its uniformity the
language supports the substantial unity of the book; in its
general character it provides the most cogent argument for a
late date.

Fragments of the Hebrew text of Ecclesiastes discovered
at Qumran have been dated in the first half of the 2nd
century B.C. The composition of the book should, therefore,
probably be put before 200 B.C.

### (d) Lamentations

The English title of the book of Lamentations is derived,
through the Vulgate (*Threni, id est lamentationes Jeremiae
prophetae*), from the θρῆνοι of the Greek Bible. The corresponding Hebrew title, *ḳînôṯ*, is applied to the book in the
Talmud (*Baba Bathra* 14b, 15a); but in Hebrew MSS and
printed Bibles the title is simply the opening word, *'ekâh*,
'How'.

Lamentations consists of five chapters, each of which is a
poem. Their subject is the sufferings of the Jews, and, more
particularly, the fall of Jerusalem to the Babylonians and
its aftermath. The formal characteristics of i, ii, iii, and iv
are striking. They are all alphabetic acrostics in the Qinah
rhythm (see above, p. 172). The metre of v is 3 + 3; and,
although it is not an acrostic, it contains as many verses as
there are letters in the Hebrew alphabet. In i and ii the poetic
lines are grouped in threes; and in iv they are in pairs. In
these three poems the first lines of successive groups begin
with successive letters of the alphabet. The lines in iii are in
groups of three, the groups being arranged in alphabetic
order; but here all the lines in a given group begin with the
same letter.[1] The letter *pe* precedes *'ayin* in ii, iii, and iv;
but in i the reverse order, which is normal, is followed.

[1] Mgr R. A. Knox's translation gives a good impression of this
arrangement.

The combination of these somewhat artificial formal characteristics with the deeply emotional content of the poems has been much discussed. The theory that the acrostic form was adopted because of the supposed magical power of alphabetic patterns is unlikely. It has been more commonly held that it is a pedagogic or mnemonic device. N. K. Gottwald, however, claims that, though facility of memorization may have played a part, the main purpose of the acrostic form is to express the completeness of grief, penitence, and hope.

Although in a general sense the poems are all 'lamentations', their literary classification is not as simple as might appear at first sight. i, ii, and iv, all reveal the characteristics of the funeral dirge (note, e.g., the recurring 'How!': i. 1; ii. 1; iv. 1; cf. 2 Sam. i. 19, 25, 27), iii is predominantly an Individual Lament and v a Communal Lament. But there is a blend of literary forms. Elements of Individual Lament appear in i. 11c ff and of Communal Lament in iii. 48 ff and in iv. 17 ff.

This adaptation and blending of literary forms is a familiar phenomenon, to which there are many parallels in the prophetic literature. It has often been said that the description of the national catastrophe of 597/587 B.C. in the terms of a dirge for the dead is an instance of a political use of the dirge form. But to this it has been objected that the subject of the dirge is not a political entity but the holy city and its sanctuary. An interesting parallel has been adduced in a lament over the destroyed sanctuary of Ur. Certainly the religious status of Jerusalem would be much in people's minds in the generation immediately following the Josianic reform.

The markedly individual character of most of iii might suggest that it differs from the rest of Lamentations in referring to private suffering and not to the national affliction of 597/587 B.C. It has, in fact, been held that the first part was originally unconnected with the other poems, and that it was brought into line with them by the addition of the Communal Lament in vv. 40 ff. But this conclusion need not be drawn. There are familiar examples elsewhere in the Old

Testament of the expression of communal experience in individual terms, a feature which is readily illuminated by the
concept of corporate personality.

Granted that the theme of all five poems is the same, it
need not follow that they were all composed at the same
time or by the same person. The vivid presentation of the
catastrophe in ii and iii suggests that they were written by
an eye-witness very soon after the events. The same may
perhaps be said of v. i and iii are usually assigned to a somewhat later date; but it has been argued that, since i describes
the attack on Jerusalem rather than its destruction, it belongs to the decade before 587 B.C.

The tradition that Jeremiah wrote the poems was probably
suggested by 2 Chron. xxxv. 25. In the Greek Bible they follow
the book of Jeremiah and are introduced by the words, 'And
it came to pass after Israel was taken away captive and
Jerusalem was laid waste that Jeremiah sat weeping, and he
uttered this lamentation over Jerusalem and said. . . .' But
the diction of Lamentations differs from Jeremiah's and the
acrostic form is not found in his prophecies. To these arguments, which are not in themselves conclusive, it must be
added that i. 21 f and iii. 59–66 are at variance with Jeremiah's pro-Babylonian attitude, that iv. 17 reflects a hope
of Egyptian help to which Jeremiah was opposed, that iv.
20 can hardly be Jeremiah's description of Zedekiah, and that
the bewildered anguish of the poems cannot easily be attributed to the prophet who had consistently predicted disaster
as the consequence of sin. Nevertheless there are some
striking similarities between parts of iii and Jeremiah's
account of his own spiritual anguish; and it may well be that
the poet drew on Jeremiah's experience.

These poems, which describe with such passionate intensity the horrors of the fall of Jerusalem and the desola-
tion which followed, have more than literary and historical
interest. In a penetrating study [1] N. K. Gottwald has argued

---

[1] *Studies in the Book of Lamentations* (Studies in Biblical Theology,
No. 14).

for their religious and theological importance, and, in particular, for their influence on Isa. xl–lv and lvi–lxvi. They come from a time when the faith of Israel had to experience the test of grim adversity. But they are not simply five laments expressing anguish and despair. The agonized bewilderment which runs through all the poems has not destroyed faith in God's purpose for His people. Events had savagely challenged the Deuteronomic doctrines of the sanctity of Zion and of God's election of Israel. The five poems in Lamentations, at least in some sort, point the way forward to later treatments of the experience of suffering.

*(e) Esther*

The book of Esther tells how a Persian king, Ahasuerus, deposed Vashti, his queen, and later replaced her by Esther, a Jewish maiden who was chosen after the most beautiful virgins in the realm had been brought to the royal harem. Esther's cousin and guardian, Mordecai, was able, through Esther, to warn Ahasuerus of a plot against his life. Later, however, Mordecai omitted to do obeisance to Haman, a noble who had been made grand vizier. Bitterly resentful against Mordecai and all his race, Haman induced the king to issue a decree that all Jews throughout the realm should be massacred on the thirteenth day of the month Adar. But, by Esther's skilful intervention and by the king's realization that Mordecai's service had gone unrewarded, the tables were turned. Haman was hanged on the gallows prepared for Mordecai, who was now appointed grand vizier. The Jews were allowed to defend themselves against their enemies, of whom they slaughtered 75,000 in the provinces on the thirteenth of Adar and 810 in Susa on the thirteenth and fourteenth. The fourteenth (in the provinces) and the fifteenth (in Susa) were celebrated as days of rejoicing; and henceforward these days are to be observed with feasting and gladness as the festival of Purim, so called because Haman fixed the date of the massacre by lot (*pûr*).

Though the book gives a vivid and generally faithful

picture of conditions at the Persian court, it cannot be taken
as an accurate record of events. Ahasuerus is to be identified
with Xerxes, who reigned from 485 B.C. till 465 B.C. Thus
Mordecai, who is said to have been deported from Judah in
597 B.C., would have been well over 100 years old when these
events took place. Other sources for the period say nothing
of the presence of Vashti and Esther at the court of Xerxes,
whose queen is known to have been called Amestris (Herodotus vii. 114; ix. 112). Nor does the choice of a Jewess, or
the manner in which Esther was chosen, agree with the law
controlling Persian royal marriages (Herodotus iii. 84).

Though the book is thus at variance with known historical
fact, it is claimed that it corresponds with certain mythological and cultic data. Haman and Vashti have been
equated with the Elamite deities Human and Mashti, and
the story said to reflect their defeat by the Babylonian deities
Marduk and Ishtar, represented by Mordecai and Esther.
Again, the story has been explained in terms of the myth
of the victory of Marduk (Mordecai) over chaos, in which,
however, Ishtar does not play a prominent part.

It is probably a mistake to try to identify the characters
with deities. The names are meant to indicate human beings;
and the story is a story about men and women, not about
gods and goddesses. But the explicit connexion of the book
with Purim makes it reasonable to look for a cultic background. Unfortunately, the meaning of the word 'Purim',
the origin of the festival, and the date at which it was introduced into Judaism are obscure.

The earliest reference outside Esther to the festival is in
2 Macc. xv. 86, where Nicanor's day, on which was celebrated
the victory of Judas Maccabæus in 161 B.C. over Nicanor
(cf. 1 Macc. vii. 49), is said to have been the day before
Mordecai's day. The patriotic spirit of Purim as described in
Esther would accord well with the national mood after the
triumphs of the Maccabees. R. H. Pfeiffer holds that the
festival was devised and its name coined by the author of
Esther in the time of Hyrcanus (185–104 B.C.) as a secular,

nationalist celebration, and that he wrote his book to explain its origin. But, since features in Purim and in Esther resemble rituals practised elsewhere, it is not surprising that some scholars have sought to establish a connexion with, e.g., the Babylonian New Year festival, the festival of Sacaea, or the Persian Fravardigan. Persia would seem to be the most probable source of borrowing; but it need not be assumed that there was only one such source. Babylonian influence may also have played a part. Nor should the cultic background and the historical inaccuracies already noted be allowed to exclude the possibility that the story has some historical basis, however small. Esther may be a counterpart of Jenny Geddes, a legendary or even a fictitious figure, associated with historical events, who symbolized intense nationalist sentiment and whose story was used to establish Purim in Jewish worship as the Jenny Geddes story was used to exclude set forms of liturgy.

The cultic application of the story made in ix. 17–19 would be an apt conclusion to the book. ix. 20–32, which shows differences of style and substance from the rest of the story, is probably an addition by another hand to explain how Purim came to be celebrated on both the fourteenth and fifteenth Adar. x. 1–3 may also be a later addition: its reference to the book of the chronicles of the kings of Media and Persia is curiously reminiscent of the references in Kings to the books of the chronicles of the kings of Israel and of Judah. In the Greek Bible there are further additions to the text, made mainly in the interest of edification.

The theme and general interest of Esther suggest that it originated in the eastern Diaspora. The language is late; and since Mordecai and Esther are not mentioned in the list of heroes in Ecclesiasticus, the book was probably written in the 2nd century, though not necessarily as late as the date proposed by Pfeiffer.

In ancient times there were doubts about the canonical status of Esther (see above, p. 16); and, though Maimonides ranked it with the Law, it has been subjected to vigorous

criticism. Luther's explosive criticism of Esther and 2 Maccabees is well known.[1] Two objections are commonly made
against the book. (1) It contains no explicit religious teaching, even when observance of the festival is enjoined. The
name of God appears nowhere in the book, and, indeed,
appears to be deliberately avoided in iv. 14. (2) It describes
the wholesale slaughter of the enemies of the Jews and exults
in their downfall.

The absence of explicit religious sentiment means that no
religious motive is associated with the massacre. Further, any
objective estimate of the book will make allowance for the
feelings (however reprehensible they may seem) of those who
were often subjected to ruthless persecution, and will also
recognize that not every detail in the Canon of the Old or
the New Testament is obviously or immediately edifying. At
all events, Esther illustrates an important trend in Jewish
life at the end of the Old Testament period: the growth of an
ardent nationalism which was not specifically religious.

## VII. APOCALYPTIC

The apocalyptic literature, of which the book of Daniel is
the only complete example in the Old Testament, is in some
sense the child of prophecy. There are important differences
between the two; but the similarity consists in the way in
which apocalyptic displays the fuller development of tendencies which are evident in the later stages of prophecy.

'Apocalypse' means revelation. The apocalyptic books
claim to tell of detailed revelations made in striking ways
to men of God. In Israel, revelation was closely related to
historical events; and both prophecy and apocalyptic are
concerned with the revelation of God's will, to which they
seek to relate the events of history. There are, however,
important differences in the ways in which the revelation is
expressed and communicated.

The prophet was primarily the man of the spoken word.

---

[1] 'Ich bin dem Buch [2 Maccabees] und Esther so feind, dass ich
wollte, sie wären gar nicht vorhanden; denn sie judenzen zu sehr und
haben viel heidnische Unart.'

The writing down of his message was secondary. The apocalyptist, on the other hand, was a writer; and it was by the written word that he conveyed his message. It was also sometimes on the written prophetic word that he based his message (e.g., Dan. ix. 2). In its literary character apocalyptic differs from prophecy; and yet it inherits the literary tendencies of the later stages of prophecy.

Again, the fact that the prophet spoke in public meant that he was known. Those Old Testament prophecies which, in their written form, are anonymous were not so when originally uttered, since presumably the speaker could readily be identified. But the apocalyptic books are pseudonymous. The writer not only conceals his identity behind his writing; he assumes the character of some ancient man of God, such as Daniel or Enoch. The reason for this convention is disputed. R. H. Charles argued that, since the age of prophetic inspiration was thought to be past, and since the Law was held to be the definitive and final expression of Judaism, the apocalyptic writings would not have been accepted as authoritative if they had not purported to come from inspired men of an earlier age. The suggestion is not very convincing. If it were sound, one would have to conclude that the apocalyptists misjudged the situation, since Daniel was the only apocalyptic work which gained sufficient standing to be included in the Old Testament. It is unlikely that they deluded many readers into thinking that their books came from the personages whose names they assumed; and it is difficult to believe that they intended to do so. Rejecting Charles's view, H. H. Rowley has suggested that the convention arose from the way in which the book of Daniel was written, the stories *about* Daniel having been circulated first, and the visions subsequently written in the name of Daniel in order to indicate identity of authorship with the stories.

Apocalyptic is characterized by the use of bizarre imagery. The prophets use symbolism freely. But, in the classical age of prophecy, the imagery used is natural. We have already noticed that in Ezekiel there are symbols which are distorted and fantastic. Something of the sort is also evident in the visions of Zechariah. This tendency in later prophecy leads to the characteristic symbolism of apocalyptic, as seen, for example, in Dan. vii, where the vision of beasts and horns is quite remote from anything in nature. This bizarre symbolism in apocalyptic is nevertheless conventional, in that certain symbols regularly represent the same things; and the symbolism thus becomes a kind of code. Allied to this is the symbolic use of numbers. In time of persecution it was an advantage to be able to convey to the initiated meanings which were not immediately apparent to others.

It is perhaps in the attitude to history that the difference between prophecy and apocalyptic is most evident, though here, again, the later phases of prophecy prepare the way for apocalyptic. Both speak of the decisive intervention of God in history. The prophet speaks to the need of his own time and traces the action of God in current events. He also predicts the future action of God, usually in the immediate, but sometimes in the more distant, future. In the later prophecies, these predictions of the distant future are more frequent, more detailed, and less obviously connected with the normal historical process. Like the prophet, the apocalyptist speaks to the need of his own time. Since, however, he adopts the role of some personage of an earlier time, what for him is actually past history is presented as future and as foreseen in a predictive vision or similar experience. Where a historical survey of this sort occurs in an apocalyptic work, the date of writing may be determined by the point at which the narrative ceases to correspond with the actual course of history (e.g., Dan. xi, where, however, the early part of the survey is sketchy and confused, presumably because it was so far removed from the writer's own day). It is in keeping with this convention that the apocalyptist represents the course of events as known and determined in detail beforehand, a view which is more obviously shared by some interpreters of the prophecy than by the prophets themselves. Further, it is typical of apocalyptic thought that history is divided into well-defined ages, a feature which resembles Zoroastrian eschatology.

Certain other characteristics have suggested foreign influence, notably the elaborate angelic hierarchy with the corresponding orders of devils which appear in other Jewish writings of the period. Such influence may indeed be present; but it is working on material which already belonged to the Israelite tradition. Moreover, the fact that the apocalyptic literature was directed to the need of loyal Jews in time of persecution links it inseparably with the life of the Jewish people.

## VIII. DANIEL

The historical setting of the book of Daniel purports to be the time of the Exile. Of its twelve chapters, the first six contain stories, mainly about Daniel and his three companions, Jewish exiles in Babylon, emphasizing their unswerving loyalty to their faith and Daniel's great gift of wisdom. The stories span the period from the beginning of the Exile until after the fall of Babylon. The remaining six chapters describe four visions, in which there is revealed to Daniel, sometimes in highly symbolic form, the course of history from the 6th century to the fourth decade of the 2nd century.

The book begins in Hebrew (i. 1–ii. 4a), but lapses into Aramaic at the beginning of the Chaldeans' speech and continues in that language in the stories that follow and up to the end of the first vision (ii. 4b–vii. 28). The remainder of the book is in Hebrew (viii–xii).

There are serious difficulties in the traditional view that the book was written in the 6th century.

1. It is in the third section of the Canon; and if it had been extant before the compilation of the prophetic section, it is difficult to understand why it was not included there.

2. Daniel is not mentioned in the record of famous men in Ecclus. xliv–l, though Isaiah, Jeremiah, Ezekiel, and the Twelve are included. The likeness between Daniel and Joseph is such that Ecclus. xlix. 15 could hardly have been written by one who knew about Daniel. Just after the middle

of the 2nd century B.C., however, there is a reference to Dan. vii in the Sibylline Oracles iii. 381–400. In 1 Macc. ii. 59, 60 (written about 100 B.C.) there are references to Daniel and his friends, which reveal a knowledge of the first part of the book. Fragments of the text of Daniel found at Qumran have been dated in the 1st century B.C These facts suggest that the book was produced before the middle of the 2nd century, but that it is more likely to have appeared after 200 B.C. than before it.

3. The linguistic characteristics of the book point to a date considerably later than the 6th century. The Hebrew is late. The Aramaic is not Babylonian but Western; and, though it cannot be dated with certainty or precision, it is later than the 5th century and probably not earlier than the 3rd. The text contains many Persian loan-words, which suggests a long period of Persian influence. There are also some Greek words, including one ($\sigma\upsilon\mu\phi\omega\nu\acute{\iota}\alpha$) which does not seem to be used in the required sense before the 2nd century B.C.

4. There are historical inaccuracies, which, taken together, cannot well be credited to a 6th-century writer. (*a*) There is no other evidence of a deportation in the third year of Jehoiakim (i. 1 f). (*b*) The use of the term 'Chaldeans' for wise men (ii. 2, etc.) is unparalleled except in later documents. In the time of the neo-Babylonian Empire the word was ethnological. (*c*) Although Jews held high office in the Persian royal service (e.g., Nehemiah), it is improbable that a loyal Jew like Daniel would have been appointed head of the priestly wise men of Babylon, or would have accepted such a position (ii. 48). (*d*) Belshazzar was the son of Nabonidus, not of Nebuchadrezzar; and he was never king of Babylon (v. 1 ff; vii). (*e*) It is impossible to make historical sense of the references to Darius the Mede, who is described as the son of Xerxes (ix. 1), and is said to have conquered Babylon (v. 31). The celebrated king of that name was not a Mede but a Persian; he was the father of Xerxes; and it was not he but Cyrus, his predecessor's father, who conquered Babylon. (*f*) The implication that a Median Empire followed the Babylonian and preceded the Persian is quite unhistorical.

5. The historical surveys in the book all lead up to the first half of the 2nd century. Moreover (and this is particularly evident in xi), the references to the earlier period are sketchy and sometimes confused; but in the treatment of the later decades there is an elaboration of detail and concentration of interest which point to the persecution under Antiochus Epiphanes (175–164 B.C.) as the situation for which the book was written. Further, the religious message of the book fits that period admirably. The stories about Daniel and his friends give guidance to faithful Jews who had to face the problems raised by an alien and pagan environment even before active persecution began; and both the stories and the visions offer comfort and hope to those who were actually facing persecution and the possibility of martyrdom.

These considerations point to the second quarter of the 2nd century as the time when Daniel was written; and, since Antiochus did not meet his death in Palestine as described in xi. 40–45 (verses which, therefore, appear to have been written before his death in 164 B.C.), the book should probably be dated shortly before that date.

But parts of the book may be earlier. Many theories, some of them quite elaborate, have been advanced, suggesting that it is not a literary unity. The main arguments in support of such views are: (a) that the book is bilingual, and (b) that the visions differ from the stories in literary character, and in presupposing a Palestinian rather than a Babylonian background, and bitter persecution rather than a situation in which mutual trust and respect between the Jews and their rulers were sometimes possible.

(a) The bilingual character of the book presents a problem for which different solutions have been offered. (1) It has been suggested that the entire book, with the possible exception of ix. 4–19, was originally written in Aramaic, and that parts were later translated into Hebrew to facilitate the inclusion of the book in the Canon. But it is in itself unlikely that Hebrew was adopted to strengthen a claim to canonical

status. Nor does this theory explain why the transitions from
the one language to the other occur just where they do.
(2) Another view is that the entire book was originally written
in Hebrew, and that part of the text which had been lost was
supplied from an Aramaic translation. This, however, is a
supposition rather than a theory which can be supported by
evidence. Moreover, if there had been such a loss it would
have been remarkable if the breaks had occurred so con-
veniently at the beginning of a speech and the end of a
section. (3) According to another hypothesis, i–vi was originally written entirely in Aramaic; and vii–xii was a later
document written (with the exception of vii) in Hebrew.
When the two were joined, the opening passage (i. 1–ii. 4a)
was translated into Hebrew. Or it is held that vii was
originally in Hebrew, like the following chapters, and was
translated into Aramaic when the two documents were joined.
Unlike the other two theories, this one presupposes that the
book is in some sense composite. But it is evident that vii is
something of an embarrassment to any such theory, since in
substance (cf. ii) and in language it is linked to what precedes
(and the view that it was originally in Hebrew savours of
special pleading), and in literary character and substance
it is of a piece with what follows. In short, the bilingual
character of Daniel provides by itself no adequate basis for a
view that the book is composite.

(b) The distinction between the stories in i–vi and the
visions in vii–xii is certainly marked. But the change from
the third person of the narratives to the first person of the
visions need not imply a change of author. The change of
geographical setting is quite appropriate if a 2nd-century
author begins by telling stories of endurance during the Exile
in order to encourage his contemporaries in Palestine. If, as
seems very probable, the stories embody traditional material,
that might explain why the foreign rulers are not uniformly
described as ruthless tyrants. The contrasts in literary character and setting are outweighed by the links in content between the two parts of the book. We have already noted

that vii is connected both with what precedes (especially ii) and with what follows. Further, the unhistorical allusions to Darius the Mede and to Belshazzar occur in both parts of the book. The trials of the persecution under Antiochus Epiphanes, to which the visions lead up, are reflected in the trials to which Daniel and his friends were subjected. Finally, the whole book displays a marked unity of spirit and purpose. Though elaborate theories of composite authorship continue to be advanced, they often assume numerous interpolations; and this of itself, apart from other considerations, tells against their cogency.

But if the book is the work of one author, it may not all have been written at one time. There are signs that the stories circulated independently of each other (e.g., the fact that Daniel plays no part in iii and the seeming chronological inconsistency in i. 1, 5; ii. 1); and it is probable that the author recorded the visions later. H. H. Rowley, one of the doughtiest defenders of the unity of Daniel, has propounded an ingenious account of the composition of the book which also provides possible explanations of its bilingual character and its pseudonymity. He holds that the stories in ii–vi, based on popular traditions, were written in Aramaic and circulated separately; that vii was written (also in Aramaic) as a sequel to them; but that the subsequent visions in viii–xii were written in Hebrew, which the author regarded as more suitable to this less popular type of literature. Finally, i. 1–ii. 4a was prefaced to the whole (replacing the original beginning of ii) in Hebrew, the language in which the more recent parts had been written. The visions were ascribed to Daniel as an indication that they came from the author of the stories about Daniel. This explanation of the pseudonymity of the book and of the transition from Hebrew to Aramaic at ii. 4 is attractive, but the reason offered for the transition from Aramaic to Hebrew is perhaps slightly less plausible. The other main contentions, that the book is the work of one author, that it was not all composed at one time, and that in parts of it the author has adapted

traditional popular material, are adequately supported by
the evidence.[1]

The Daniel about whom the stories are told and in whose
name the author of the book speaks cannot be identified with
any known figure of the Exilic age. A Daniel is mentioned in
Ezek. xiv. 14, 20, and xxviii. 3. Evidently he is regarded as a
paragon of righteousness and wisdom. But the reference cannot well be to a 6th-century contemporary of Ezekiel, since
Daniel's name is linked with those of Noah and Job, which
implies that he is a figure of ancient tradition. Further
evidence is provided by an epic poem among the 14th-century
documents discovered on the site of the ancient city of Ugarit
(Ras Shamra). This tells of Dan'el, son of Aqhat, who treated
the widow and the orphan with compassionate righteousness.
The spelling of the name agrees with that in Ezekiel, but
differs slightly from that in the book of Daniel. It is very
probable that Ezekiel's references to Daniel go back to the
ancient traditions embodied in the Ugaritic poem (note that
Ezekiel xxviii presupposes that Daniel is well known to the
Tyrians). But it is doubtful whether the book of Daniel owes
anything to the same stream of tradition. The stories are so
obviously Jewish in character, 6th-century in setting, and
2nd-century in application, that, if anything at all is derived
from Ugarit, it can be little more than the name and the
general characteristics of wisdom and righteousness.

In common with much of the literature of the later Old
Testament period, Daniel appeals for unswerving loyalty to
the Law. It represents the attitude of the religious party

---

[1] The prayer in ix. 4–19 has been regarded by some scholars as an
interpolation, on the ground that it does not fit its present context very
well. xii. 11, 12 is also regarded as an addition or additions.

In the Greek Bible (both LXX and also the version of Theodotion
which at an early date supplanted the LXX text of Daniel in Christian
usage) the following additional material appears: the story of Susanna
(prefixed to the book); the Song of the Three Holy Children (consisting
of the Prayer of Azarias, details about the fiery furnace, and the
Benedicite, following iii. 23); and the stories of Bel and the Dragon, with
a short narrative about Habakkuk (following xii. 13). These sections are
included in the Apocrypha.

(Hasidim), and appears to be rather critical of the nationalistic Maccabean movement, to which it refers as 'a little help' (xi. 34). The writer looked for a divine intervention rather than for military victories. Before that supreme crisis, which is to usher in the new age, history is divided, as in other apocalypses, into successive ages dominated by different world powers. The part played by angelic figures in interpreting visions (vii. 16; viii. 16; ix. 22) and acting as patrons of specific nations (x. 13, 20, 21; xii. 1) is also in keeping with apocalyptic teaching. The reference in xii. 2 f to resurrection (even if it is not universal and only temporary) is an important step in the development of the Jewish belief in life after death. The description in vii of 'one like a son of man' is probably the first appearance in Jewish literature of a concept of great importance in later apocalyptic and in the Gospels.

## IX. Ezra, Nehemiah, 1 and 2 Chronicles

The Hebrew Canon ends with the books of Ezra, Nehemiah, and 1 and 2 Chronicles, in that order. But it is clear that the books of Ezra and Nehemiah are the sequel to Chronicles, and that the four books form, in some sort, a literary unity.

(1) A comparison of the end of 2 Chronicles and the beginning of Ezra shows that there is an overlap and that 2 Chronicles ends with an unfinished sentence, which is completed in Ezra. Ezra and Nehemiah, the closing parts of the entire work, were added to the Canon first. Later, when 1 and 2 Chronicles were added, the latter was made to end abruptly at the point just indicated.

(2) Although the material is far from homogeneous, and there is ample evidence of the incorporation of literary sources, the editorial portions reveal the same stylistic features and the same interests and outlook.

If, then, we take the four books as a whole, in the order in which they appear in the English Bible, the following is the general plan of the contents:

(a) 1 Chron. i–ix. A genealogical survey from Adam to Saul and his house.

(*b*) 1 Chron. x–xxix. The story of the monarchy from the death of Saul to the death of David.

(*c*) 2 Chron. i–ix. The reign of Solomon.

(*d*) 2 Chron. x–xxxvi. From the division of the kingdom to the return from Exile.

(*e*) Ezra i–vi. The return and the restoration of the temple. The work of Zerubbabel and Jeshua.

(*f*) Ezra vii–x. The reforms of Ezra.

(*g*) Neh. i–vii. The rebuilding of the wall by Nehemiah.

(*h*) Neh. viii–xiii. The reading of the Book of the Law under Ezra's direction. Further measures taken by Nehemiah.

The period up to the fall of Jerusalem is covered in the Pentateuch and the Former Prophets. It is, therefore, interesting to note the significant differences in the way in which the story is told. In Chronicles the story does not really begin until we reach the death of Saul and the beginning of David's reign: the earlier period is covered by genealogies and lists. It is only the death of Saul that is recounted: his reign is otherwise passed by. The history of the Northern Kingdom (including the stories of the northern prophets, Elijah and Elisha) is omitted. Even in the story of David's reign there are some remarkable gaps: the events between Saul's death and the capture of Jerusalem are not recorded; nor is there any narrative parallel to the brilliant Court History of David (2 Sam. ix–xx; 1 Kings i–ii).

There are also several important additions. These appear, for example, in the lists in 1 Chron. i–ix and in the list of David's heroes in 1 Chron. xi. 10–47 (cf. 2 Sam. xxiii. 8–39). There are significant additions to the story of the bringing up of the Ark to Jerusalem in 1 Chron. xv and xvi (cf. 2 Samuel vi), emphasizing the importance of the presence of the Levites. Interest in the priests, the Levites, and the temple is also evident in 1 Chron. xxii. 2–xxix. 30, which owes only xxix. 23a, 27 to 1 Kings, in 2 Chron. i. 3b–6a, which justifies Solomon's sacrificing at Gibeon by the view that the sacred

tent and the altar were still there (cf. 1 Kings iii. 4–15), and
in the expansions of the account of Jehoshaphat's reign in
2 Chron. xvii. 1b–19; xix. 1–xx. 30.

These are only a few of the many additions to the substance of the earlier canonical books. The most important
addition is, of course, Ezra–Nehemiah, which is also characteristic in its interest in the restoration and regulation of the
life of the Jewish community.

Verbal parallels make it clear that the Chronicler used the
earlier historical books. That he drew on other sources is
evident both from the additional material and also from the
many explicit references to such sources. We hear of 'the
book of the kings of Israel and Judah' (2 Chron. xxvii. 7;
xxxv. 27; xxxvi. 8), 'the book of the kings of Judah and
Israel' (2 Chron. xvi. 11; xxv. 26; xxviii. 26; xxxii. 32), 'the
book of the kings of Israel' (2 Chron. xx. 34), 'the words
(acts, records, chronicles) of the kings of Israel' (2 Chron.
xxxiii. 18), and 'the commentary (midrash) of the book of
the kings' (2 Chron. xxiv. 27). It is very unlikely that the
variety of titles represents an equal variety of sources.
Indeed, it may well be that only one work is referred to
in these different ways: '(the midrash of) the book of the
kings'.

Other titles mentioned suggest that prophetic records have
been drawn upon: 'the words of Samuel the seer', 'the words
of Nathan the prophet', 'the words of Gad the seer' (1 Chron.
xxix. 29), 'the words of Nathan the prophet' (2 Chron. ix.
29), 'the words of Shemaiah the prophet', 'the words of
Iddo the seer' (2 Chron. xii. 15), 'the words of Jehu the son of
Hanani, which are included in the book of the kings of Israel'
(2 Chron. xx. 34), 'the words of my (the ?) seers' (2 Chron.
xxxiii. 19), 'the prophecy of Ahijah the Shilonite' (2 Chron.
ix. 29), 'the visions of Iddo the seer' (2 Chron. ix. 29), 'the
vision of Isaiah the prophet, the son of Amoz, in the book
of the kings of Judah and Israel' (2 Chron. xxxii. 32), 'the
commentary (midrash) of the prophet Iddo' (2 Chron. xiii.
22), to which list should be added the statement that Isaiah

the prophet, the son of Amoz, wrote 'the rest of the acts of Uzziah, first and last' (2 Chron. xxvi. 22). Here, again, it need not be assumed that each title represents a separate source, or, indeed, that this list is entirely independent of the other, particularly since the words of Jehu and the vision of Isaiah are both said to be included in the book of the kings of Israel. The prophetic sources referred to in 1 Chron. xxix. 29 and 2 Chron. ix. 29 are most naturally explained as the relevant parts of our books of Samuel and Kings. It may well be that the other prophetic titles refer to various parts of (the midrash of) the book of the kings, though 2 Chron. xxxiii. 18, 19 may indicate that the royal history did not include 'the words of the seers'.

Noth has shown that the Chronicler's account of the reigns of David and Solomon is derived from Samuel and Kings, and that the differences are to be attributed, not to other sources, but to the Chronicler himself. We may reckon, then, with the use of our canonical books of Genesis–2 Kings, supplemented, *for the period after Solomon,* by (the midrash of) the book of the kings, which was possibly an expanded version of the canonical books of Kings.[1] There are also signs that the Chronicler drew on the canonical prophetic literature (Isa. vii. 9 in 2 Chron. xx. 20, Zech. iv. 10 in 2 Chron. xvi. 9, and Jeremiah in the account of the fall of Jerusalem in 2 Chron. xxxvi).

Not unnaturally, other sources provided material for Ezra–Nehemiah.

1. The presence of autobiographical passages describing the work of Ezra and Nehemiah suggests that personal memoirs have been used. This is abundantly evident in Neh. i. 1–vii. 73a and in parts of xi–xiii, though editorial revision is evident in these latter chapters. Parts of the chapters dealing with Ezra also appear to be based on a private record (Ezra vii. 1–10, 27–x. 44; Neh. vii. 73b–ix. 38). But the

[1] The term 'midrash' is not to be understood in its later sense (narrative edited and adapted in the interests of edification) but simply in the sense, 'study', 'inquiry', 'work'.

memoirs of Nehemiah are more distinctive and more extensively used than those of Ezra, which appear to have been
subjected to more drastic editorial treatment. Indeed, it has
been argued that the narrative portions written in the third
person about Ezra are stylistically indistinguishable from the
autobiographical passages and that both are to be attributed
to the Chronicler (or Chroniclers), whose work, however, was
based on traditions of Ezra.[1]

2. As in Chronicles, lists are prominent. In Ezra ii and
Neh. vii. 6–72 there is a list of those who returned with
Zerubbabel from exile. The fact that it occurs twice is
probably an indication that it was included in two different
sources used by the Chronicler. Ezra viii. 1–14 is a list of
those who returned with Ezra; and Ezra x. 18–44 records
those who had married foreign women. Neh. iii enumerates
those who co-operated in the building of the city wall. Neh.
x. 1–28 is a list of those whose names were added to a solemn
undertaking. Neh. xi. 1–36 relates to the population of
Jerusalem and includes records of the surrounding area.
Neh. xii. 1–26 contains lists of priests and Levites. These
documents raise difficult questions of content, context, and
date, too detailed for discussion here.

3. Letters and other official documents have been included
in the record. The decree of Cyrus in Ezra i. 2–4 has often
been dismissed or drastically criticized as unauthentic. In
form it no doubt owes much to the Chronicler; but its substance need not be rejected as mere invention. In vi. 3–5
there is quoted a decree of Cyrus authorizing the rebuilding
of the temple. By contrast with i. 2–4, this document gives
details about measurements and materials. It purports to
come from the Persian royal archives, where it is said to have
been found in the reign of Darius I, when an attempt was
made to interfere with the work of restoration which was
organized by Jeshua and Zerubbabel. It is part of a section
of the book, written mainly (iv. 8–vi. 18) in Aramaic, in
which data about Jewish rebuilding and attempts to stop

[1] A. S. Kapelrud, *The Question of Authorship in the Ezra-Narrative.*

it have been assembled with a bewildering disregard for chronology. iv. 1–5 tells of local opposition to the rebuilding of the temple from the reign of Cyrus till the reign of Darius I (522–486 B.C.). iv. 6 mentions opposition during the reign of Xerxes I (485–465 B.C.); and iv. 7 jumps forward to the reign of Artaxerxes I (464–424 B.C.), to which also belong the incidents described in iv. 8–23, where the Chronicler quotes letters between the Jews' opponents and Artaxerxes about the rebuilding not of the temple but of Jerusalem and its walls. In iv. 24 we are back again in the reign of Darius I, at the point indicated by iv. 5. The story then continues, including (a) a letter from the opponents of the Jews to Darius, (b) the decree of Cyrus which was brought to light by the command of Darius, and (c) the reply of Darius. Finally, vii. 12–26, which is also in Aramaic, gives the royal authorization for Ezra's mission.

The Chronicler's dependence on his sources is evident in Ezra–Nehemiah, not only from the way in which he uses them, but from the gaps in his narrative, above all in the sudden jump from the time of Jeshua, Zerubbabel, Haggai, and Zechariah to the mission of Ezra, and the absence of even a summarizing survey of the intervening period. We have already noted that his use of sources in Ezra iv is chronologically confusing. His chronology has been subjected to more serious criticism. It is widely held that he has reversed the order of Ezra and Nehemiah.

He dates the beginning of Ezra's mission in the seventh year of Artaxerxes (Ezra vii. 7), and Nehemiah's first coming to Jerusalem in the twentieth year of Artaxerxes (Neh. ii. 1). If, as has been traditionally assumed, both references are to the reign of Artaxerxes I (464–424 B.C.), then Ezra's coming to Jerusalem is dated in 458/7 B.C. and Nehemiah's in 445/4 B.C. But many scholars believe that Ezra belongs to the reign of Artaxerxes II (404–359 B.C.), and therefore that Ezra vii. 7 refers to 398/7 B.C. The following are the chief arguments.

(a) Nehemiah's first task was the rebuilding of the walls of

Jerusalem. Ezra ix. 9, however, appears to imply that, when
Ezra arrived, the walls were already built. But the word for
'wall' in ix. 9 is not that used in the Nehemiah narrative,
and its meaning here has been disputed.

(b) Ezra x. 1 implies that Jerusalem was populous, and
therefore belongs to a later and more settled time than Neh.
vii. 4. But Ezra x. 1 describes an assembly, and does not
represent the entire population of the city.

(c) Ezra's measures against mixed marriages (Ezra x. 3,
11) are more extreme than Nehemiah's (Neh. xiii. 25), and
therefore later. On the other hand it has been claimed that
Ezra's policy may have failed (for which there is no evidence),
and that this may have led Nehemiah to adopt more moderate
measures. But it is difficult to see what general grounds there
are for thinking that severe measures either precede or follow
a less radical policy.

(d) The sections attributed to the Nehemiah memoirs do
not refer to Ezra; and, although Nehemiah is mentioned in
association with Ezra in Neh. viii. 9 and xii. 26 and again
in x. 1, this may be the result of editorial revision. It is
at all events a striking fact that neither leader plays any
significant part in the accounts of the other's activity, as
might have been expected if they had been contemporaries.

(e) In Nehemiah's time the high-priest was Eliashib (Neh.
iii. 1); but Ezra appears to have been a contemporary of
Johanan, Eliashib's grandson (Ezra x. 6; Neh. xii. 11, 22);
and the Elephantine papyri show that a Johanan was high-
priest in Jerusalem ca. 410 B.C.

(d) and (e) are undoubtedly weighty arguments. But, although the case for the late dating of Ezra has been widely
accepted,[1] the traditional view is still supported by many
who feel that the alternative requires too drastic handling of

[1] According to alternative forms of this view, Ezra came to Jerusalem
in the twenty-seventh, thirty-second, or thirty-seventh year of Artaxerxes I, i.e., later than the beginning of Nehemiah's work, but in the
same reign.
The extreme theory, held by C. C. Torrey and G. Hölscher, that the
figure of Ezra is an invention of the Chronicler, is generally rejected.

the documents and that the Chronicler probably lived too
near to the age of Ezra and Nehemiah to be guilty of so
serious an error.

The date to which we assign the Chronicler's work depends
in part on the view taken of the nature and extent of the
editorial revision which the book has undergone. Several
scholars have maintained that there is evidence of two stages
in the production of the book. Rothstein held that the first of
these was about 432 B.C. and the second about 400 B.C.,
and that some additions were made later. A. C. Welch, who
denied that Ezra–Nehemiah came from the same hand as
Chronicles, argued for a first draft of Chronicles *ca.* 520 B.C.,
followed by a later recension under the influence of the
Priestly source in the Pentateuch. von Rad has analysed the
work into a stratum influenced by D and another by P.
S. Granild has sought to show that editorial additions to
the Chronicler's work include the material about Nehemiah.
By contrast with the hypothesis of two main strata, it has
been maintained, notably by W. Rudolph, that there is evidence of only one author (whom Rudolph dates *ca.* 400 B.C.),
though additions continued to be made for well over two
centuries.

The language points to a late date; but no precise chronological conclusions can be drawn from it. The reference to
the coin known as a 'daric' (1 Chron. xxix. 7), which was so
named after Darius I, suggests a date fairly well on in the
Persian period. In 1 Chron. iii. 19–24 the Davidic genealogy
is brought down to the sixth generation [1] after Zerubbabel;
and the list of priests in Neh. xii. comes down to about
400 B.C.; but the evidence of both passages has been rejected
by Rudolph on the ground that they are later additions.
If we regard Ezra–Nehemiah as an integral part of the
Chronicler's work, then, on the traditional dating of Ezra's
mission, the book must be later than Nehemiah's second
governorship (i.e., no earlier than about 430 B.C.); but, on
the later dating of Ezra, it must have been written some time

[1] In the Greek Bible to the eleventh.

after 397 B.C. It seems reasonable to assign it to the 4th century.

As has often been observed, the Chronicler is less useful as a recorder of past history than as a witness to an interpretation of history and a religious outlook which were characteristic of the age in which he lived. But this appraisal requires qualification. The narratives about the events after the Exile, and particularly those about Ezra and Nehemiah, contain information of very great historical interest and importance. But it remains true that the Chronicler's history is highly selective and interpretative. He shows a special interest in the Law, the cult, and the Levites. In this, and in his fondness for lists, his work resembles the Priestly material in the Pentateuch. Yet it should be noted that his interest is in the Levites rather than in the priests, and that it is David (and the Davidic line) and not Moses who is presented as the great agent of God's purpose for Israel. Judah, Jerusalem and its temple, and the community which centred its life there are leading themes in the story which he has to tell, which reaches its climax in the restoration of that community and its separation from corrupting alien influence. Rudolph has rightly pointed out that the Chronicler should not be dismissed as a mere ritualist or legalist, and that his emphasis on faith and prayer link him with the true prophetic tradition, though he expresses little or nothing of the eschatological hope.

## NOTE

In the Greek Bible, Ezra–Nehemiah appears as 2 Esdras. I Esdras, sometimes called the Greek Ezra, is a rendering of 2 Chron. xxxv; xxxvi; Ezra with some rearrangement and a long insertion; and Neh. vii. 73b–viii. 13a. This is the 1 Esdras of our Apocrypha. In the Vulgate it is 3 Esdras, the books of Ezra and Nehemiah appearing as 1 and 2 Esdras. The 4 Esdras of the Vulgate (which is not included in the Greek Bible) is the 2 Esdras of our Apocrypha.

# VII.—LITERARY FORMS AND LITERARY HISTORY

THE Old Testament contains the fragmentary remains of a national literature. In earlier chapters of this book the attempt has been made to examine the contents and structure of the several books and to trace the process of their composition. We now consider what the material contained in the Canon reveals of the character and development of ancient Hebrew literature. This may be done in two ways: (a) by studying the literary genres which appear in the Old Testament, and (b) by attempting, so far as is possible, to sketch the history of Hebrew literature in the Biblical period and to relate it to the history of the nation.

The chief formal distinction is that between poetry and prose. Hebrew poetry has certain well-defined structural features and others which are more open to dispute. These have already been discussed (pp. 171–173). It must suffice here to survey briefly the main types of poetry.

In the study of literary types it is customary to give attention to (a) form, and (b) setting in life (*Sitz im Leben*). Both these factors are of great importance; but it is unwise, and indeed impossible, to carry through a rigid classification. Poems which, because of their subject, must be considered together (e.g., war poems) do not always reveal the same formal characteristics; and literary forms appropriate to one setting in life may be adapted to another (e.g., the prophets' use of forms such as the lament to convey their message about national events). Nor is it easy to distinguish between sacred and secular literature. Much that would to-day be regarded as secular was in ancient Israel intimately connected with religion.

224

This is particularly evident in some of the most ancient poems in the Old Testament, which are connected with war. The brief poetic formulas associated with the movement of the Ark (Num. x. 35, 36) probably marked the beginning and the end of campaigns. Something of the sort is also seen in the opening words of Psalm lxviii. The vivid glimpse which we get of a decisive point in Joshua's victory over the five kings (Joshua x. 12, 13) may well be part of a much longer poem describing the battle, similar in character to the Song of Deborah (Judges v). The entire incident of Balak and Balaam (Num. xxii.–xxiv) illustrates the use of maledictory incantations against the enemy. The brief snatch of poetry in 1 Sam. xviii. 7 is a sample of the songs in which victory was celebrated. Exod. xv. 21 is a similar song of triumph, though Israel had not actually been engaged in battle. The anthology of martial poems in which Num. xxi. 14b, 15 is said to have been included (The Book of the Wars of Yahweh) may well have contained many more war songs than those which have survived. It should be noted that these poems are classed together because of their subject and not because of any formal characteristics which they share. Formally, some of them would be classed as curses, thanksgivings, and the like.

A few traces of work songs have survived. Num. xxi. 17, 18 is usually interpreted in this sense; and there are some allusions to harvest songs, e.g., in Isa. xvi. 9, 10 and Jer. xxv. 30. But again it is not possible to associate with such songs any common formal characteristics. This also holds good of the drinking songs to which prophetic denunciations bear witness (Isa. v. 11–13; xxii. 13; lvi. 12; Amos vi. 4–6).

A much richer representation of the songs of love and marriage has been preserved, mainly in the Song of Songs, including antiphonal and dramatic elements as well as description, narrative, and words of appeal. The Psalter contains a magnificent poem for a royal wedding (xlv); and some parts of the prophetic books may be adaptations of this genre.

In 2 Sam. i. 19–27 and iii. 33, 34 we have two laments, both attributed, probably rightly, to David. This type of poem was sometimes imitated by the prophets and applied to national disasters (e.g., Jer. ix. 19; Amos v. 2); and it is clearly the main literary model for Lam. i; ii; and iv. Among its characteristics are the opening (and sometimes recurring) 'How', and descriptions of the qualities of the dead and the sadness of their end.

A prophetic text which in some ways resembles the lament and yet expresses mocking triumph rather than grief is the superb poem in Isa. xiv. 4–21, to which the term *māšāl* (which more commonly denotes a pithy saying) is applied. Similar taunt songs are found elsewhere in the prophetic books (Isa. xxxvii. 22–29; xlvii; Hab. ii. 6–19).

Some of the most important poetic genres are those which were used in the cult. The main classes have been discussed above (pp. 175–177).

In the Wisdom literature the most familiar literary unit is the short proverbial saying, to which the term *māšāl* is applied. The book of Proverbs, from x onwards, consists almost entirely of such *mešālîm* in the familiar 3 + 3 metre (cf. also Jer. xxxi. 29; Ezek. xviii. 2). But it should be noted that not every pithy saying of this kind is recognizably poetic in form (e.g., 1 Sam. x. 12). Such utterances appear to have been used for moral instruction. The same purpose was served by more elaborate compositions of the type found in Prov. i–ix, to which the term *māšāl* may also be applied.

The riddle (*ḥîdâh*) is beautifully illustrated in Judges xiv. 12–18. Prov. i. 6 suggests that it was allied to the *māšāl*; and it must have been used as a medium of instruction in Wisdom. It is interesting to note that when the Queen of Sheba visited Solomon, the wise man *par excellence*, she tested him with riddles (1 Kings x. 1).

A didactic purpose is also present in the fable, of which we have a clear example in Judges x. 8–15.

As the *māšāl* was the characteristic form in which the teaching of the Wise was imparted, the typical media of priestly and prophetic instruction were *tôrâh* and the prophetic oracle respectively. *Tôrâh*, which was not always poetical in form, contained guidance on ritual and morals. A clear illustration of *tôrâh* given in response to a specific request occurs in Hag. ii. 12–14. From such answers a body of tradition would be built up over successive generations. Interesting instances of *tôrâh* in liturgical form are found in Pss. xv and xxiv. 3–6, where the conditions of access to the sanctuary are formulated.

The prophetic oracle expresses the message which was imparted to the prophet in the revelatory experience which has often been described as ecstasy. It is sometimes introduced by the words, 'Thus saith Yahweh', or 'Hear the word of Yahweh', and ends with the expression 'oracle of Yahweh' (cf. p. 100). Where these or similar expressions are used, the prophet commonly speaks for Yahweh in the first person. The message is usually presented as an utterance which the prophet has heard; but sometimes he describes a vision which he has seen; or there may be a blend of the two (Amos vii. 1 ff). The message may contain prediction, rebuke, or command, or a combination of these elements. Indeed, the prophets employ for their purposes a wide range of literary forms: dirge, taunt song, thanksgiving, etc.

The narrative prose of the Old Testament may be assigned to several different categories. The classification depends in some sort upon the relation of the various categories to historical truth. But it is important to bear in mind that some of the names applied to these categories (such as 'myth' and 'legend') are not to be understood in the loose sense of common usage, which practically equates them with falsehood or fiction.

The term 'myth' is used in several different senses. For our present purpose it will suffice to describe it as a story about the gods. As such, myth is at home in a polytheistic setting; and the character of Hebrew religion was less hospitable to it. Nevertheless, many mythological elements have survived in the Old Testament; and there are also stories to which the term may be applied with some degree of appropriateness. The creation narrative is the obvious example. Comparison with its Babylonian counterpart shows how such material could be transformed by the religion of Israel. The transformation is less obvious in Gen. vi. 1–4.

The saga or legend is not pure fiction. It has a historical core, but has been amplified and refashioned in the process of tradition. There is much saga material in the stories of the patriarchs and in the traditions of Israel's history before the institution of the monarchy. By some the term 'legend' is applied particularly to such stories when they deal with religious persons, places, and usages. There are, for example, sanctuary legends, which tell of the foundation of specific shrines or of important events in their history (e.g., Gen. xxviii. 18 ff). Narratives which record traditions about the doings of the prophets (such as the Elijah and Elisha cycles) are sometimes classed as prophetic legends. But the use of the term should not be allowed to obscure the great historical value of some of these stories, in the narration of events, the delineation of character, the description of social conditions, and the presentation of religious crises. Aetiological legends explain the origin of local topographical names and features, religious usages, and the like (e.g., Gen. xvi. 14; xxxii. 32).

The German word *Märchen* is used to denote a story the aim of which is to amuse rather than to instruct or edify. The usual rendering, 'fairy tale', is misleading, for the supernatural need not enter into it. Though the Old Testament is more concerned with edification and instruction than with amusement, many traces of *Märchen* have been found in it (e.g., in the Joseph story and in the account of Balaam's ass). But, on the whole, what we find is not complete examples of *Märchen*, but elements which are characteristic of the genre.

Somewhat more elaborate in structure and of rather greater length are the short stories Ruth and Esther, in both of which an element of instruction or edification may be present. The Joseph story, which has a quite definite didactic purpose, may be classed with them. To these narratives the German term *Novellen* is often applied.

It has often been observed that the Old Testament reflects an interest in and grasp of history as distinct from chronicle to which it is not easy to find parallels in the ancient Near East. Certainly it both provides interesting examples of the variety of Hebrew historiography and also gives evidence of the wide range of source material available to the Hebrew historians. We have noted above the superb quality of the Court History of David (p. 80), the great achievement of interpretative historiography in the Deuteronomistic history (pp. 93–96), and the highly selective and edificatory narrative of the Chronicler (pp. 215–223). Behind the extant historical books there must have lain, not only the vivid popular traditions of the saga type, but also a mass of official and semi-official annals (e.g., the books of the chronicles of the kings of Israel and Judah, which are mentioned in 1 and 2 Kings, and the sources mentioned by the Chronicler), of statistical records (e.g., the many lists in Samuel, Kings, and Chronicles–Ezra–Nehemiah), and of personal memoirs such as those of Ezra and Nehemiah. Autobiography is also represented, as we have seen (pp. 101, 103) in the prophetic literature.

The historical books include a number of speeches, varying in character from the pungent utterances of Jotham (Judges ix. 7–20) to the farewell speeches of Joshua (Joshua xxiii and xxiv) and Samuel (1 Sam. xii). But it is not surprising that Hebrew rhetorical prose is found at its best in Deuteronomy (especially i–xi), which has a markedly hortatory character, or that the books of Jeremiah and Ezekiel, which are associated with the same period and with the generation or two immediately following, contain many speeches or sermons in prose (cf. p. 126).

Both the historical and the prophetic books contain examples of letters, quoted in whole or in part. These are mostly

from royal personages: Jezebel's message to the authorities
at Jezreel (1 Kings xxi. 9, 10); the request made on behalf of
Naaman by the king of Syria (2 Kings v. 6); the correspondence between Jehu and the guardians of Ahab's sons (2
Kings x. 1–6); the correspondence in Aramaic between the
opponents of the Jews and the Persian kings, Artaxerxes
and Darius (Ezra iv. 7–22; v. 6–vi. 12); the letter (also in
Aramaic) of Artaxerxes authorizing Ezra's mission (Ezra
vii. 12–26). In the prophetic corpus there is the memorable
letter of Jeremiah to the Jewish exiles in Babylonia (xxix.
4–23), to which are appended part of a letter from Jeremiah
to (or about) Shemaiah, and part of a letter from Shemaiah
(xxix. 24–32). In these letters the opening formula of saluta-
tion of address is only sometimes given; but we may note
the recurring use of 'and now' to introduce the main part
of the letter. Our stock of ancient Hebrew letters was enriched
in 1935 by the discovery at Tell ed Duweir (the ancient
Lachish) of a number of ostraka containing letters from the
last days of the kingdom of Judah.

It has been noted above that the *tôrâh* of the priests was
not always in poetic form. Some reference must now be
made to the great mass of legal material contained in the
Old Testament. One important formal distinction is that
between casuistic and apodictic laws. The former are of the
type, 'If thou . . .', 'If a man . . .' (e.g., Exod. xxi. 2–11),
which is familiar from other law codes of the ancient Near
East. Laws of this kind are probably part of Israel's Canaanite
inheritance. The apodictic type, which appears to represent
an indigenous Hebraic tradition, is of the form, 'He who
strikes (participial construction) a man so that he dies shall
be put to death' (Exod. xxi. 12), or, 'Thou shalt not kill'
(Exod. xx. 13).

Both the above types are admirably illustrated in the Book
of the Covenant. The Priestly stratum of the Pentateuch
contains many cultic regulations, doubtless intended for
those who were responsible for the ordering of worship.
These are sometimes introduced or rounded off by some such

formula as, 'This is the law of the burnt-offering' (Lev. vi. 9, Heb. 2). Such cultic directions probably go back to pre-Hebraic cultic practice; but this conclusion is not derived from considerations of literary form.

It is impossible to reconstruct in any detail a history of Hebrew literature in the Biblical period. There are too many uncertainties of analysis and of chronology. But certain broad lines of development may be discerned.

The first decisive turning point is the establishment of the Davidic monarchy. From being a confederacy of tribes, Israel became a state with a cultural life which owed much both to the Canaanite environment and also to Hebrew national and religious self-consciousness. The process must have begun in some measure during Saul's reign; but it was David who made possible its rapid development. During the earlier period the Israelite traditions had been formed and orally transmitted; but it is unlikely that much had been committed to writing. Under David the establishment of national independence and unity, the improvement in the standard of living, and the influence of Jerusalem as a cultural centre must have stimulated the development of a national literature. The mere existence of a royal court would lead to the compiling of royal records. But formal annals were not the outstanding literary production of the time. It must have been soon after the end of David's reign that the great Court History was written (see pp. 76 f., 80). Something of the same spirit is evident in the work of the Yahwist, who is regarded by some as the first great historian in Israel, on the ground that his range is wider and his interests less biographical than those of the Court Historian. But he is usually assigned to a date after the Disruption (see p. 34).

David has been traditionally regarded as the father of Hebrew psalmody and as the author of a considerable part of the Psalter. His skill as a poet and musician is adequately attested by the narratives about his life; and the laments in 2 Sam. i. 19-27; iii. 33, 34 are no doubt correctly ascribed to him. It is not easy to find strong and definite evidence that he composed any of the poems in the Psalter. But the new impulse given to the cult by the establishment of the monarchy cannot have been without its effect on the composition of liturgical poetry. This is in keeping with the current tendency to assign a considerable number of the extant Psalms to the pre-exilic period.

The cosmopolitan character of Israelite culture in Solomon's reign is evident from the account which is given of it in Kings. There is, therefore, a certain appropriateness in the traditional association with Solomon of the Wisdom literature, which had important cosmopolitan affiliations; and it is not unreasonable to suppose that some part of the extant material dates from Solomon's reign.

The Disruption led to the separate transmission of the traditions and annals of the northern and southern parts of the country. All that now survives in the Bible has come down through southern channels, by which there was transmitted such northern material as survived the fall of Samaria and the extinction of the Northern Kingdom. It is not surprising that E, the northern source in the Pentateuch, is inadequately represented, and that only a few psalms can be attributed to the Northern Kingdom with any degree of probability. Accordingly, it is all the more noteworthy that we have the remarkable series of narratives in 1 Kings xvii–2 Kings x, which give so vivid a picture of Northern Israel. These chapters are related to a series of crises: the Syrian wars, the religious conflict produced by Jezebel's policy, and Jehu's *coup d'état*. The prophetic narratives which form the bulk of them have no southern counterpart at so early a date. But in both kingdoms the activity of great prophets in the 8th century led to the formation of the earliest collections of prophetic teaching combined with prophetic narratives. The substance of what is now the book of Hosea was presumably brought to Judah soon after the fall of Samaria and preserved in prophetic circles along with the traditions of southern prophets. In the same way, what survived of the historical and legal records of the Northern Kingdom would be transferred to the south, and the two streams of literary tradition become one.

During the Assyrian domination of Judah for rather more than the first half of the 7th century, loyal adherents of the national religion were in a hazardous position. But with the waning of Assyrian power, there came a great national and religious revival which had important literary effects. Deuteronomy contains much ancient material, which was probably refashioned in the dark days of Manasseh; but it was the formative document of this age of transition and prompted other literary activity. Whether or not we accept Noth's view of the Former Prophets, that great corpus of interpretative history reflects memorably the outlook and standards of the Deuteronomic reformers.

The age of reform also saw the revival of prophecy in the activity of Zephaniah, Nahum, Habakkuk, and Jeremiah. Jeremiah's dictation of many of his utterances heralded a period in which prophecy became more consciously literary. This, together with important changes of emphasis in pro phetic teaching, helped to prepare the way for the transition to apocalyptic. Some of these tendencies are already evident in Ezekiel and Deutero-Isaiah. In the prophets of the Persian period certain interests clearly become dominant: the ordering of the life of the restored Jewish community by the Law, the ordering of its worship, and the hope of a decisive divine intervention. These interests determine much of the literary activity of the period. During the Exile and the early Persian period the collection, revision, and arrangement of laws produced the Priestly Code, which was finally combined with the earlier legal collections. Though there are good grounds for thinking that the monarchy was the great creative age of Hebrew psalmody, the compilation and arrangement of the Psalter took place in the post-exilic period, when the Psalms were being used in the ritual of the second temple. The hope of a decisive divine intervention and of a cosmic transformation is prominent in the latest phases of prophecy and in apocalyptic, in which the faith of Israel, confronted by the last great crisis of the Old Testament period, finds a new mode of expression.

The eschatological hope is noticeably absent from two important parts of the later literature of the Old Testament. The work of the Chronicler, in which the records of the past are edited and adapted so that the life of the holy community may be fitly presented, betrays no interest in the final crisis of human history. The Wisdom literature, of which a considerable proportion probably belongs to the later period, reveals an interest in the destiny of the individual rather than that of the nation, the human race, or the cosmos. It lacks the perfervid nationalism that is characteristic of so much post-exilic writing.

It is in these later reaches of the Old Testament that we realize most keenly that the limits of the Canon are a quite artificial frontier in the historical study of Hebrew literature. Even if we leave out of account the vast literature of the post-Biblical period, apocalyptic, Wisdom, and the later forms of historiography are all amply represented outside the Canon. But it is with the Old Testament alone that the present work is concerned.

# VIII.—THE OLD TESTAMENT AS CHRISTIAN SCRIPTURE

The fact just noted, that the Old Testament is a mutilated literary torso, brings us back to the point from which we started (p. 9). It is not primarily as a literary anthology that it must be understood. Important literary influences are discernible in its growth. But its existence and the definition of its contents are, above all, the result of religious factors. If, as a collection, it has any meaning, it is a religious meaning. The religious authority of the Old Testament has been recognized in differing ways in Judaism and Christianity. Since the present volume is one of a series on Christian theology, it is appropriate to consider the relation of literary criticism to the status of the Old Testament as Christian Scripture. In its widest sense this subject raises a number of questions, such as the use of the Old Testament in the formulation of doctrine and the religious interpretation of the text of the Old Testament. But we are here concerned with the subject as it is raised by the modern study of the structure and growth of the Old Testament books. If their character and composition are such as modern scholars hold, is the case for their inclusion in the Canon of Christian Scripture affected? [1] It is, of course, possible to argue that

[1] No attempt is made here to review the arguments for and against the inclusion in the Canon of the books of the Apocrypha. Because of the approach adopted above, this would be more appropriately undertaken in a review of their contents and composition. But the following points may be noted. (1) The term 'Apocrypha' does not denote an absolutely fixed corpus. (2) The authority of the books included in it has been and is differently estimated in different branches of the Church. (3) None of the books of the Apocrypha is quoted as Scripture in the New Testament.

their canonical status is established by ecclesiastical authority, irrespective of scholarly theories. But there can be
no absolute divorce between the scholarly study of Scripture
and the religious interpretation of its meaning and recognition of its authority. Certainly the progress of criticism has
had important effects on Protestant thought about the Old
Testament.

The Old Testament was the original Bible of the Christian.
Church; and, in spite of Marcion's determined onslaught on
it and the depreciation of it by heretical sects, it has continued to form an integral part of the Christian Scriptures.
Seeming or real discrepancies between the teaching of the
two Testaments have traditionally been explained, either
by the method of allegorical interpretation or by the view
that the two parts of the Bible represent two dispensations
in God's dealings with men.

As critical study developed, it seemed to many to be an
attack on the authority of the Bible, partly because books
formerly regarded as unities were attributed to more than
one writer and traditional views about the age and authorship of others were rejected. This was a natural but erroneous
confusion of authority with authorship. But something more
than authorship was involved. The analysis and dating of
the literature were allied with a reconstruction of the history
of Israel's religion in terms of development (see above,
pp. 2 f.). This made it easier to explain the theological and
moral differences between the Testaments, but also invited
the judgement that the Old Testament recorded an outmoded level (or outmoded levels) of religion, and therefore
that its theological authority was open to challenge. As a
source of evidence for a historical development it was indispensable; but as part of the Christian Scriptures it was an
anachronism.

It has often been remarked (cf. above, p. 3) that general
agreement with the theories of literary analysis which were
widely accepted in the latter part of the nineteenth century
does not necessarily commit one to the views about the history

of Israel's religion which were associated with them. But, if the general approach adopted in the above chapters is sound, we may go further. Admittedly the Pentateuch provides evidence of different phases in Hebrew religious faith and practice. But, together with the variety, there is also a constant: a confession of faith in God's saving acts on behalf of His people. This is present in individual passages, in the substance of the major sources, and in the framework of the completed compilation (cf. above, p. 56). It is not merely one element in the content of the Pentateuch but its theme. But for this factor the Pentateuch would not exist at all.

This faith in the purpose and action of God in history appears repeatedly in many other parts of the Old Testament, not simply as an element in the content of the books, but as the factor which explains the selection of the material and why the books were produced and preserved. The great selective and interpretative corpus of history writing can be understood only in terms of this faith that God's saving acts created Israel, and that the continuing life of Israel, with its triumphs, its crises, and its catastrophes was under the guidance and judgement of God. Again, the prophetic literature, with its wide range of moral teaching and of future vision, is knit together by the conviction that the God who acted signally in the past is at work in contemporary events, and is directing them towards the consummation of His purpose. Apocalyptic expresses the same faith with a different emphasis.

In some parts of the Old Testament this conviction is less evident, or even appears to be absent, notably in the Wisdom Literature, with its more reflective approach to the problems of conduct and of the lot of man. But even there, where international affinities are particularly evident, and where we miss explicit references to the historic traditions of Israel's faith, the influence of that faith is none the less present. It provides the context for the ethical teaching of Proverbs, for Job's inner conflict, and even for the scepticism of Ecclesiastes. Parts of the Psalter celebrate the mighty acts of God; but the collection as a whole expresses the varied worship of the community which had been created by them.

There remain elements in the Old Testament (e.g., the Song of Songs) whose place in the Canon still raises problems; but, taking the collection of books as a whole, we may say that it would not have come into existence but for this faith in the action and continuing purpose of God in history. It bears witness to that action, and to the life, worship, thought, and hope of the community which that action created. Recognizing this, we also recognize varying levels of belief within the Old Testament and important differences between the teaching of the Old Testament and that of the New. But, when all such differences have been established, the Old Testament is linked with the New, because the New Testament itself expresses, and owes its existence to, a similar faith in the redemptive action of God in historical events, and, further, because the New Testament writers, in citing the Old Testament as Scripture, see in it a record of the divine purpose in history, which reaches a climax in the life, death, and resurrection of Jesus. These facts establish an important theological continuity between the two Testaments, even if we cannot always accept the traditional Christological exegesis of some Old Testament passages. Both collections owe their existence to faith in certain historical events as saving acts of God; and both reflect the life of the communities which these events created. According to the New Testament writers, these events form one series. Thus, to reject the Old Testament as an integral part of Christian Scripture involves an important qualification of the authority of the New Testament.

It is necessary to distinguish this relationship between the Testaments from another which is widely and rightly recognized. There is much in the New Testament which could not be understood without the Old. It provides the necessary background and the appropriate local colour. This is undeniably true. It is also true of the extra-Canonical intertestamental literature. But the New Testament writers use the Old Testament, not only as scenery for the drama of salvation, but as the record of earlier acts in that drama. Jesus Himself, who used the Old Testament Scriptures with sovereign freedom, understood His own work as their decisive fulfilment. His use of them remains the supreme sanction of their place in the Christian Bible.

## APPENDIX

In the period of more than a century since the Graf-Wellhausen hypothesis was presented and widely accepted there have been many modifications and criticisms of it. Since 1970 several important studies have appeared which, if the arguments presented in them are accepted, require not simply modification but the rejection of the hypothesis.

R. Rendtorff has argued that the theory that the Pentateuch contains continuous narrative sources (J, E, P) must be rejected. Adopting a traditio-historical approach he concludes that the larger complexes contained in the Pentateuch (Primeval History; Patriarchal Narratives; Egyptian Bondage and Exodus; Sinai Narratives; Settlement in Canaan) were not the work of individual authors but arose from the amalgamation of small units of tradition into larger complexes which were further enlarged and finally combined into a whole.[1]

An important feature of some recent studies of the Pentateuch has been the assigning of much of the material (or all of it in its present form) to a later date than was formerly done. This is argued in a study by H.H. Schmid of material commonly assigned to J. Schmid compares passages such as the promises to the patriarchs, the call of Moses, the plagues of Egypt and incidents in the wilderness with others generally agreed to be of later origin, notably the Deuteronomic History. He argues from the similarities that J is to be dated, not, as von Rad held, in the time of Solomon, but in the same period as the Deuteronomic literature, a conclusion which also differs from the views of scholars who have suggested dates later

[1] R. Rendtorff, *Das überlieferungsgeschichtliche Problem des Pentateuchs* (1977).

240

than the reign of Solomon but still in the pre-exilic period.[2]

R.N. Whybray argues forcibly against the alleged evidence used by earlier generations of scholars in their attempts to solve the problem of the Tetrateuch/Pentateuch: varying use of divine names, alleged variations in style, duplicate narratives and the like. He concludes that one author produced the Tetrateuch, using material derived from folklore 'with substantial additions of his own invention'. This author's literary method was in accord with 'the canons of the historiography of his time' (viz., the sixth century), by which Whybray means the methods employed by fifth-century Greek historians such as Herodotus.[3]

In a profound and wide-ranging study J. Van Seters has surveyed historiographic material from ancient Greece, Mesopotamia, Egypt and elsewhere in the ancient Near East and has related his findings to Old Testament historiography, including the Tetrateuch.[4] One of the important conclusions which he draws is that there was Greek influence on Hebrew historiography, notably on the Yahwist, whom he dates in the exilic period, and on the Deuteronomist, to whose work he regards the Court History as a post-exilic addition.

Whybray and Van Seters are at one in emphasising the importance of Greek influence on Hebrew historiography, in dating in the exilic period material which had previously been regarded as pre-exilic. In their work and in that of the other scholars mentioned above there is a formidable array of criticisms of the methods used and the conclusions reached by the source-criticism, form-criticism and traditio-historical criticism of earlier writers, but no single unified view has emerged. Moreover some of the attacks made on the evidence

[2] H.H. Schmid, *Der sogennante Jahwist, Beobachtungen und Fragen zur Pentateuchforschung* (1976).

[3] R.N. Whybray, *The Making of the Pentateuch: A Methodological Study* (1987).

[4] J. Van Seters, *In Search of History: Historiography in the Ancient World and the Origins of Biblical History* (1983). See also his *Abraham in History and Tradition* (1975).

used in identifying and separating the alleged sources J, E and
P (different divine names, varying vocabulary and style,
duplicate accounts of the same events) are not wholly
convincing. The dating of the Yahwist in the exilic period is
unconvincing, since nothing in it reflects the experience of the
fall of the kingdom of Judah and the Exile, nor is it
conceivable that an author of the exilic period, when Edom
was regarded as Israel's vindictive enemy, could have
described the voluntary humbling of Jacob and his family
before Esau. The documentary hypothesis of the
Tetrateuch/Pentateuch doubtless needs to be reconsidered and
revised in the light of recent work; but it is premature to
discard it and consign J, E and P to the wastepaper basket.

In the study of the prophetic literature (the Latter Prophets)
the main tendencies in recent study have been (a) to date
much of the material later than has been customary, (b) to
question the historical accuracy of narratives about the
prophets, and (c) to draw attention to the presence of inner-
biblical interpretation in the texts. These tendencies appear
prominently in the work of O. Kaiser and R.P. Carroll.[5] Kaiser
argues that the formation of Isaiah i-xxxix extended over a
long period. A good example of his approach is found in his
treatment of vi.1-8, 18, which he argues took shape in stages
following the fall of Jerusalem in 587. More difficult questions
of composition and interpretation arise in the discussion of
xiii-xxxix. Since Kaiser holds that the redactors were not
concerned to preserve the prophet's actual words, he
maintains that even in xxviii-xxxi no passage should be
ascribed to Isaiah which can be explained in terms of a later
age. Similarly, xxxvi-xxxix are held to provide no reliable
information about Isaiah. The so-called Isaiah Apocalypse
(xxiv-xxvii) is attributed to the fourth-second centuries. Later
Jewish eschatological belief is held to have influenced the

[5] O. Kaiser, *Isaiah 1-12. A Commentary*, 2nd edition (1983); *Isaiah
13-39. A Commentary*, 2nd edition (1980); R.P. Carroll, *From Chaos to
Covenant: Uses of Prophecy in the Book of Jeremiah* (1981); *Jeremiah.
A Commentary* (1986).

composition of the book. In *From Chaos to Covenant* Carroll claims that we can know little or nothing about the prophet Jeremiah or Baruch. The 'Chaos' of the title is that caused by the Babylonian invasion. The traditions preserved in the book were a response to the needs of the community and to its hopes, and underwent a complex redactional process. This general view of the nature of the book is applied in detail in his commentary. Carroll holds that only a small part consists of authentic poems of Jeremiah. The bulk of the book comes from Deuteronomic editors of the exilic and post-exilic periods. Carroll regards the Septuagint version as an earlier edition than the present Hebrew text.

The debate about the prophetic literature continues.

# SELECT BIBLIOGRAPHY OF WORKS IN ENGLISH

## 1. Introduction to the Literature

R.E. Clements, *A History of Old Testament Study* (1976). A brief and lucid presentation of the main areas of Old Testament literature and theology.

O. Eissfeldt, *The Old Testament, including the Apocrypha and Pseudepigrapha and also similar works from Qumran. The History of the Formation of the Old Testament*, tr. by P.R. Ackroyd (1965, 1976). Detailed, comprehensive and fully documented.

G. Fohrer, *Introduction to the Old Testament*, tr. by D. Green (1970).

J.H. Hayes, *An Introduction to Old Testament Study* (USA 1979; UK 1982).

O. Kaiser, *Introduction to the Old Testament. A Presentation of its Results and Problems*, tr. by J. Sturdy (1975).

W.H. Schmidt, *Introduction to the Old Testament*, tr. by M.J. O'Connell (1984). Includes a brief survey of the history and social history of Israel.

J.A. Soggin, *Introduction to the Old Testament*, tr. by J. Bowden (3rd edition 1989). Comprehensive, detailed and fully documented.

Essays on recent developments in the study of the following areas of Old Testament literature are contained in G.W. Anderson (ed.), *Tradition and Interpretation* (1979): Pentateuchal Problems (R.E. Clements), Old Testament Historiography (J.R. Porter), Prophecy and the Prophetic Literature (W. McKane), Apocalyptic (E.W. Nicholson), Wisdom (J.A. Emerton), The Psalms and Israelite Worship (J.H. Eaton).

The series 'Old Testament Guides' published by Sheffield Academic Press consists of first-rate introductions to the books of the Old Testament.

## 2. Special Subjects

*A. Problems of Method*

J. Barton, *Reading the Old Testament: Method in Biblical Study* (1984).

R.J. Coggins, *Introducing the Old Testament* (1990).

K. Koch, *The Growth of the Old Testament: The Form-critical Method*, tr. by S.M. Cupitt (1969).

B. *The Pentateuch*

On the older critical position:
A.T. Chapman, *An Introduction to the Pentateuch* (1911).
D.C. Simpson, *Pentateuchal Criticism* (1924). Brief and clear.

On more recent developments:
M. Noth, *The Laws in the Pentateuch and Other Studies*, tr. by D.R. Ap-Thomas (1966), pp. 1-107; *A History of the Pentateuchal Traditions*, tr. by B.W. Anderson (1972).
G. von Rad, *The Problem of the Hexateuch and Other Essays*, tr. by E.W. Trueman Dicken (1966), pp. 1-78.
See also the Appendix to this edition of the present work.

C. *The Historical Books*

M. Noth, *The Deuteronomistic History*, Foreword by E.W. Nicholson (1981); *The Chronicler's History*, tr. by H.G.M. Williamson, with an Introduction by the translator (1987).
J. von Seters, *In Search of History* (1983). An examination of Old Testament historiography in relation to that of neighbouring countries.
H.G.M. Williamson, *Israel in the Books of Chronicles* (1977).

D. *The Prophets*

J. Blenkinsopp, *A History of Prophecy in Israel* (1984).
E.W. Heaton, *The Old Testament Prophets* (1961).
J. Lindblom, *Prophecy in Ancient Israel* (1962). A masterly, detailed treatment of all aspects of prophecy. Ch. IV deals with the composition of the prophetic books. Reprinted 1963 with enlarged bibliography.
R.B.Y. Scott, *The Relevance of the Prophets. An Introduction to the Old Testament Prophets and their Message* (revised edition 1967).
C. Westermann, *Basic Forms of Prophetic Speech*, tr. by H.C. White (1967).

E. *The Psalms*

C.F. Barth, *Introduction to the Psalms*, tr. by R.A. Wilson (1966). A good, brief survey.
J.H. Eaton, *Kingship and the Psalms* (1976).

H. Gunkel, *The Psalms*, tr. by T.M. Herner with an Introduction by J. Muilenburg (1967). This is Gunkel's article on the Psalms in the 2nd edition of *Die Religion in Geschichte und Gegenwart*.

S. Mowinckel, *The Psalms in Israel's Worship*, 2 vols., tr. by D.R. Ap-Thomas (1962, reprinted in 1 vol., 1982). A superb, comprehensive survey.

H. Ringgren, *The Faith of the Psalmists* (1963).

C. Westermann, *The Praise of God in the Psalms*, tr. by K.R. Crim (1965).

*F. The Wisdom Literature*

G. von Rad, *Wisdom in Israel*, tr. by J.D. Martin (1972). A masterly, comprehensive study.

R.B.Y. Scott, *The Way of Wisdom in the Old Testament* (1971).

J. Wood, *Wisdom Literature: An Introduction* (1967).

*G. Apocalyptic*

S.B. Frost, *Old Testament Apocalyptic: Its Origins and Growth* (1952).

P.D. Hanson, *Old Testament Apocalyptic* (1987).

H.H. Rowley, *The Relevance of Apocalyptic: A Study of Jewish and Christian Apocalypses from Daniel to the Revelation* (3rd edition 1963).

D.S. Russell, *The Method and Message of Jewish Apocalyptic* (1964); *Divine Disclosure* (1992).

*H. The Canon and the Authority of the Old Testament*

G.W. Anderson, 'Canonical and Non-canonical' in P.R. Ackroyd and C.F. Evans (eds.), *The Cambridge History of the Bible*, vol. 1 (1970), pp. 113-59.

J. Barr, *Holy Scripture: Canon, Authority, Criticism* (1983).

J. Barton, *Oracles of God: Perceptions of Ancient Prophecy in Ancient Israel after the Exile* (1986).

J. Bright, *The Authority of the Old Testament* (1967).

S. Mowinckel, *The Old Testament as Word of God*, tr. by R.B. Bjornard (1960).

# INDEX OF REFERENCES

* See footnote to page 30.

247

# INDEX OF REFERENCES

# 257

# INDEX OF AUTHORS

258

# GENERAL INDEX

A (History of the Ark),
73 f., 81
Aaron, 21, 24, 30, 35,
45 ff., 60, 169
Aaronic Blessing, 50
Ab, Ninth of, 12
Abdon, 64
Abel, 15, 31
Abimelech (King of
Gerar), 31, 34
Abimelech (Son of
Gideon), 64 f., 67 f.,
77
Abiram, 31
Abner, 79 f.
Abraham, 19, 23, 24 f.,
31, 33 f., 37, 45, 47,
50
Absalom, 72, 76
Accadian literature, 198
Achan, 57
Acrostics, 158 f., 172 f.,
200 f.
Acts of the Apostles, 95
Adam, 45, 215
Adonijah, 72, 76, 81
Adonis-Tammuz, 194
Aetiological narratives,
60, 62, 228
Ages, doctrine of, 209,
215
Agur son of Jakeh, 189
Ahab, 85 f., 91 ff.
Ahab, Acts of, 85, 87,
158
Ahasuerus, 203 f.
Ahaz, 106, 108, 142, 155
Ahijah, 88, 217
Ahimaaz son of Zadok,
77
Ai, 57, 59, 61 f.
Aijalon, 57
Akiba, 16, 192, 195
Alexander, 110, 137,
160, 168
Alexandria, 199

Amalek, Amalekites, 35,
50, 71
Amaziah, 148
Amenemope, 188
Amestris, 204
Ammon, Ammonites, 71,
74, 131, 148, 162
Amnon, 72, 76
Amorites, 36, 44, 63 f.
Amos, 37, 101, 127, 141,
144, 148 ff., 157, 163,
170
Amos, Book of, 148 ff.
Amoz, 106, 217
Anathoth, 121, 123
Angels, 36, 209, 215
Anthropomorphism, 32,
47
Antiochus Epiphanes,
211
Apocalyptic, 139, 147 f.,
153, 167, 206, 233 f.,
237
Apocrypha, 16 note, 18,
235 note
Apodictic law, 37, 230
Aqhat, 214
Arabia, 109
Arab tribes, 152
Aramaic literature, 198
Aramaisms, 146, 195,
200
Artaxerxes I, 16, 220,
230
Artaxerxes II, 220
Asaphite psalms, 173,
180
Ashdod, 109
Asher, 58, 63
Ashurbanipal, 121
Asia Minor, 5
Asshur, 50
Assyria, Assyrians, 38,
45, 91, 106 ff., 121,
142, 149, 153, 158,
160, 162, 174, 233

Assyrian law, 37
Athaliah, 89
Atonement, Day of, 20
Aufklärung, 2
Autobiographical nar-
ratives, 100 f., 103,
105, 125 f., 142 f.,
148, 166, 229
Autumn festival (see
also Tabernacles) 53,
115

Baal, 144
Babel, Tower of, 31 ff.
Babylon, Babylonia,
Babylonians, 5, 90,
108 ff., 113, 116 f.,
120, 121 ff., 130,
134 ff., 154, 156, 160,
166, 177, 182, 200,
202, 205, 209 ff., 230
Babylonian Job, 187
Babylonian law, 37
Balaam, 21, 31, 35, 50,
225, 228
Balak, 21, 225
Baruch, 102, 124 ff.
Bathsheba, 72
Beer-sheba, 23, 34, 37
Behemoth, 184
Belshazzar, 210
Benjamin, 58, 65 .,
69
Berechiah, 165
Bethel, 23, 31, 34, 37,
42, 62, 88, 166
Bethlehem, 150 f.
Bildad, 183 ff.
Bilingual character of
Daniel, 212 f.
Biographical narratives,
100 f., 103, 105, 125 f.,
142, 148, 163
Boaz, 190 f.
Bothweil Brig, 62
Bride of Christ, 144